John Abbott

About the Author

A NNE F ISHER writes the "Ask Annie" career advice column that appears biweekly in *Fortune* magazine. She is the author of *Wall Street Women* and has written for *Inc.*, the *New York Times*, and *Barron's*. She lives in New York City.

Also by Anne Fisher

Wall Street Women

If My Career's on the Fast Track, Where Do I Get a Road Map?

*Surviving and Thriving
in the Real World of Work*

ANNE FISHER

Quill
An Imprint of HarperCollins*Publishers*

"There is no use trying," said Alice. *"One can't believe impossible things." "I dare say you haven't had much practice,"* said the Queen. *"When I was your age, I always did it for half an hour a day. Why, sometimes I've believed as many as six impossible things before breakfast."*

—LEWIS CARROLL

Believe nothing, no matter where you read it or who has said it, not even if I have said it, unless it agrees with your own reason and your own common sense.

— BUDDHA

Question authority.

—BUMPER STICKER, UNITED STATES, CIRCA 1968

THINK.

—THOMAS J. WATSON SR. (FOUNDER OF IBM)

Contents

A Very Short (Honest!) Introduction

Stop, please! Don't turn the page!

If you're like me, you usually skip the introduction. You're busy! You're pressed for time. You want to get to the juicy parts! But if I may be so bold, I'd like to grab you by the sleeve for a minute here, to tell you just a couple of things about how to get the most out of the pages that follow.

First, this is a peculiar book because unlike most career-advice manuals, it's written by somebody who makes no claims to being a career expert. What I am, though, is a pretty good reporter, which means only one thing: I know how to listen, not just to what people say, but to what they might mean by it, and how that fits into a much bigger picture that is changing at the speed of light. Everything in these pages comes from conversations with hundreds of consultants, coaches, lawyers, executives, recruiters, managers, and other experts I've interviewed for my magazine and Web columns. Some of their best and most candid thoughts are—at first glance anyway—surprising.

Beyond that, I get many dozens of letters every week from people in midcareer who tell me about their experiences—including what they now wish they'd done differently, and why. Quite often, as you know if you've ever visited the scribble board at my Web site (www.askannie.com), the best—most sensible, most seasoned—advice to one reader comes not from an expert or from me, but from another reader. I've included some of those insights in these chapters and, if you've got anything to add (or argue with), I hope you won't be shy: E-mail me at askannie@fortunemail.com.

Second, I'd like to explain something quickly about the structure of this book: In the interest of clarity, I've divided it into sections that roughly correspond to the chronological stages of a typical career (if indeed there is such a thing these days as a typical career—but more about that shortly). However, this is a pretty arbitrary way of organizing these ideas, with the weird result that you may find something useful where you might not have thought of looking for it. For instance, if you've already been in the workforce for many years, you might flip right past the first section, addressed to new college grads. But there is some stuff in there that might help any job hunter—such as just what employers are really seeking that they're hard-pressed to find among job applicants now (pages 33–41), and why conducting a job search entirely over the Internet is so often an exercise in frustration (pages 45–51). Likewise, if you haven't yet got anyone reporting to you, you might not read chapter 5, "Now That You're the Boss . . ."—even though it's got a shimmering little gem of an insight, thanks to my *Fortune* colleague Peter Petre, into how Thomas Watson Jr. built a global computer empire in part by listening very, very carefully to people he didn't like (page 204). Then there are items of universal interest such as—you'll appreciate this, I'll bet—why you should take a real vacation, without a cell phone or a laptop, at least once a year without feeling the least bit guilty about it (see "The Great American Stress-out," pages 148–160).

All this is simply to say that the best way to proceed might be to ignore the section headings in the Contents table and check out the chapter headings and the Index instead.

But really, why read this book at all?

Well, as you already know (am I preaching to the choir now?), careers are strange and bewildering these days, whether you're twenty-two or thirty-two or fifty-two. Nobody is too sure anymore what's going on, which does keep things lively. It's even safe to say that if you aren't at least a little confused, you're just not paying attention.

Consider: We are caught up in the most turbulent and contra-dictory job market in at least thirty years—arguably much longer, indeed, since the Industrial Revolution, but let's skip the full his-tory course, and there won't be a quiz. I'm not a fan of statistics that are manipulated to make a point (or, as Mark Twain famously said, "There are three kinds of lies. Little lies. Damn lies. And sta-tistics.") Even so, in times of tremendous upheaval, some numbers can show us patterns of activity over areas of the world that are too broad and inscrutable for any of us to visit on our own. There is hardly a day when I don't get a few interesting stats on my desk, about where the jobs are, what companies need, how the economy is changing, which way the wind is blowing.

Ever watch the Weather Channel? Don't you love how they keep playing those perky little background tunes while predicting thunderstorms and tornadoes? When Hurricane Floyd was pum-meling the East Coast in September 1999, the local forecast for the beach town where I happened to be vacationing kept saying that the "current weather" was "partly cloudy." In communities flooded to the roofs of three-story houses (those that still had roofs) and hammered by relentless gales, this understatement—while it did little to inspire confidence in the forecasters—was at least good for a badly needed laugh.

The Weather Channel's radar is an apt metaphor for job-market–watching at the turn of the century: You can be directly underneath one of those green areas on the "real time" weather screen and see not one drop of rain. Or you could find yourself on the happy side of a high-pressure zone—according to the map, that is—and be drenched in seconds or pelted by hailstones. Even the most up-to-the-minute, state-of-the-art predictions can't account for every sudden squall or shift in the wind's direction.

So in that spirit of enlightened caution, let's look at the job-market map. Beginning in the mid-nineties, unemployment fell to record lows, enabling lots of people to move from good jobs to even better ones. No question, it was a powerful high-pressure zone, building from both Wall Street and Silicon Valley, with isolated highs in the Great Plains, converging to produce generally fair skies over most of the heartland. Even so (here come the hailstones), by mid-1999, the U.S. workforce had seen sixteen straight months of layoffs—more than at any time since 1993—with each month's figures (averaging about 63,000 every thirty days) mounting higher than in the same month a year earlier.

As companies continue to restructure, reengineer, and merge, layoffs will always be with us, but it sure can get confusing. Look, for instance, at Atlanta, Georgia, in many ways a perfect microcosm: In 1999, the city's go-go economy generated 113,600 new jobs, more than any other metropolitan area in the United States. Yet by early 2000, although new jobs were still being created at that prodigious pace, Lockheed Martin had announced a total of 2,800 layoffs, BellSouth was planning to cut 1,300 local jobs, and Coca-Cola, long an economic and social mainstay, said it would lay off 2,500 people—a stunning 40 percent of its Atlanta-area workforce. So how would you describe Atlanta's job market? How about mostly sunny with the occasional tornado? For better or worse, that's become a typical forecast in lots of other places, too.

At the same time, another remarkable trend has picked up momentum: In a typical month in 1999 (the latest figures available as of this writing), according to the U.S. Bureau of Labor Statistics, thirteen million Americans changed their employment status. That is, they left home or school to seek work, bailed out of the labor force for good, landed a new job after a period of unemployment, or started looking for work after they quit or were laid off (or fired).

Now, thirteen million people changing direction every month is hard to imagine. But it's only the beginning, because the Labor Department admits that that figure is a very low estimate. It doesn't count workers who left one job and began working at another within one month, which, while unfortunately far less common than in the boom years, still happens with some frequency even in a recession. And then there are the virtually uncountable hordes who choose to change jobs or even careers—from, say, marketing to sales or vice versa—within the same company. In all, the Labor Department says that 40 percent of all U.S. employees, or about fifty million people, are doing something different for a living within any given year than they were doing twelve months earlier. Picture it: fifty million people, in the United States alone, cleaning out their desks and moving on, every single year.

The job market even just seven or eight years ago was like baseball (or like baseball used to be)—orderly, elegant, slow, maybe a little dull at times, but, after all, comfortingly familiar and freighted with more than a century's tradition. If you were talented and lucky, you got to the Series. Now? It's more like a vast videogame, say Quake III in the "death match" stage: frenetic, solitary, unpredictable, played in a murky, quirky, perennially shifting landscape where nothing is ever quite what it looks like, and there is never quite enough light to see by. Total defeat can come from nowhere at any moment. So can triumph.

Are you ready for this? Is anybody?

ANNE FISHER
Sullivan County, New York

If My Career's on the Fast Track, Where Do I Get a Road Map?

CHAPTER ONE

So You've Graduated from College. Now All You Need Is ... More Advice?

One of the hardest things in life is to know what you want out of life—as opposed to what you feel you ought to want, what your parents and siblings and society and whoever else may expect of you. If you can allow yourself to trust those little movements round your gut that tell you when something is interesting or exciting, they will tell you where to go.

—JOHN CLEESE

Okay, I know: If you're a recent successful (or even halfway presentable) product of a U.S. institution of higher learning, you're already stuffed full of more advice—most of it well-meaning, some of it astute—than you could possibly absorb in a lifetime, or would want to. Everybody's got an opinion, or a bias, or a factoid: teachers, friends, guidance counselors, friends, parents, friends, campus recruiters, friends, professors, friends (you know I'm repeating friends because their opinions tend to count most, for better or worse, at each step of the way) . . . and then there's the Web. Hey, is there anything you don't know yet? You've looked into your options; you've listened (at least some of the time); you've worried; you've plotted; you've studied; you've planned. You've partied. You're good to go.

Right?

Well, maybe. And maybe not.

Congratulations! You're a Scarce Resource

Weird as things are, cheer up. You do have certain advantages. That college degree really is (surprise!) every bit as valuable as your parents kept telling you it would be. Three-quarters of Americans aged eighteen to thirty-four don't have one, and that is significant. JobTrak.Com—a vast on-line job-listing service for college students, MBAs, and the alumni of more than nine hundred U.S. colleges (www.jobtrak.com)—reported that as of graduation time in 1999, employers were holding out 317 percent more jobs for new college grads than they had just one year earlier. Let me repeat that, because it is astounding: Between 1998 and 1999, on-line job listings for people fresh out of

> **Q.** After three years of college, I dropped out to deal with a family crisis. Now I'm afraid to put on a résumé and job application that I only "attended" college. Do employers check to see whether you really graduated?
>
> **A.** Yes, most do. Never lie to a potential employer about anything, but especially not about this. You'd be far better off explaining why you left school than pretending to have graduated. If you have plans to complete your degree in your spare time, say so. Who knows—you might even find a job with a company whose tuition-reimbursement program will pay for the rest of your courses.

college rose 317 percent. The number of new grads during the same period, according to the National Center for Education Statistics, went up just 7.2 percent. I'll save you the trouble of punching that into your calculator: The ratio of jobs to grads was 44 to 1. And 1999 was no fluke. In January 2000, job postings for new grads were 40.3 percent higher than that 317 percent leap. Sometimes, the sky really is the limit.

So if you've got lots of great offers to choose from, it's thanks to an imbalance between supply and demand that has lately reached historic proportions. Never forget that economics is classically defined as the study of the allocation of scarce resources. Hmm. *Any* scarce resource is implied, and not just (as later definitions have narrowed it down) money, but also—and no less important—time, effort, talent. You yourself, as an energetic, bright college grad, are a scarce resource right now. Even better, you're likely to remain one for a while: The absolute number of people in the full-time workforce who are between the ages of twenty-five and thirty-four has declined about 12 percent since 1990, and demographers say that—thanks to low birth rates in the mid-to-late seventies—the age group will continue to shrink for several more years. The U.S. Bureau of Labor Statistics predicts that by 2006, the number of available jobs will have risen by 19 percent since 1996—while

Q. I'm about to graduate from college and I still have no idea what I want to do for a living. My major is economics, but I've taken a lot of English courses and love to write. I also have pretty good computer skills and have studied music seriously for years. Is there any hope for such a jack-of-all-trades?

A. Sure there is! If you haven't already done so (and I suspect you haven't), head over to your school's career-placement office and tell the people there what you just told me. They can give you a bunch of aptitude tests, and maybe a few sessions with a career counselor, to help you figure out which direction to take. If you've studied economics and love to write, you might end up as a business journalist. (That's how I got here.) There are worse fates.

the workforce grows by just 11 percent. The most severe shortage of skilled workers is expected to hit in 2005. "All you have to do is look at the numbers," says Ray Marcy, former chairman and CEO of worldwide human-capital consulting firm Spherion (formerly Interim Services Inc.). "Seventy million Baby Boomers are heading toward retirement, and only about 45 million Gen-Xers are stepping into their shoes. So twenty-first-century employees will experience a version of paradise as companies clamor for them, offering top dollar, stock options, and beefy bonuses as ammunition." Paradise? Wow.

This isn't a big news flash to many of my readers, who are twentysomething years old, swamped by opportunities, and wondering which way to turn—a lovely problem to have. Yep, you're hot stuff. You're in demand. You're what everybody's after. You're young, you're cool, you're happening. You're also likely to be far less expensive than somebody older.

Want to choose wisely? First comes an exercise in empathy and imagination. Do your best to see yourself as prospective employers see you. (And if you can cultivate this skill now, it will serve you well throughout the rest of your career—and your life—even if you work for a hundred companies and live to be ninety-nine. But more about that later.) The people who are interviewing you are making at least one big assumption about you: As they see it, even if you're not a techie, you probably know something about computers. You're not intimidated by new technology. And you're eminently trainable. So don't be

Q. As a recent liberal-arts grad (comparative lit and European history), with no real exposure to computers, I now find myself at a disadvantage in the job market. How can I overcome my technophobia?

A. As quickly as possible, I hope. Get a tech-savvy friend to give you a crash course in basic computing, or take a formal class. Once you've done a bit of Net surfing, and maybe even bought yourself a home computer to play with, you may find you're hooked. Even if not, you'll feel less intimidated.

too surprised if, in a job interview that is supposed to be for a position in sales or finance or public relations, you suddenly start hearing lots of questions about how good your computer skills are. That's because companies are desperate for people well versed in information technology—or failing that, able and eager to learn.

And no, desperate is not too strong a word. Can I get away with a few more statistics here? The Information Technology Association of America says that about 354,000 high-tech jobs are going begging, and that number is projected to rise to more than 1.5 million by 2005. Managers in a survey by infotech staffing firm Darwin Partners think that estimate is low. Ninety percent of these folks report that projects are delayed or unfinished because of a lack of skilled workers. Other polls echo the same dismal theme, with executives in one study confiding they could increase annual sales by an average of $353 million if only they could get the right people—

and keep them for longer than thirteen months, which as of January 2000 was the standard tenure of a technical professional at any given U.S. company (down from eighteen months in 1999). The shortage is so acute that the infotech industry, and people from all kinds of companies you wouldn't think of as high-tech (railroads, for instance), are pushing hard to import as many techies as possible from India, China, and anywhere else they can be found—no easy feat, given current U.S. immigration policy.

Q. I'm just finishing up my bachelor's in business and plan to get an MBA later on. But all my work experience so far has been as an executive secretary and senior administrative assistant. I'd like to go into public relations or marketing, but will I be typecast as a secretary? Should I not mention my past jobs?

A. Once you have a bachelor's you can just conduct your job search the same way any other new college grad would do. Go ahead and reveal your previous jobs, and include in your résumé a brief description of what you learned from them. If you worked for very senior executives, you may well have gained far more valuable experience than you think.

Compare that thirteen-month turnover among tech people to the job market just a generation ago, when most valued employees stayed with one company for thirteen years or more. Clearly, to attract and keep good employees, companies are having to change their attitudes, and their approach—sometimes with great reluctance. "What we need is a good recession," an embittered recruiter once told Sara Preston, career services director at Bentley College, in Waltham, Massachusetts. Oh, really? Preston's reply, according to a letter she wrote to *Fortune:* "Students [and new grads] want job content, chances to develop skills, and real responsibilities. *It is not about laziness or greed.*" (Italics hers.)

Happily, you, as one of the nonlazy and nongreedy, are in a position (because you are a scarce resource, remember) to expect—and ask for—what you want. A survey by global staffing firm OfficeTeam found that in the struggle to attract and keep best young talent, companies are handing out more (and more fun) benefits, including casual-dress policies (82 percent of those employers polled), flexible work schedules (53 percent), profit-sharing and stock-option plans for the rank and file (51 percent), and the option of telecommuting (43 percent). Some companies go still further. For example, a software outfit in Alpharetta, Georgia, gives every single employee, right on down to receptionists, a brand-

Q. I'm graduating in June 2002 with a bachelor's in business. My problem is that I'm going bald at a very fast rate, which is something that runs in my family. To fit into corporate America, should I shave my head and be fully bald, or not? (This is not a joke.)

A. These days, there really is no such thing (or place) as "corporate America." Cultures, and hence fashions, vary wildly from one industry to another, or even among companies in the same industry. In general, in a "creative" business like high-tech, publishing, or advertising, the look you're considering would be just fine. (In fact, heck, why not add an earring?) But in a more conservative field, like banking, it would probably be a bit too radical, in which case you'd do better to hold on to whatever hair you've got.

new leased BMW for his or her own personal use. You may not be as lucky as that. Even if you're in white-hot demand, getting some material goodie that you really want is easier if you can make a persuasive case that your perk of choice would help you do the job better. Example? Lots of people who yearn to work from home, at least part of the time, have sold the idea to higher-ups by pointing out (accurately) that it's far easier to concentrate in a quiet room in the house than in an office cubicle, with its constant racket from adjoining cubes.

> **Q.** I'll be graduating soon with a bachelor's in business. My grade point average is a 3.3—okay, but not great. How much does a GPA matter in landing a job?
>
> **A.** It matters, of course, but not as much as certain other things. Practical work experience—summer internships, part-time jobs, even volunteer work—can count heavily in your favor, especially when combined with good references and your own insights into what you learned from them. Most important, though, is your attitude. Energy, enthusiasm, and willingness to learn can make you shine despite your ho-hum GPA. Go for it!

And while you're asking for what you want, don't forget to take care of what you need. One theme, in the reader mail I get, never stops astonishing me: People with great skills, in their twenties, who would be welcome at just about any forward-looking company in the civilized world, ask: "I just got this great job offer but the interviewer didn't say anything about health insurance. Is it okay to ask for health insurance?" Honey, puh-*leeze*. I have to say, with all that one hears and reads about the legendary Arrogance of Youth, what really floors me is the rarely-if-ever-noted Timidity of Youth. In late 1999, the U.S. Census Bureau reported that a record percentage of Americans—16.3 percent—lacked any health coverage at all, even though one in four of the uninsured were earning upward of $50,000 a year; and this at a time when, the

OfficeTeam survey said, 46 percent of employers were trying to attract new workers by offering better-than-ever medical and dental benefits. Part of the explanation for this apparent discrepancy is that a huge number of new jobs each year are being created in small start-up companies, many of which tend to offer skimpy, if any, health coverage. At large, well-established companies, if the interviewer doesn't mention health insurance, it's because he or she assumes you know it is part of the package.

No matter where you sign on, *read the paperwork* they hand you before you commit yourself to anything. If by some unlikely chance these documents contain no mention of medical insurance, for heaven's sake, speak up. And, at a start-up, do not hesitate to push for some kind of coverage, even if it's major-medical only. No matter how young and healthy you are, you could still be flattened financially by a serious illness or an accident, piling up truly terrible debts it could take years to pay off. Stuff does happen. Why take the chance?

Two Great Debates: Big versus Small, and Love versus Money

What do you want to do for a living, and why?

Or, to put it more precisely, what's your best guess right now? With so many people changing jobs so often, "job hopping"—a derogatory term, once upon a time—has become acceptable and even chic. The odds are good that you won't be in one place for long. Technology adds an intriguing wrinkle, an element of total mystery. Not long ago, after an on-line discussion with some of my Web readers who were still in their teens and already anxious about career choices, Gabrielle Solomon, senior editor of *Fortune*'s Web site, sent me an e-mail that said, in effect, that these kids were worrying too soon: "My job, for instance, didn't exist when I graduated from college ten years ago. So how could I possibly have known I'd be doing it?"

Maybe your true calling hasn't been invented yet. Maybe you will be the one to invent it.

Still, the choices you make now, from the available feast, will likely have important consequences later. So let's look at the two biggest either-or questions that people ask me, even now that the late-nineties Internet bubble has popped: Given a range of job offers from which to choose, should I start my career at a big established company or a "hot" start-up? And should I take a job

> **Q.** After I graduate in May 2001, I want to go on for an MBA and eventually work in the hotel business. But is investing two more years in my education worth the time and money, or should I venture out into the real world with just the four-year degree?
>
> **A.** Well, since most good B-schools require five to seven years of "real world" work experience before they will even look at your application, that is a decision that has already been made for you. So do go out and get a job. Once you've been working for a while, you may realize you don't really need an MBA anyway.

I think I'd love doing, or go for the one that pays more?

A related question, and one that makes me a little uneasy when I hear it: What are the fast-growing careers of the future? This is a perennial query from readers who are hoping not to miss out on the Next Big Thing. (Or the next New New Thing. Or whatever it's called these days in Medialand.) It's a desire with roots that run millennia deep, all the way down through the ancient human wish to know the future. The corresponding human truth: Nobody knows the future. When I first started writing the column, I would call eminent labor economists, with strings of advanced degrees and decades of job-forecasting experience, and I would earnestly ask the jobs-of-the-future question, and I soon noticed an interesting thing: The more perspicacious and wise the expert, the louder he or she would laugh. And for good reason. Of

Q. Is there any such thing as a surefire code word or phrase that will get me the entry-level job I want? What do interviewers really want to hear?

A. Alas, there is no magic bullet. However, as a general rule—and despite this squeaky-tight job market, where even brand-new employees are increasingly able to call the shots—all job interviewers have one thing in common: They hope to get an idea of what you expect to contribute to the company's success (rather than the other way around). So be sure and focus your remarks on just what you'll be bringing to the party.

course, plenty of researchers purport to have the future of jobs all figured out, at least in the short term, and a few of them have written interesting books about it (five of which are listed in the Appendix). But beware. Predictions about growth rates for any given industry—and, by extension, the future demand for any particular skill—are always a rough sketch, never a definitive blueprint.

The kinds of experience most likely to lead to the Big Payoff have been changing every few years. In 1989, for instance, executive-recruiting giant Korn/Ferry International surveyed hundreds of CEOs around the globe and found that the surest path to career glory was through the finance department. The bosses viewed international experience as strictly optional. Marketing was nowhere. But when Korn/Ferry repeated the same survey eight years later, marketing took top honors, with 37 percent of CEOs stressing its importance as a career booster. International expertise came in second. Finance, once supreme, had tumbled to a distant third.

So what? Well, consider just one current example of how slippery the "hottest" skills can be: One of the biggest things going in the late nineties was enterprise resource planning (ERP), a management system that integrates all facets of a business, including planning, manufacturing, sales, and marketing, often using software applications like SAP, Oracle, PeopleSoft, and Baan. Human-resources consultants Hewitt Associates reported in mid-1999 that ERP expertise would practically guarantee you an average annual raise of 10 percent to 20 percent, way above the 3 percent to 5 percent pay hikes that everybody else was getting. Terrific! So why not go off and steep yourself in ERP technology, right? Well, maybe. But bear in mind that many, many other people are rushing to do the same thing. By the time you finish your training and get some real work experience in ERP, you might find that your hard-won skills—although they will never be totally useless—are no longer such a hot commodity. As one techie told me rather wistfully, "Just a couple of years ago, if you could write HTML code, it automatically got you half a dozen great job offers. But now, so many people can do it, all you get is a merit badge."

Of course, advising people not to invest too much energy in chasing the latest high-tech rainbow is about as popular as warning California homesteaders in 1849 that most of the "gold" in the creek beds is really just pyrite. Everybody, in every era, expects to beat the odds and strike the mother lode—as of course a very few did, and still do. (This is the same hope that keeps people buying lottery tickets, even though anyone with an ounce of sense knows that these are an excise tax on the mathematically challenged.) From the mid-nineties until early 2001, as bankers and venture capitalists tripped over each other in their eagerness to hand millions to anyone with a halfway plausible idea for an Internet business, and when some (actually quite a few) initial public offerings made overnight tycoons out of entrepreneurs whose companies were still years away from turning a profit, only incorrigible killjoys were counseling caution.

Call me a killjoy. Or a plain capitalist. They amount to the same thing, because if you took Economics 101, you recall that in a market economy, there is a little thing called the business cycle,

Q. I graduated from college last fall and am considering taking a job with a dot.com start-up. As one of just about a dozen employees who will be doing most of the work in getting the company up and running, how many stock options am I entitled to?

A. "Entitled to"? Ha ha! Here's a news flash: As an employee (not a partner or owner), you aren't entitled to anything but what your bosses offer you. You can insist on negotiating for options, of course, but don't be surprised if you have to trade them for a cut in pay. Are you sure you want to?

which has a disconcerting way of ensuring that every boom is followed by a bust. With Internet start-ups, the first (but not necessarily the last) bust came in the form of a massive shakeout among Internet companies that pummeled high-tech stocks, draining $1 trillion from the nation's money supply in April 2000 alone, and pushing the formerly high-flying Nasdaq down to a net loss for the year by late July. Tech start-ups, the erstwhile darlings of the New Economy, suddenly found that landlords didn't want to rent to them; ad agencies were far less eager to help launch campaigns without up-front payment (and glitzy advertising had been, after all, what many Internet companies' buzz was built on); and investment bankers who had formerly scrambled to take them public were suddenly not returning phone calls. Several thousand people got laid off, although many of them quickly found new jobs. Vast numbers of stock options turned into worthless paper.

This came as a tremendous shock to many people, largely because, if my colleagues in the press will forgive me for saying so, most newspaper and magazine articles about Internet businesses had zeroed in on the ones that were making tons of quick cash and creating dozens or hundreds of instant millionaires, which is a bit like purporting to cover the gambling industry by profiling only the players who hit the jackpot. A few observers did warn that many tech stocks, and by extension their issuers, were too hot not to cool down. Silicon Valley insiders Anthony and Michael Perkins, who founded and now run the high-tech trade magazine *Red Herring,* wrote a book called *The Internet Bubble,* which portrayed the rush into "hot" Internet stocks as a gigantic roulette game that most individual investors—and employees—were almost certain to end up losing. Meanwhile, Federal Reserve Chairman Alan Greenspan rumbled ominously about the stock market's "irrational exuberance."

Well before all that, even some venture capitalists, whose business is about taking calculated risks, had begun to get nervous. Ann Winblad is a partner in Hummer Winblad Venture Partners, a San Francisco–based venture capital firm that has helped fund renowned start-ups like Berkeley Systems, Liquid Audio, and Pets.com. Asked by a reporter in late 1999 who "the big on-line winners" would be, Winblad replied: "The real question is going to be, 'Who are the first big losers?' " She predicted that droves of Internet companies would go out of business within five years, and sure enough, early tremors showed up just a couple of months later, when a frantic holiday shopping season separated the winners from the losers in e-tailing in a big way.

So what does all this mean to you as you attempt to plan a career? For one thing, as Candice Carpenter, founder and former CEO of iVillage, a successful Internet start-up that has nonetheless seen its share of turbulence, presciently told *The Wall Street Journal* some months before the shakeout hit: "[T]he idea that everyone should quit corporate jobs and join dot.coms is ludicrous. There is a reason you make a lot of money in this space if you succeed: It's a big risk."

There's nothing inherently wrong with risk. Without risk, there's no change, no growth, no movement—in short, no capitalism. But in your own career, you need to think carefully about timing. Think of your skills and experience as a stock-market investor. Over time, you want to balance some Blue Chips with some more aggressive small-caps—not start out with all high-risk IPO shares, which would in effect have you gambling far more than you can afford to lose. Every inside source (including many venture capitalists who, from the point of view of strict self-interest, ought perhaps to pipe down) will tell you that only one in ten start-ups ever recoups its burn rate, defined as the costs incurred between initial bright idea and actual money in the bank, whether that be revenues from a viable product or service or (Nirvana!) proceeds from an IPO. As a green young thing willing to work long hours with few or no benefits and at sweatshop pay, you would be part of the burn rate—sheer overhead in an almost unwinnable (at least for you) game of shoot-the-moon.

As for the usual hook with which these companies reel you in, let's be really clear about one thing. A stock option is just a piece of paper, or a blip on a screen. It has no value until it vests and hits its strike price. This isn't a primer on securities and their discontents, but if you don't know what vesting is, or what a strike price is, or what has to happen before an option is worth exercising . . . well, don't jump at any Internet job offers just yet.

Jack Welch, CEO of General Electric and no slouch at wealth

> **Q.** Can a person legally challenge a company for not hiring him or her for a particular job even though he or she is qualified? I didn't get a job that I know I'd be perfect for, and a friend of mine tells me I should sue. Is he right?
>
> **A.** I'm guessing your friend isn't a lawyer or he would know that the dominant principle of U.S. employment law is "employment at will," meaning that companies can hire (or fire) anyone they please, for any reason or for no reason at all. It may not seem fair, but there it is. Among the few exceptions to employment at will is if you believe you were not hired because of your race, sex, religion, or (in some places) sexual orientation. But this can be extremely difficult to prove, and why would you want to start out your career with a big nasty lawsuit anyway? Forget about it and move on to a company that will appreciate what you have to offer.

creation, may have put it best: "I know a train's going to come through this building one day. I just don't know where it's coming from." Neither do you. So right now, you want to think about building experience and a reputation (the "brand called You," as Tom Peters calls it) that will carry you through any economic weather—or, to extend Welch's metaphor just a bit, no matter which direction the train comes from, even if you happen to be sitting on the tracks.

For that purpose, you could do a lot worse than to go to work for a Big Company, at least for a while. In fact, traditional, lumbering Fortune 500 dinosaurs are evolving (or should that be e-volving?) so quickly—and small tech companies are beginning to behave so much more like bigger, better-established ones—that the whole Big versus Small debate could soon, and happily, be obsolete.

As my colleague Jerry Useem wrote in *Fortune* (November 8, 1999), "[W]ith a leader firmly established in most Internet categories, it's getting awfully pricey to launch a credible startup from scratch—unless that startup happens to have the brand name and resources of, oh, a $38 billion corporation." Case in point: Procter & Gamble, long an archetypal Big Name, which is now pushing to be among the most aggressive and innovative of e-marketers. Joining P & G now isn't what it was in the old days, when a young assistant brand manager took years to work up to any meaningful or exciting work. "Within three years of joining the company, I was running a $110 million business . . . [and my assistants now are] using the Internet to change how consumer product companies learn from, and market to, consumers," wrote a P & G brand manager named Kevin J. Burke, at corporate headquarters in Cincinnati, in a letter to *Fortune*. "Silicon Valley hasn't cornered the market on exhilarating, high-impact careers."

Hardly. Even General Motors and Ford, towering icons of the

Q. I'm looking for my first job out of school, but I already know I want to start a family within a few years and would like to work flexible hours when I do. How can I target my job search?

A. One way would be to focus on the companies featured on *Fortune*'s annual list of the "100 Best Companies to Work For" (archived at *www.fortune.com*). Take a look, too, at *Working Mother*'s yearly ranking of family-friendly employers (www.workingmother.com). These companies are in the forefront of helping their employees balance work and life, but it's a trend that many other companies are busily pursuing too. Why? Not out of the goodness of their hearts, Lord knows, but in order to attract (and keep) people like you.

Old Economy, expect to do almost all of their purchasing online by the end of 2001. GM spends $87 billion a year, working with about 300,000 suppliers. Ford, which spends only slightly less, has teamed up with Cisco Systems to speed up the process of wiring more than forty thousand of its suppliers to the Internet. At the same time, dozens of old-line companies, like Chase Manhattan, AT&T, and The New York Times Company, are mulling ways to build up, and extract more profits from, their on-line businesses. Wall Street has started referring to these hybrid companies as "bricks and clicks": Bricks-and-mortar stalwarts, even if only

metaphorically, whose on-line ventures are heating up. "A few years ago, everyone in the dot.com world was a maverick, but now it's becoming mainstream," notes Paul Danos, dean of Dartmouth's Tuck School of Business. "The establishment is metamorphosing, and the dot.coms are becoming part of the establishment."

One clear sign he's right: Internet companies are beginning to adopt establishment-style personnel practices. A study in early 2000 by the Association of Internet Professionals, using data collected from more than 2,500 dot.coms, found that "technology careers increasingly mirror positions in traditional corporate America," with techies now tending to follow "a formal and structured career path." In far greater numbers, dot.coms have begun paying people with standard salaries and bonuses, not stock options; and senior management ranks are filling up with MBAs from the top business schools who are trained to worry about uncool stuff like actually making a profit. How traditional can you get?

There are even more down-to-earth reasons to consider starting your career at a big established company. Dale Winston, chairman of New York City–based executive search powerhouse Battalia Winston, notes that you are probably going to change jobs in a few years no matter where you start out. Recent Labor Department data have shown that the median job tenure for U.S. workers aged twenty-five to thirty-four is just 2.7 years. By age thirty-two, the average worker has had nine full- or part-time jobs. So let's assume you don't plan to stay with your first employer for more than four years at the outside. You don't want your next employer to look at your résumé and say: "Who?"

Explains Winston: "Do you want to be ready for a big opportunity when it comes along? Great. I have clients coming to me every day who say, 'I want someone with premier-company experience.' That is, they want an operations person who has spent a few years at, say, General Electric, or a CPA who started out at a Big 5 firm. No one is saying you have to spend your whole life at a big company if you later decide it isn't for you. But you'd certainly be wise to get

Q. I've been offered sales jobs at two different pharmaceutical companies. The positions and pay are practically identical, but one company is about to merge with a big competitor and the other isn't. Should that affect my decision?

A. I'll probably catch some flak for this, but I think it should. A company that is heading for a merger is usually a pretty volatile environment, with lots of people getting shuffled around, reassigned, and even (very frequently) laid off. Since you say that the two jobs are similar in every other respect, I'd go with the company that is staying independent.

that 'brand name' on your résumé—and take advantage of the enormous range of opportunities and resources that big companies can offer, including the chance to learn from people with solid real-world experience. You might think of it almost as an on-the-job graduate degree, or an apprenticeship."

A few years at a diverse and deep-pocketed Big Company is a kind of employability insurance. It is, and may always be, far easier to move from a large, well-established company to a smaller, less stable one than the other way around.

Something else to bear in mind, if you've got student loans to pay off: The Bureau of Labor Statistics reports that in 1993, white-collar employees at large companies (five hundred or more employees) earned 33 percent more than their counterparts at small companies (fewer than a hundred employees). By late 1999, that gap had widened to 47 percent. So while you're unlikely to become an instant millionaire no matter where you work, a large outfit is less likely to expect you to starve.

One further thought: If you do decide to take the leap into an e-venture, try your best to check out the company carefully. A twentysomething Chicago reader of my column wrote recently: "I found out the hard way—after I had already quit my job at a big-name company to go to a start-up—that the exciting new opportunity I had been wowed by was a put-up job. In my first few weeks there, I was expected to set up phony tax records, mislead new investors about how 'hot' we really were, and 'get rid of' customers who kept demanding what they had paid for. I now realize that the trouble with start-ups is precisely that they have no track record—and you have no real way of knowing, until it's too late, what you are setting yourself up for." Of course, most start-ups are honest (if sometimes inept, but that's usually fixable). Still, before you join one, do some serious asking around. How good are the people in charge? Have they run profitable businesses before? What's the buzz about them in their own industry, among former colleagues, suppliers, and customers? Ask for a detailed copy of their business plan. If they're getting any dough from venture capitalists, they do have one, in writing, that goes at least five years out. Study it carefully. Ask questions.

What's that you say? Your new would-be bosses don't want to show you the business plan, or at least describe it to you in detail? Hmmm. If they don't trust you, are you sure you trust them?

This question points up yet another advantage to joining a company, whether very large or less so, that has already gone public. The U.S. Securities and Exchange Commission requires publicly held companies to publish 10Ks, annual reports, quarterlies, and all kinds of other stuff about what they're doing, why, where, and how profitably. So it's a relative breeze to find out quite a lot—which is generally a good idea before any job interview. The more detailed your knowledge about what a company has been doing lately, and (even better) what it hopes to be doing in the future, the more credibly you'll be able to describe how you see yourself fitting in. Annual reports and other such juicy documents are available on the Web at www.sec.gov/edgarhp.htm. Don't forget to visit each company's Web site, a terrific way to get a quick, accurate, and sometimes surprisingly detailed sense of just what you might be getting into if you worked there.

"Love what you do. Success requires passion."

So says Carleton "Carly" Fiorina, CEO of Hewlett-Packard. The first woman to run a really huge company ($47 billion in annual sales, 123,000 employees), Fiorina walked away from an estimated $50 million in stock options when she left her old job as head of the $20 billion global-services division at Lucent. She'll do all right at H-P too, of course—but it's plain from interviews with her that she made the change because the new job is a bigger challenge, and "tough challenges are more fun."

Fun? Do real, live, wildly successful grown-up executives really plan their careers around *fun*? You bet they do—and so should you. There's a practical reason for it: If you don't love what you do, you won't be terrific enough at it to compete against those who do. "The passionate ones are the ones who will go the extra mile, do the extra work, come up with the fresh, outside-the-box idea," says Phyllis Woods, a senior consultant at career-counseling firm Drake Beam Morin in Seattle. "To get ahead today, your first question shouldn't be, 'Where are the hot jobs now?' It should be, 'What can I get passionate about?' "

By the time you read this, you will probably have at least a vague notion of where you'd like to work. You may already have interviewed with campus recruiters, or been in touch directly—perhaps through Internet job boards like www.careermosaic.com—with a few of the important players in your chosen field. If so, congratulations. You're on your way. But maybe you're just not all that excited about what you've been planning to do, and you need to find your passion. This isn't always easy, especially before you've graduated and gotten a real job, or even in your first couple of years of full-time work. I get lots and lots of letters from people who studied, say, finance for four years, and are now all set to take a job that is, theoretically anyway, just perfect. But they still have a nagging feeling that they'd really rather be doing something else entirely, they're not really sure. So, what should they do now? A complicating factor is that most of us are, or think we might be, pretty good at more than one thing—finance and writing, or product design and sales.

If you're wavering on the choice of a career, let me ask you something: Have you made an appointment to talk with someone at your school's career-placement office? Every college has one—

even community colleges and other two-year schools—and most are equipped to do an excellent job of helping students figure out what direction to take. Yet too many people either never darken the job counselors' doorways at all, or else just swing by now and then to check out the job listings and campus recruiters' notices tacked to the bulletin boards in the hallways. If you're really unsure what you want to do for a living, making an appointment to discuss it with a counselor could be the smartest move you'll ever make.

Career-placement counselors will usually begin by giving you a series of "tests"—and I put that in quotes because, unlike on the tests you're used to taking, there are no right or wrong answers. These quizzes, which are generally quite detailed and extensive, take three basic forms: personality inventories, designed to figure out generally what kind of person you are; interest inventories, which are aimed at pinpointing what kind of work might appeal to you; and aptitude tests, which can provide valuable clues as to the kind of job at which you'd excel. Once you've taken the tests, your counselor will sit down with you and explain the results. Then the two of you can do some brainstorming about what kind of work you should be seeking, and how best to start going after it.

A widely used personality test is the Myers-Briggs Type Indicator (MBTI), based on the work of Carl Jung, which can identify you as one of sixteen possible personality types—and, based on

> **Q.** If you filled out an application for a job and then discovered that you left something out, how can you get that information to the employer (who is two thousand miles away)?
>
> **A.** There's no reason why you can't write a brief note to the person to whom you gave the application, explaining what you left out. Identify yourself clearly, so that whoever reads your addendum knows which application it belongs with. I sense that you're afraid this will make you look absentminded or flaky, but don't worry. It may actually give you a good chance to remind the job interviewer of your application—and by extension yourself.

that, suggest what kind of career would fit you best. Another test you may well be taking is the Strong Interest Inventory. This is a very cool exercise because it matches your interests with those of highly successful people in different occupations, with an eye toward seeing what you have in common with those folks and hence where you might be happiest and most productive.

By the way, one of the reasons why your college tuition is so high is that your school offers these career services. I am not kidding. Later in life, when you're perhaps thirty-five or forty and wondering about changing jobs or careers, you may end up taking these tests again (although naturally your answers will probably be somewhat different by then), and going through the ensuing brainstorming sessions too. The big difference is that, later on, a professional career coach will most likely charge you a few thousand bucks for the privilege. So why not take advantage of this now while it's available to you for free?

Let's say your test scores show that you would indeed, as you may have suspected, be good at more than one thing. (My scores, as a college senior, predicted that I'd become either a teacher or an entertainer. I think I turned out to be a little bit of both.) Don't worry. Go after a job that promises the opportunity to use at least one of your major strengths—and then, once you've gotten your feet wet, keep an eye out for ways to use your other talents. One of the truly terrific things about the new world of work is that, to a far greater extent than in the past, it encourages "crossfunctionality," which is consultantese for "learning how to do more than one thing." In the best and brightest companies now, people work in relatively small teams designed to throw different disciplines together—engineering, manufacturing, finance, marketing, sales—and see what develops. This is eminently practical, as it tends to avert a situation (frightfully common in the old days) where, say, the engineers design a product that the marketing people can't sell. Or everybody agrees on a new product except the finance people, who point out when it's already too late that the plan isn't cost-effective.

Crossfunctional teams save companies a lot of time, money, and trouble—but even more important from where you sit, they let you work closely with people in other disciplines and learn from them. At Intel, Paul Otellini, an executive vice president in charge of worldwide sales and marketing, once told me that his company's approach is "like a flea market. First, you look at everything that's going on in the company and find what intrigues you." Then you work for a series of small, temporary teams that come together to work on specific short-term projects, so that engineers get to pick the brains of marketers and finance mavens, and vice versa. "This gives you breadth. You learn by doing," says Otellini. "The interested and the interesting get together and spark ideas."

Intel may be a bit ahead of the pack, but most companies now offer some way of exploring various areas and working closely with people who do more than one thing. And, for people with great aspirations (including, you, of course), the broader the range of exposure and experience, the better. Start now, in your very first interviews with prospective employers, to seek out ways to put as many of your skills, talents, and interests to work as you possibly can. After a discussion in my column about how to gain crossfunctional skills, I can't tell you how many letters I got from readers in their thirties and forties who wished they had started their careers by seeking out more varied assignments. "I see now," wrote a marketing manager in his mid-thirties, "that I should have been thinking about this when I first joined my company's management training program. Now, with thirteen years in marketing, I'd like to branch out, but it's hard to be taken seriously in some other area when you've been pigeonholed as 'a marketing guy.' "

Don't get pigeonholed. Flex your wings a bit—even if it takes a while to find an employer who will encourage you to do so. "In the first company where I worked, the human-resources people really resisted letting anyone contribute in more than one area. They wanted to keep people in tidy little categories," wrote a woman in her forties. "I bought into that—until I came to the place where I work now and discovered that it doesn't have to be that way. Wish I had known sooner that I'm actually just as good at customer-service management as I was at finance—and I enjoy it a lot more, too."

Let's say you're interested in, and trained for, a given field or discipline, but you just aren't sure whether it's really for you. It's understandably hard to commit yourself to something without a clue to what it would be like day in and day out. If this is your dilemma, let me suggest a shortcut to enlightenment that career counselors call "informational interviewing." As the phrase implies, the goal here is not a job or a reference (although those sometimes arise incidentally), but simply a chance to gather as much information as you can get about what working in a given field really entails.

First, do a bit of homework and identify a couple of people who are doing what you think you'd like to do. For instance, suppose you're interested in television production. A search on the Web, a glance through a few trade publications like *Variety,* and even just grabbing a pencil to jot down the names of production companies as they zip by on your TV screen will give you lots of producers who are clearly succeeding at this game. Call a couple of them and ask if, just for information's sake, you could have a few minutes of their time to ask some questions. (Ideally, if you don't live on either coast, be prepared to travel: Informational interviewing is far more illuminating in person than by phone or e-mail.) The kinds of things that might be good to know: What is this person's average day like? What time does it start, and end?

How many meetings? Do they carry a beeper? Have to travel much? How much travel is on short notice or no notice? What do they enjoy about the work, and why? Likewise, what is the part they like least? Is it something that would rankle you, too? What skills or personality traits do they think have helped them the most in this line of work? (And have you got those qualities?) Ask about anything that concerns you, even if it seems dumb. Nobody's on trial here.

Don't be shy. As long as you make it clear that all you're after is time-tested wisdom, most people even very high-ranking, very busy people—will take the time to talk. Indeed, many successful people enjoy talking about themselves so much that you may find the hard part is getting them to stop. As Linda Srere, CEO of giant ad agency Y & R New York, told me: "Anybody just starting out should not hesitate to ask for insights from people they think might be role models for them. You would be surprised at how rarely I say 'no' to some young person who wants advice or guidance. People at my level understand the importance of taking the time to do this." So go for it. Who knows? Plucking up the nerve to quiz somebody in your chosen field might lead you to head off in another career direction altogether, sparing you many miserable years in the wrong job. This sometimes happens with very young attorneys who spend a day observing what goes on at big Wall Street law firms.

Q. Please settle an argument. I am considering taking a job (my first out of school) for which I was offered what I think is a generous salary plus very good benefits. My friends tell me that employers expect you to ask for more money, even if they're already offering a lot, or else you will look like a chump. I say they're wrong. What do you say?

A. I'm with you. Holding out for more, under these circumstances, won't make you look smart—just greedy. This is especially true since, if you'll pardon my saying so, you haven't really done anything yet. Later in your career, when you can point to a solid track record of achievement, employers are likely to tolerate (or even expect) a bit of greed. But not just yet.

Now, back to passion. Suppose you're like a reader named Alison, whose letter a while back kicked off a great debate on my Web site about love versus money—whether to take a job you believe you could really love, or go for the less interesting one that pays better. This is a harder question than it may appear to be, because it requires you to figure out what really matters to you. And, in the New Economy, where there are no guarantees, you may have to do this kind of internal inventory over and over again. Just ask any forty-eight-year-old who's been replaced by a twenty-eight-year-old with less than half the experience, at about half the pay. What makes you happy? What can you not live without? What must you have in your life to be your own best self, and what is just someone else's idea of success?

Clearly, this all goes far beyond mere dollars and cents, and there are no right or wrong answers. The only real mistake you might make would be in not being honest with yourself—or just not thinking about it at all.

Money is wonderful. It is useful. It is fun. I'm very fond of money. Still, even a great thing can be overrated—and, in our superheated consumer-driven culture, it so often is. Think about it. In late 2000, the Census Bureau reported that U.S. median household income was at an all-time high. Every region of the country saw significant increases in pay over the previous two years. While the government's researchers were quick to acknowledge that millions of Americans still struggle to make ends meet, there's nonetheless no question that we as a nation are better off than ever before by almost any quantitative measure you could name.

Cool! Now, let me ask you: Do people seem happier than ever before? Do they get along better? Do we seem content with how well we're doing? Has there been, for example, a drop in the suicide rate? (No, there certainly hasn't—quite the contrary, in fact—but that is a subject too grim to dwell on here.) To put it in a really corny way, does money buy happiness? Look around you. Watch TV. Read the newspapers. Listen to people talking about their lives.

What do you think?

Ideally, of course, you'd choose a career you can get passionate about that also happens to pay well—but Alison's dilemma was a stark either-or, which is what makes it interesting to ponder. If you're facing a similar choice, neither I nor anyone else can tell you which way to go. Instead, just a couple of thoughts. First, consider what you are selling in the labor market: your time and effort, and lots of both. The poet John Ciardi once remarked that "a man is what he does with his attention." If you devote enough time to something, no matter with what degree of ambivalence, that thing becomes in a real sense your self. Be very careful what price tag you put on it.

And make no mistake, in the course of a career, you will spend a lot of time at work—about forty thousand hours over twenty years, assuming you work only eight hours a day and take weekends off and two weeks' annual vacation. Of course, your real hours on the job are likely to be far more than that. One recent national survey put the average

Q. Every job interview I go to seems to include the question "Where do you see yourself in five years?" I'm fresh out of school, about to get married to someone whose career may require a lot of moving around, so this question really throws me. Is there a standard answer?

A. No, there is no standard answer. In fact, believe it or not, this question—which, as you've noted, is ubiquitous—was designed by some human-resources genius to elicit from you a creative riff that will give your inquisitor a glimpse of your True Self. Instead, it's just making you nervous. The trick is not to take it so literally. Nobody is looking for a precise job description (or marital status, or address) dated five years from today. Still, you must have some ideas about where you would like your career to go, and what kind of job you expect to be doing in the future. Jot these down. Then, in your next interview, explain how you think your goals and your prospective employer's might mesh.

workweek among white-collar folk at 49.2 hours, and 48 percent of these people said they are working more hours now than they did five years ago, with no letup in sight. Moreover, although conventional wisdom has it that life is short, it's actually pretty long. If you start a career at age twenty-one and work until you're sixty-five (and many Americans keep working well past that age), you're looking at forty-four years, or nearly half a century.

Now, obviously, taking a high-paying job that doesn't interest you—selling your self short, in other words—in your twenties, as a relatively quick way to pay off school loans or get a car, doesn't mean you're stuck with a ho-hum career for life. But habits have a wicked way of outliving their usefulness. If you let yourself get into the habit of making decisions based solely on short-term financial consequences, you're letting the tail wag the dog. It will become a hard pattern to break, and could lead you to wake up one morning ten or fifteen or twenty-five years from now and wonder just what the hell you thought you were doing.

I hear this all the time from readers who make lots of money—enough to pay the very best shrinks—but who look at their lives and question why they bother. One reason for their discontent is that measuring all of life in financial terms means that you never quite catch up. There will always be someone richer than you are, and once you've gone far enough down the Yellow Brick Road, the more money you have, the more you think you need—until finally you find yourself (as someone once said about Hollywood) spending money you don't have to buy things you don't need to impress people you don't like. Eeek.

Many people eventually get very tired of this and change careers in midlife. Sometimes they even do something radical, like run off to join the Peace Corps or pick up a hammer for Habitat for Humanity. A wholesale reevaluation of ends and means at, say, age forty-five or fifty is certainly one solution. But why spend a couple of decades slaving away in the wrong profession before you figure out what's for sale in this world and what isn't? Far better to think about it now.

If there is something you are passionate about, pursue it. There will never be a better time than right now for you—young, optimistic (I hope), unencumbered by stuff like mortgages and college-savings funds for your own as-yet-unborn kids—to follow a dream, even if you have to do it in your spare time for a while. And there may never be a more welcoming, or more forgiving, environment for your ideas than this rapidly expanding economy that seems endlessly hungry for innovation. Examples of people who have made a gigantic footprint in the world just by doing what truly fascinated them are too numerous to list, but let's take just one: A Harvard dropout who spent all his time fiddling around with computers, at a moment (the mid-seventies) when an obsession with electronics was so exceedingly odd as to be almost certifiable. You may have heard of him. His name is Bill Gates. He's doing okay now, and not just because he happened to get rich. He still loves what he does for a living, after all these years. He's a lucky man, but also (and more relevant, for the rest of us), a singleminded one. He knew what he cared about, and never let anybody else sway him with some dumb remark like: "Billy? You still messing around with them fool computers? When are you going to get a real job?"

While we're—more or less—on the subject of money, a few words about how to approach the subject in a job interview. Scarce resource though you are, you're still something of an unproven quantity at this stage of things. Naturally, you haven't yet got the kind of leverage you'll have later on when it comes to salary negotiations. So it would be unwise, and possibly self-defeating, to get your salary expectations up too high. Consultants KPMG surveyed 1,743 college students in late 1999, asking them what they thought their first job would pay. Forty-two percent said "$50,000 or more," up from just 17 percent who aimed that high in the same survey a year earlier.

Now, the reality check: The actual average starting salary in 1999, according to the National Association of Colleges and Employers, was $35,668—and that was for economics and finance majors. If you majored in, for example, history or English, expect to start lower.

It's never a bad idea at any stage in your career to do some homework and get an idea of what the going rate is, in your geographic area, for the kind of job you want. Check out Web sites like *Salary.com,* talk to recruiters, take a look at newspaper want ads. You might also find out if trade associations in your industry keep up-to-date tallies of salaries at various levels in different parts of the country. Keep in mind that after taxes, your take-home pay will be about 28 percent lower than your gross salary, and don't forget to compare benefits—investment plans, tuition-reimbursement programs, and the like—when comparing job offers. Once you've gotten a clear sense of what kind of pay to expect, be a bit cagey: On job applications—often the first place where the issue of money arises—don't commit yourself to a specific figure. Instead, fill in the blank with a word like "open," "negotiable," or "competitive." You want to seem flexible and realistic. You'll also avoid accidentally underpricing yourself.

Fresh out of school, before you've established a track record of achievement, your bargaining power is obviously pretty limited. Don't lose any sleep over it. As long as the job you want pays enough to feed you, clothe you, and take you out to a movie once in a while, forget about money for the moment and concentrate instead on where the job is leading and how you can build a future on it. After all, any career is likely to be a long, long road. So try to base your early decisions not on how comfortable the first few steps are, but on how well you'll like the destination. Says Peter Veruki, executive director of career planning at the Jesse H. Jones School of Management at Rice University: "The point of your job search [right out of school] is not salary negotiation. It's finding a job you'll be happy with, that you'll grow with, and that will allow you to be yourself. If your starting salary isn't the one you dreamed about, but the job presents the right opportunity, think about the possibility of commanding a higher salary once you've had the chance to prove yourself invaluable to the organization." And you do intend to be invaluable, right? I thought so.

Veruki also says this: "Trust your instincts. If you're dissatisfied with the employer [during the interview process], don't bet that the situation will improve after you start." Sometimes, money, or the promise of it, is just a way of lulling you into not thinking about what else is going on—such as a job that won't challenge you or use your best talents to the fullest. Pay attention.

Very often, the sharpest insights in my columns come straight from real live *Fortune* readers, like dispatches from the front lines of the business wars. So, before we leave the topic of money (for now; there'll be more about it in later chapters), let's hear from a few of those correspondents:

•Cathy: "I'm forty-six, a corporate lawyer who started out with a degree in political science. I like what I do, but I have not done nearly the kind of exploration [of career options] that I would have liked to do. . . . We seem to have it backwards. We get our training, often very specialized, at a time in life when we have little or no experience to tell us what else might be out there for us. I suggest that students investigate various careers while still in college or fresh out of it, by taking part-time jobs or internships, and by talking with people they know—friends, family—in fields of interest.

But also understand that you may find yourself back in school, later in life, to train for a field you really love."

•Yin: "When I graduated, it was the middle of a recession, and jobs were scarce. But in hindsight, I'm glad I took a job that didn't pay all that well but that has provided me with a lot of marketable experience and training. One thing I know for sure: You have to like your job because there is no such thing as 'enough' money. Last year, to bring me up to the level of some newly hired managers in my company, I got a 20 percent raise. [The average raise for managers in the United States that year, 1998, was just 4 percent.] Now I have to laugh at myself, because I find myself hoping for another raise soon. When money becomes the main standard, it's never high enough."

•Chris: "After two decades in a lucrative career that was, and is, not really what I wanted to do, I've learned two things. First, what you keep and invest is more important than what you earn. If you earn a lot and spend it all, it's just as if you never had it to begin with. And the second thing is related to that: When you're unhappy in your job, you do tend to spend more of what you make, or even more than you make, in order to 'reward' yourself for doing something you dislike. It becomes a vicious circle. I try to explain this to my kids, but I think they'll have to learn it the way I did—that is, the hard way."

•Randy: "I 'sold out' a decade ago, but here's what I've realized lately. A job, no matter how great a career it might lead to, is not a complete life. Don't apply 100 percent of your energy and devotion to any one thing. Leave some space in your life for music, art, sports, exploring, learning. Do your best at your job, but reserve at least a portion of your best self for your private loves. The irony is, this will give you what you need to be a bigger 'success,' with broad perceptions and the ability to communicate with many different kinds of people."

Hear, hear.

Just What Are Employers Looking for, Anyway?

Every bookstore in America, not to mention sites like Amazon.com or Barnesandnoble.com, has got lots of guides on how to write a winning résumé, how to draft a killer cover letter, and how to wow a job interviewer by anticipating—and acing— the tough questions ("What do you see yourself doing ten years from now?" "Pretend you have to fire me. How would you do it?"). Yet, rather oddly, very little has been written about what it is that companies really hope to find in a new hire. It goes without saying that you need the requisite education and skills to do a particular job: You're presumably not bothering to apply for a finance job if all you know or care about is programming, or vice versa. And at this point in your career, your résumé is a pretty brief document: You were born, you went to school, you probably held some part-time jobs or internships, and now here you are. A plain chronological rendering, spelled correctly, with brief descriptions of what you've learned in your work life so far, will do fine.

But let's suppose that a couple of dozen other applicants—or maybe a couple of hundred—are vying for the job you want. Assuming everyone else has the same basic education and background that you do, how can you stand out? What would make an interviewer pick you—or not? If you know what employers, at

Q. In the age of electronic job seeking, is a written résumé (on paper) outdated? We had a career adviser at my school who made us agonize over functional vs. chronological résumés and what color paper to use. Was this a waste of time?

A. To answer your first question first, no. There are plenty of people making hiring decisions who would rather see your résumé on paper than on a computer screen. Your best bet is to submit both a cyber-résumé and a paper version, so people can read about you in whatever form they choose. (Of course, the impression you make in person counts most anyway.) As for your second question, I don't know. If you didn't learn anything useful, then I guess it was.

any company, in all industries, really want, you've got a big advantage. Luckily, as the skilled-labor shortage drags on, plenty of very smart people have devoted vast resources to figuring out just what the tiebreakers really are. And here's a surprise: Even at bleeding-edge high-tech companies, the aptitudes employers crave are much the same as in the Old Economy—only, interestingly, somewhat more so. The Big Three: (1) a knack for problem solving and a certain dogged self-motivation; (2) the ability to listen well and get along with other people; and (3) strong communication skills. Yes, this means reading and writing well, in plain English. Imagine that.

Caliper, a human-resources consulting firm in Princeton, New Jersey, surveyed executives at a thousand U.S. companies and asked them: What do you really need in your new hires that you are having trouble finding? Problem-solving talent was the number one answer, by which the managers responding meant: If we give you a Serious Situation to fix, can you figure it out? Assuming that you have the technical skills and we give you the resources, do you have the imagination—and the dedication—it takes to worry this thing like a dog with a bone until it is resolved? A close second in the Caliper survey was conscientiousness. Do you know what a deadline is, and will you consistently meet same? Do you understand your responsibilities to other people—especially colleagues and customers? Will you try your best to do a good job even when you're having a bad day?

Problem solving and conscientiousness were selected by these one thousand hiring managers more than twice as often as any other quality, although "open to new ideas" and "versatile" ranked pretty high, too. And—somewhat predictably, in light of the rest of this survey—"ability to handle stress" was a must-have. Says Harold Weinstein, Caliper's COO: "Employers don't want to hire people just to carry out routine tasks. Computers can do that."

Ah. The more sophisticated technology we have at our disposal, in other words, the more fully human we have to be. This is the paradox behind a big push, in many companies now, to teach "people skills"—listening, getting along with others, persuading people to try a new approach—to techies. Says Marilyn Condon, a senior consultant at Minneapolis-based training powerhouse Personnel Decisions International: "Tech experts now are really internal consultants to their companies. And as such, they need more than just technical savvy if they're going to succeed. They need leadership skills, client-relations skills, a whole range of competencies in areas that used to be considered 'soft.' "

Reams of research back up what she's saying, including a fascinating study by OfficeTeam of where the U.S. workforce is headed. Called "Office of the Future: 2005," the project based its conclusions on interviews with 1,400 corporate chief information officers and found that 77 percent of them believe "increased use of technology will require workers to communicate more articulately and effectively"—not less so—than they do now. "It's kind of ironic, isn't it," muses Lynn Taylor, an OfficeTeam vice president who directed the study. "The proliferation of technology really is the main factor making so-called 'soft' skills essential to an employee's success."

Q. I keep hearing that the best way to find a new job is by networking through family members and friends, that it all depends on "who you know, not what you know," etc. But I just graduated last spring and I don't know anybody yet in my chosen field. Am I doomed?

A. Good grief, of course not. Lots of studies have shown that the more senior you are in a given industry or company, the more likely it is that you will have gotten your big-honcho job through some kind of informal channel, a phone call from the friend of a friend or some such. But that network of connections—acquaintances, pals, people who owe you favors— takes many years to build. Not having those contacts now is certainly no cause for alarm.

That's partly because being able to e-mail a hundred, or a thousand colleagues at once means that just that many more people will notice if your skills aren't so great: "If you can't express ideas clearly, persuasively, and with a certain flair for diplomacy, technology allows you to reveal these shortcomings very quickly, and to ever-wider audiences." Yikes.

The OfficeTeam study pinpointed six key "soft" skills that employers say they need: problem solving, ethics, open-mindedness, persuasiveness, leadership, and educational interests (as in, willingness to pursue training and acquire knowledge in unfamiliar areas). "These abilities can be even more difficult to develop than technical expertise, because they are so intangible," says Taylor. "Typically, people build up these skills over time, through experience, observation, and instinct. Colleges just don't teach these things."

At this juncture, you haven't had too much time yet in which to do this kind of skill building, although certainly some people are innately gifted at, say, problem solving, or leadership, or learning new things. The Caliper and OfficeTeam findings' biggest implication for you right now? I'll bet you've already figured that out: If a previous part-time job, or internship, or other experience has given you an edge in any of the six key areas aforementioned, it couldn't hurt to mention it on your résumé or (when appropriate) in job interviews. A very common interview question goes something like this: "Oh, I see you interned at Ostrich Corp. last summer. What did you learn there?" Think this over before going into an interview: Was there an instance where you figured out a new and better way to do a particular task (problem solving), or perhaps a time when you organized a companywide team of interns that then held a softball tournament to raise money for charity (leadership)? Naturally, be sure to mention any new technical skills you acquired, too, because your willingness to keep learning is vital. If you analyze all of your experience so far in terms of the six key "soft" skills, and then describe yourself that way to interviewers (without any undue embellishment, please), you may find that you stand out from the crowd quite nicely.

Filmmaker Woody Allen once said that "90 percent of success is just showing up." I'd amend that to say that 90 percent of success is getting along with the people who show up next to you. The Society for Human Resource Management studied the causes of performance problems in the workplace and found that in more than 65 percent of cases, "problem employees"—many of whom ended up getting fired— didn't lack technical skills or motivation, but rather suffered from "strained relationships" with co-workers.

As if that weren't scary enough, another study, by the Bureau of Vocational Guidance at Harvard, shows that for every person who loses a job because of poor-quality work, two more are sacked because they just can't deal successfully with other people. Taylor is right that colleges don't teach these things—but maybe it's time they started.

A major reason for "strained relationships" at work: lousy communications. If you can stand one more survey on this subject, I'd like to note that 80 percent of executives in a poll taken by recruiting firm Select Appointments North America ranked "listening" as the most urgently needed—and the most lacking—skill among new hires. "Interpersonal skills," or a knack for getting along well with others, ranked second, followed by "problem solving." "Technical" ranked fourth. Weird, huh? Why does the ability to listen outweigh even sought-after technical skills? "While technology forces workers to communicate more often with more people, more quickly than ever, managers in particular must be able to hear what others are saying," the study said, "since they spend about 60% of their day listening to their staff and to customers."

How good a listener are you?

And how good a writer? It really does matter. The ubiquity of e-mail has brought with it a widespread rash of casual misspellings, bizarre or nonexistent grammar, and sometimes cryptic abbreviations, and these are okay for dashing off a quick note to a friend. But in a business setting, where you're hoping to impress others with your great ideas, presentation counts. An e-mail proposing a new sales scheme, or explaining a new computer program, or outlining a new marketing strategy is no different from a memo on paper: If you expect anyone to take it (or you) seriously, it has to be well thought out, well written, and concise. The more people you hope will see it—and the higher up they are in the organization—the more true that becomes.

So few people bother to write well these days that if you do, you'll be a standout for that reason alone. Says Gary Blake, who runs a training company called the Communication Workshop in Port Washington, New York, "When I go around the country talking with clients in big companies, I am astounded at the number of managers who bewail the fact that nobody who works for them can write a simple paragraph. You can have the greatest ideas in the world, but they're no good to your company, or your career, if you can't express them clearly and persuasively."

Want to impress a job interviewer? Write a cover letter that tells in concise, vivid, and accurate English why you think you'd be great for the job you want. Paula Goodman, a vice president and senior recruiter at Citigroup in New York City, says that strong writing skills are "a definite tiebreaker. If I have two job candidates in front of me, equally qualified except that one writes well and the other doesn't, I'll hire the one who does—every time."

Goodman isn't the only one to do so. A survey by Robert Half International of the one thousand largest employers in the United States found that 96 percent say employees must have good writing skills to get ahead. Writing well does pay better in the long run, in real dollars and cents, than being sloppy about it, as some very detailed research has shown. Stephen Reder, a linguist at Portland State University in Oregon, has worked closely with the U.S. Department of Education in studying how American adults' verbal proficiency (or lack thereof) affects their long-term economic success. Reder found that among people with a two- or four-year college degree, those in the highest quintile of writing ability earn on average three times more than the group with the worst writing skills. Jumbled reports and murky memos just won't get you very far, no matter what other great skills you may possess.

Of course, plenty of people graduate from college with lackluster writing ability. And, even if you got good grades on term papers, business writing is a different proposition, where brevity, clarity, and relevance are vital. If you have reason to believe you're already a pretty good business writer, skip ahead to the next section. For those who aren't so sure, may I offer a crash course here? Richard Pinsky, whose eponymous New York City–based firm conducts one- and two-day writing seminars for clients like Pfizer, Merck, Merrill Lynch, BBDO Worldwide, and Fleet Bank, maintains that good corporate prose springs from ten basic steps that are logical—and that is their strength. "That which is logical soon becomes obvious," says Pinsky, "and that which is obvious soon becomes instinct." Here's an abbreviated guide to Pinsky's system:

•Take your time. Writing too hastily is usually a mistake. "Unlike diving into a frigid pool, when writing it is often best to think about it first," Pinsky notes.

•Be sure you know what you are trying to say, and why. "What is your message, and why are you conveying it? If you aren't sure, no one else will be, either."

•Don't, as we say in the journalism racket, bury the lead. Put your main point right up front, so as to be sure your (presumably busy) readers will see it.

•"Don't chatter." Pinsky observes that much writing is cluttered up with unnecessary asides and unimportant details: " 'Related' is not the same as 'relevant.' Knowing what to leave out is as important as knowing what to put in."

•Remember those outlines you had to do in school, where (A) logically preceded (B), which was followed by (C)? No? Well, never mind: Organize your writing so that one point logically leads to another in a way that will make sense even to someone who is only devoting about half of his or her attention to your memo—as will likely be the case nine times out of ten.

•Consider your audience. What are they really interested in? Do you need to tell them all about quarterly sales figures, if all that counts to them is earnings per share? This implies that you might have to write, perhaps, three memos instead of one in order to tailor your message to particular readers. But if you can effectively reach three audiences instead of none, it's worth the trouble.

•Watch your tone. Some people like a few jokes with their facts and figures. Others don't—and then there's the question of which jokes will fly and which will land with a thud (or, perish the thought, land you in court). If you suspect you may be tone-deaf to these nuances, play it straight.

•Don't leave 'em guessing. "This isn't a mystery novel," says Pinsky. "Good business writing anticipates readers' questions and answers them immediately."

•State your purpose. Unless you are sure it is crystal-clear (for example, a memo on a particular topic to someone who specifically requested it), mention why you are addressing this to the person(s) in question—and, when applicable, what is supposed to happen next.

•Before you send it, polish it up a little bit. Line up the margins; check the spelling (or have a computer program do this, but beware: Computers will confuse "their" and "there" every bit as readily as some humans do). Try to make sure the thing looks as if a grown-up had written it. Neatness counts.

All this takes practice, and no one expects you to be brilliant at it overnight. Still, the sooner you start, the better—because naturally your first piece of great business writing ought to be a wonderfully succinct and lucid cover letter explaining why the company of your choice would be making a real mistake not to hire you.

Do Manners Matter?

As if urging you to write well weren't old-fashioned enough, I'm about to get positively antediluvian and posit an idea that is so moldy it's radical. But as long as we're on the subject of what employers really want, I'd be remiss not to mention that good manners do matter—and, to judge from the mail I get from corporate recruiters and other hiring managers, they're in woefully short supply. Three more-or-less random, and entirely typical, laments from job interviewers, plucked straight out of my e-mailbox:

•"Annie, what is it with 'kids' these days? I feel like an old fogy asking that, but honestly, I've been interviewing new college grads for some time now and can't figure out what they could be thinking. They show up late—sometimes hours late—for interviews, slouch in the chair, won't look you in the eye, and don't seem to know what a handshake is. As for clothes, let's not even go there. My company has adopted 'casual dress,' but some of what the kids show up wearing is incredible. How do they expect to get hired?"

•"I just got finished interviewing fourteen candidates, recent grads of topnotch schools, and as bright as they all are, their attitudes astonish me. I know (only too well) that the job market is weighted in their favor, but the arrogance I see is just amazing. They don't listen, just want to make demands. Also, has combing one's hair before a job interview become passé?"

•"Do you get other complaints about the new crop of entry-level applicants, or is it just me? I'm a recruiter for a major consulting firm and, since we are a client business, we need people who are not only smart and energetic but also have strong social skills. It is so discouraging to have to turn down a brilliant candidate, as I just did this morning, because he was so rude to me and the two other interviewers here that I shudder to think of the damage he'd do if we let him loose among the clients."

Lots of employers, especially but not only in client-oriented businesses, are so concerned about recent hires' lack of polish that they're shipping "the kids" off to seminars where they're supposed to learn basic etiquette (at the company's expense). As manners trainer Susan Bixler, founder of Atlanta etiquette consulting firm Professional Image Inc., told *The Wall Street Journal:* "All that training that used to be done at the family dinner table is just not being done there now. Both parents work, and kids are busy with extracurricular activities. And kids aren't going to learn manners from other kids." With everybody in a typical household now grabbing a quick microwaved meal before they rush out the door again, nobody's instructing anybody on the difference between a salad fork and a dessert fork, the proper way to eat a roll, or where to put your napkin when you leave the table. So companies find themselves picking up the slack. Marjorie Brody, who runs Brody Communications Ltd., based near Philadelphia, in Jenkintown, Pennsylvania, says corporate requests for manners training are rising by 50 percent a year.

Q. After three interviews with a company I was interested in, I was offered a job somewhere else that interests me even more. Now the first company has made me a firm offer. How should I tell them that I've decided to take the other one?

A. Very carefully. After all, you may want to work for this company at some point (maybe sooner than you think), so you don't want to burn any bridges. Ideally, in person—but by letter if you're too chicken—do explain that after much thought, you've decided to pursue another opportunity right now. But you very much appreciate the chance to have met with this really interesting organization, you wish everyone there all the best, and you hope they'll keep in touch with you in the future. The more gracefully you handle this, the greater the likelihood that if you ever do want to work there, they'll welcome you warmly—or at least return your phone calls.

For you, the implications are clear. If you're already presentable in polite society—or can manage to make yourself so by studying up on it a bit—you've got a distinct edge over the Animal House crowd. It's no coincidence that many job interviews now include a lunch or dinner, either in a corporate dining room or at a restaurant with real linen tablecloths and no pizza on the menu: Your manners are being judged along with your credentials.

At the risk of expounding what ought to be obvious (but apparently isn't always), even if you've got straight A's from an Ivy League school and are otherwise white-hot stuff, behaving like a jerk in a job interview could still cost you the job you want. So do arrive on time, or even a few minutes (not more than ten) early. Wear something clean, pressed, and at least nominally businesslike. Say "please" and "thank you." Sit up straight. Make eye contact. Shake hands when arriving and before you leave. Speak clearly, but not at great length, and don't whine about any previous negative work experience you may have had. A job interviewer is not a therapist, and bad-mouthing former employers is the quickest way to mark yourself as a "problem employee"—not the kind anyone wants to risk hiring.

Now, back (briefly) to the topic of empathy. Good manners are nothing more or less than the outward sign of your ability to put yourself in someone else's place and treat him or her as you would like to be treated. Before you go into a job interview, take a few minutes to imagine what your prospective employer is really after. If you've studied up on the company by reading its annual report and visiting its Web site (you have done that, haven't you?), you must have gotten some sense of what kind of culture prevails there. Is teamwork seen as paramount? Then you need to come across as someone who can work effectively in a team, not as a prima donna who's going to want all the glory. Does the company place a premium on innovation? Then you need to think of some instances from your past where you came up with a novel solution to a problem. In other words, to paraphrase John F. Kennedy, be prepared to talk about what you can do for the company, not just (or even mainly) what the company can do for you. And keep it succinct and to-the-point. As you no doubt learned in the past four years of sitting in classes, the human attention span is pretty short.

Most important, and most often overlooked: Follow up each interview with a short thank-you note. This doesn't need to be more than four or five sentences, thanking the interviewer for his or her time and interest and reiterating your enthusiasm for the job, with maybe a very brief reminder of why you think you'd be great for it. The note should be handwritten on paper and mailed, not e-mailed. Like most vestiges of old-fashioned good manners, the thank-you note serves several purposes at once. For one thing, employers tend to see it as an indication of attention to detail. And for another, if an interviewer has spoken with several people who all share roughly the same qualifications, your note could be the tiebreaker—the extra fillip that makes you stand out in his or her mind as someone who'd be a pleasure to have around. And that is never a bad thing.

A Few Words About Job Hunting On-line

As a member of the first generation of job hunters to have the World Wide Web at your disposal, you know it can be a powerful tool. But like anything else, it's only as effective as the use you make of it, and here's where plenty of people are running into a brick wall. First (surprise!), a few statistics: In 1998, just 17 percent of Fortune Global 500 companies actively recruited on the Internet. Today, more than 70 percent do, and that figure is mounting by the hour. And the Net isn't just for entry-level folks.

Exec-U-Net, a nationwide networking organization for senior executives (defined as managers earning $100,000-plus annually), reports that the percentage of big cheeses who surf the Net looking for a new job rose from 64 percent in 1998 to over 90 percent in 2000. *Computer Economics* estimates that there are more than five million résumés on the Internet as of this writing. (Of those, www.monster.com alone posts—also as of this writing—more than 1.6 million.)

Hmmm. Mighty big numbers. Maybe too big. Debbie Hansen, who manages on-line recruiting at Gateway, spoke for thousands of her beleaguered peers when she told a trade newsletter in mid-1999: "Internet recruiting right now is a mixed blessing. We've been overwhelmed." Added Leslie Fagenson, director of global human resources at Merrill Lynch, "We spend too much time processing candidates when we should be finding them and evaluating them." As a result of the flood tide of résumés, job hunters often get nowhere fast. A Yankelovich Partners survey says that 40 percent of people who have been job hunting on-line say that posting a résumé on a job board is "equivalent to sending it into a black hole." More than 50 percent of those polled say their on-line job search has "seldom or never" led to an interview for a job that matched their qualifications.

"The on-line job market is still fragmented and the process is haphazard, and that greatly reduces the chances for successful matches between an employer and a job seeker," says Neil Fox, chief information officer at Management Recruiters International, a giant global search firm based in Cleveland. "Most job sites today are based on a traditional classified ad model. Jobs are posted and candidates are essentially left to their own devices to follow up on potential opportunities. Many people don't even get past the application process—and if they do, the artificial intelligence used on the sites is based on an automated 'key-word' system and is usually not sophisticated enough to truly match the best candidates to a particular position. So there is a lot of wasted effort involved."

Why am I telling you this? Simply to reassure you. If you're among the legions of frustrated folks who've sent on-line résumés into the aforementioned "black hole," don't feel bad. It's probably not your fault. The technology, marvelous as it is, is still seriously buggy. Not surprisingly, companies are working hard to remedy the problems and make more timely contact with candidates (such as you) who really would make great employees, if only you could be picked out of the crowd. Fox's own firm, MRI, is taking a typically innovative approach. One new project is a site, www.BrilliantPeople.com, that links job seekers directly with one of five thousand recruiters in a thousand offices worldwide. The headhunters then make sure the right candidates hook up with the right employers. Instead of receiving thousands of résumés that have to be sifted through, companies get just those that have already been eyeballed by an actual human being and evaluated in connection with a specific job that needs to be filled—thus immeasurably boosting the odds that a real-world match will happen. Says Fox, "We're trying to take the sheer luck out of on-line job hunting." Efforts in that direction are bound to accelerate because companies are far too

Q. Can you please tell me what in the world I'm supposed to wear to job interviews? Every company seems to have a different dress code, so I always feel I'm wearing the wrong thing no matter what I put on. Help!

A. You're not alone. No less an authority than dress-for-success guru John Molloy (author of several gazillion–selling books on what to wear to work) admits that the whole clothing question has gotten pretty mystifying lately. He recommends a wee harmless bit of spying: "The day before your interview, go stand around in the lobby or parking lot of the building where your interview will be. The best times are early morning and late afternoon, when lots of people are coming and going. Take note of what they're wearing. Then dress accordingly." Good luck.

hungry for new talent to let so much of it slip through their fingers for too long.

If the Net, like any new technology, just needs some pretty extensive tinkering to make it do its best work, then the obvious question right now is: What should you do in the meantime?

The consensus among the experts I've talked to: Go for quality, not quantity. "Don't even think about mass-mailing—or e-mailing, or faxing—your résumé," says Hank Stringer. "Right now, résumés are not the principal currency of career transactions." Stringer is the founder and president of Hire.com, an e-cruiting firm based in Austin, Texas ("Silicon Gulch"), whose clients include IBM, General Instrument, and MCI Worldcom. Instead, "networking with people in a field of interest, or at a company you have your eye on, is still the best way to get a great job." Where to start? The smartest companies these days, Stringer notes, have Web sites where job seekers can learn about the organization, and vice versa: "Employers are building relationships with candidates by allowing them to anonymously answer questions about themselves and their ideal job without requiring a résumé. The company then keeps the individual updated on news and opportunities that may be of interest." A few examples of employers with these interactive sites: General Instrument, LSI Logic, Microsoft, IBM, MCI Worldcom, Sprint, US West, Eli Lilly, and Electronic Arts.

Stringer adds that a targeted approach, where you are in touch one way or another with just a few companies—rather than sending out hundreds of résumés like so many shots in the dark— "puts you in control of the process. It allows you to focus." That, in turn, increases the chances that a company you like will focus on you, too.

William Schaffer, head of European wireless marketing at Sun Microsystems and author of a terrific book called *High-Tech*

Careers for Low-Tech People, agrees with Stringer: "It's naïve to think that you can just post your résumé on a job board and get a great job. Companies are swamped with so many applicants—especially, but not only, for tech jobs—that they are actually looking for ways to screen *out* the résumés that don't address the company's particular needs. And the ones that get screened out first, which is to say most of the résumés out there now, are the ones that are too general. They're not targeted to any specific job, so they're not useful." To get your dream job, Schaffer says, "you really need to make connections at the company—through your health club, your church, it doesn't matter how—and find out the kind of details that will help you tailor your approach to particular opportunities in that company." He adds that "all you really need is your first job there. Then you can move around. But to get in the door, you need to get to know the people."

What? Old-fashioned face-to-face networking as the path to a great job in the New Economy? Engage in actual conversations with real human beings? Leave the safe, silent glow of the computer screen and maybe go dancing? (Or at least lunching.) Bizarre, perhaps, but also strangely appealing, don't you think? The more things change, the more they stay the same. Lots of current research backs up Schaffer's point. One Yankelovich survey of human-resources honchos found that more than two-thirds are frustrated with on-line recruiting techniques that don't let them meet candidates in person until fairly late in the process. Says David Dunkel, CEO of an on-line recruiting firm called kforce.com, "Hiring managers still place tremendous value on face-to-face interactions. On-line classifieds have opened new avenues for reaching job applicants, but they preclude the kind of personal contact that managers really need in making good hiring decisions."

In other words, they want to get a look at you. They want to

> **Q.** I'm about to start my first "real" (full time, salaried) job, and I'm curious about something. If you had to pass on just one piece of advice on which to build a career, what would it be?
>
> **A.** I've always liked Albert Einstein's dictum: "If A equals success, then the formula is $A = X + Y + Z$. X is work. Y is play. And Z is, Keep your mouth shut." Now, obviously (and luckily), he didn't keep quiet about relativity, but I think what he meant was that real success springs from deep wells of thought that are easily disturbed by excess noise. If you make it a habit to listen, observe, and reflect more than you speak, you can't go too far wrong.

hear you speak and check out your body language. They want to see what you're wearing. One of the biggest imponderables: How well will you fit into the corporate culture at the place where you're applying? Interviewers need to get some sense of what your personality is like, and that's almost impossible to convey except in a face-to-face encounter. Gerard Roche, CEO of executive-recruiting behemoth Heidrick & Struggles, once told me that he decides whom to hire by chatting with the candidate for a while and then asking himself: "Could I stand to be stuck in an elevator with this person?"

No wonder then that according to the Yankelovich poll, although human-resources people report being "inundated" with on-line résumés, they still hire only one in ten new employees as a result of an on-line contact. Think about that: just one out of ten. So nine out of ten people who actually get hired are those who call up and make an appointment, show up in person, shake hands, and sit down for a little talk—just as in the days before the Internet existed.

This is not to discourage you from casting your net on the virtual waters. Go ahead and post résumés on job boards if you want to. Just don't expect miracles. As Craig Sawin, CEO of career-development powerhouse Drake Beam Morin, wrote in a letter to *Fortune:* "The Internet may be an invaluable door opener in a job search, but the decision to hire a candidate still rests largely on human contact. . . . [T]he in-person interview is still the ultimate dealmaker—or deal breaker."

It probably always will be. After all, the people hiring you won't be working, day in and day out, beside an electronic résumé or a collection of key words artfully arranged on a computer screen. They'll be working with a breathing, living human being: you. So decide on a small cadre of companies you'd really like to work for. Then, go show 'em what you've got.

And hey—enjoy. You are embarked on a great adventure.

CHAPTER TWO

Moving Up:
How to Travel Vertically
in a Horizontal World

*Career . . . — n. 1. An occupation or profession followed as one's life-
work. 2. A person's general course of action through some or all of
life. . . . 3. A course, esp. a swift one. 4. Speed, esp. full speed.—v.i. 5.
to go at full speed.*

—WEBSTER'S COLLEGE DICTIONARY

*The U.S. Constitution doesn't guarantee happiness, only the pursuit of
it. You must catch up with it yourself.*

—BENJAMIN FRANKLIN

Let's indulge, briefly, in a New Age visualization exercise. It has a point that even non-Californians can appreciate. Close your eyes and picture an object that embodies the
word "career." If you joined the workforce fifteen or twenty
years ago, you're probably hard-wired, as the techies say, to

visualize your working life as a predictable series of narrow and distinctly separate rungs that lead straight up (or down)—in other words, a ladder. Well, friend, in most companies now, the ladder has been chopped up into little pieces and tossed out. A team of sanitation engineers disposed of it at dawn while you were dreaming.

This development has left lots of people groping for new ways to picture a career path. A Dallas consultant named Price Pritchett, whose clients include GE, Kodak, and Southwest Airlines, suggests a web: "Even the word 'career' sends too linear and limiting a message. Work today is about expanding your web by making more connections (knowing more people) and spinning stronger strands (gaining more experiences and skills). A web is flexible, expandable, and you can always tear it down and build a new one somewhere else." John Humphrey, CEO of executive-training powerhouse Forum Corporation, talks about a toolbox: "The old ladder was a rigid, immovable thing. Now, the question is, what skills have you got in your toolbox, so that you can carry them anywhere and ply your craft?" Says Bill Gray, head of human resources at Harley-Davidson: "We try to discourage people from thinking in vertical terms. We see it more as widening your circle of influence."

Metaphors matter because they shape our unspoken, and often unconscious, expectations. If you still see yourself as climbing a ladder, then the web weavers, toolbox toters, and circle wideners are probably running rings around you. They're also probably the ones getting "promoted" in the new sense of the word—making more money, yes, and also getting the chance to work on the most exciting projects and lead the most dynamic teams. To them, titles mean little; it's pay and quality of work that count.

In the old days of corporate empire building, you got rewarded for managing more people. You could follow a clear set of rules, be a good organization man (and managers were, of course, almost always men), and practically be handed a new title every few years. Big companies could afford to operate this way, back then. But after almost two decades of reengineering, cost cutting, outsourcing, flattening of organizations, consolidating of industries, and breakneck competition from the Internet, the opportunities for old-fashioned promotions have shrunk. "I don't like the word 'promotion,'" says Gerard Roche, CEO of Heidrick & Struggles. "It implies that you believe you're automatically in line for a bigger job. You're not."

In the new game, people float from project to project, team to team. Job definitions often become blurred, so that titles have less and less meaning. What matters is what you know and how well you apply it to the business (your "value added," as management wonks put it). Those who play this game well are the ones most likely to rise up and grab one of those increasingly scarce and lucrative jobs at the top. (Of course, despite the decline of old-style hierarchies, every company still has a top level, although the trappings of power are often distinctly less imperial than they used to be.)

So much rapid change, and the resulting uncertainty, have given rise to some truly wacky notions—some of which end up getting repeated, straight-faced, by "experts" who really should know better. The biggest canard to date, which I'd like to dispel right here and now: In the New

> Q. My team leader has just hired someone from another department who has only a one-year technical degree. Everyone else has a four-year degree. Yet the new guy is being paid the same as the rest of us. What should we say to our boss?
>
> A. What makes you think you should say anything? If you go whining to your boss about this, he will probably think you're a jerk. He may also point out that this new person, while lacking your credentials, has certain skills (not to mention attitudes) that you don't. Are you sure you want to have that conversation? This sounds to me like a perfect opportunity to mind your own business.

Economy, since we can't rely on old-fashioned corporate hierarchies, we're all responsible for developing our own careers (true so far). Besides that, more and more people are working in teams, where responsibility for results is (ideally, anyway) shared equally among the members of the group. Therefore, it follows logically that the word "boss" is no longer useful because no one really has a boss anymore. Ha! This is nonsense, and could lead anyone who believes it to make some stupendous—and utterly needless— mistakes. So let's get one thing straight: Anyone who works for a paycheck has a boss. Heck, the CEO of a Fortune 500 company has a boss. Granted, it's not one person, it's a collective entity made up of the board of directors, shareholders, and big institutional investors, to say nothing of the press, Wall Street analysts, employees, unions. . . . When you stop and think about it, a CEO has so many different and demanding constituencies to answer to, it makes having a boss who is just one or two people (as most of us do) seem like a day at the beach.

The word "boss" has become unfashionable. You've no doubt noticed that it is frequently replaced by euphemisms like "team leader" and "project facilitator." That doesn't mean that the reality has somehow vanished into thin air. In these pages I use the B word as convenient shorthand meaning (1) a person (or collection of persons) who is empowered to listen to your ideas and help you reach your goals by encouraging you to do your best work at whatever you are best at, or who can by the same token throw roadblocks in your path and thwart your efforts to move ahead; and/or (2) whatever person or entity decides whether you get your next paycheck and directly influences the size of it.

This is purposely a broad definition, because in any career these days there are going to be times when success—or even survival—will depend on identifying just who your boss really is. At certain moments, it could be someone right beside you on the organization chart, a teammate or a peer in another department whose output could make or break yours. It could even be someone "below" you, a key subordinate or a team whose cooperation is essential and whose resistance or hostility could spell disaster.

At the same time, of course, your boss is always whomever you officially report to—and who has reached a level in the company that you may be aiming to reach or surpass. Even in this horizontal world, where webs, circles, and toolboxes have replaced ladders, it's still possible to move up—especially if you're willing to start by looking inward.

Take a Good Look at Yourself: The Art of Self-evaluation

When it comes to sizing up our own job performance, most of us think we're from Lake Woebegon, Garrison Keillor's mythical town where "all the children are above average." Indeed, one memorable study I saw a couple of years ago showed that when people in a typical U.S. corporation were asked to rate their own work according to whether they belonged in the top quartile, the second, the third, or the fourth, fully 75 percent put themselves in the top 25 percent group—which, even if you're no statistician, you can see is a mathematical impossibility. It's nice to have a positive self-image, and confidence is a fine thing—except that, alas, if you go around blissfully assuming you're doing great, you could be in for a nasty surprise one day soon. Rob Norton, a human-resources executive at pharmaceutical giant Pfizer, calls it "that awful shocker of a Friday afternoon"—the moment when totally out of the blue you're summoned into some higher-up's office and told that your services are, um, no longer deemed essential.

This happens most often, and most traumatically, in times of intense and continuous change—like now. Says Bob Kaplan, a founder of management consulting firm Kaplan DeVries in Greensboro, North Carolina: "It's like a marriage where you go along day to day without really seeing your impact on the other person, and then one day your spouse says, 'I want a divorce.' And you're totally in shock." And here's the really intriguing part: The higher up you are on the organization chart, the more likely you are to be clueless until it's too late to do anything about saving yourself.

Your only protection is to have a clear sense of your own value to your company. But figuring that out is, like so much else these days, largely up to you. Consider for a moment what 150 CEOs revealed when asked, in a survey by executive-training company Manchester Inc., why they had recently canned senior managers—executives who had been just one level, or at most two, below the chief executive's office. In many cases, the CEOs said, the firees were lacking in skills like team building and strategic thinking. But 77 percent of the CEOs also confided that the newly departed were in desperate need of an impartial, no-holds-barred performance evaluation. So why didn't they get one from the very top dogs who eventually fired them? Explained Manchester cofounder Molly Shepard, who oversaw the research: "Most senior people just don't have the skills, or the desire, to convey bad news." In other words, the big bosses wimped out.

It isn't unusual. Joseph Gibbons, a consultant at Towers Perrin who has put together evaluation programs for clients like AT&T, Union Carbide, and Citigroup, explains it this way: "When you get on the 'high potential' list in a lot of companies, you have your last formal evaluation as a middle manager. Above that, it's all a matter of relationships—you and the Big Guy are *buddies.*"

Even if you haven't yet attained that rarefied club, where the CEO is just too close a pal to tell you the truth about yourself, you may be on your own when it comes to an honest appraisal of your work. At most companies—even those that have formal evaluation programs in place—your real standing is seldom revealed through official channels, because most bosses are no better than the CEOs in the Manchester study when it comes to delivering constructive criticism. But are you up to a rigorous self-assessment? Says Molly Shepard: "Unfortunately, because we all have a need to cling to the familiar and safe, most people will not go looking for bad news—even if hearing it could save them."

She offers four surefire tip-offs that your personal stock is sinking fast: (1) You've stopped being invited to important meetings; (2) your boss suddenly won't make eye contact with you or avoids you altogether; (3) your peers know more than you do about

Q. I hate to sound like Rodney Dangerfield, but I get no respect. I've been in the e-commerce business for four years and a senior executive for two, but I'm only twenty-eight. Now I'm trying to move from a start-up to a larger company and I'm finding that people ignore my experience and skills and just focus on my age. What can I do besides just wait to get older?

A. It sounds like you're applying to the wrong companies. At real high-tech leaders (think Microsoft, Intel, Cisco Systems, not to mention high-flying Silicon Alley start-ups whose executives' average age is about twenty-four), your youth—coupled with your accomplishments—would be seen as a big advantage. Just keep looking until you find a company that appreciates what you've done and can do, irrespective of the date on your birth certificate. You wouldn't really want to work for any other kind of outfit anyway, would you?

what's going on; (4) responsibilities are taken away from you under the guise of repositioning the business. This last pretext, Shepard says, "turns out to be b.s. ninety-nine percent of the time."

Nancy Friedberg, an executive coach who works with a New York City career-counseling network called the Five O'Clock Club

Q. I'd like to write brief (and very sincere) thank-you notes to both of the people above me who recently helped me get a big promotion. But I'm hesitating. Won't it seem like I'm kissing up?

A. No. Says Bill Strickland, an executive communications coach in New York City: "It's really unfortunate that common-sense politeness is so often lost in the sharp-elbowed, almost barbaric competitiveness of so many companies today. It's important to thank people properly, with a short note, and I strongly encourage all my clients not to forget."

(www.FiveOClockClub.com), suggests sitting down with a pencil and paper—or a laptop—and writing out a list of your accomplishments over the past twelve months. Examine these in very specific terms. First, what did you do? Then, whom did it please? (The client, your boss, the CEO?) Why was it great? (What did they like about it? If you don't know, go and ask them.) How much money did it bring in? (If the answer is a negative number, that might be viewed as a problem.) And then, if you were forced to find another job tomorrow, what could you say about your achievements that would persuade a potential employer to hire you? If you were trying to "sell" yourself to a new employer, what is it about your performance over the past year that you would, um, be careful not to mention or to emphasize? Why? These last two questions are essential, because the odds are that whatever you'd prefer to conceal from an imaginary job interviewer is probably already glaringly visible to the people above and around you. The more honestly—ruthlessly, even—you can admit your shortcomings to yourself, the better. The purpose here is not to make you feel bad or self-conscious (nobody's perfect, and beating yourself up will get you nowhere), but rather to pinpoint specific errors, either of omission or commission, that you don't want to repeat.

Another vital element in any self-appraisal is a frank answer to this question: Is your company changing faster than you are? If so, do the people around and above you see you as unable, or unwilling, to keep up? Notes Tod White, an organizational psychologist in Princeton, New Jersey, "For many of us, the old standards and values—loyalty, long years of experience, a sense of history—are simply not wanted anymore. If you have a boss who is trying to change the mission and culture of the company"—and nowadays, who doesn't?—"actively supporting that boss will help you get ahead, almost independent of your skills in other areas. Resisters, again regardless of how good they are at the technical aspects of their jobs, will get left behind."

Is this a polite way of saying that a little politically motivated bootlicking goes a long way? Yes and no. Says Joe Gibbons: " 'Politics' has become a dirty word to a lot of people, but all it really means is being there when the decisions get made and understanding the people who are making them." You have to be sincere, though. If you really don't agree with where the organization is headed, or how it plans to get there, your best bet is to think about finding another job—because the odds are that sooner or later you'll be leaving anyway, voluntarily or not.

To avoid your own personal Friday Afternoon from Hell, you have to look up from the piles of work on your desk, peer past the specific skills and habits that got you where you are, and focus on

Q. I'm trying to find a job in my boss's hometown, where she knows everybody worth knowing in the business community. How can I go about doing this without her finding out? Or should I just tell her I'm looking?

A. Well, now, let's use our imaginations for a minute here. Suppose your boss happens to be chatting with some old chum who says, "Oh, by the way, [insert your name here] just interviewed for a job with us the other day. What do you think of him?" Your surprised and annoyed boss is unlikely to come out with a flattering reply. Far better she hear the news from you than from somebody else—and who knows, this could start an interesting conversation about why you're dissatisfied where you are. Maybe she'd rather fix the problem than lose you.

the big picture. Where do you fit in it? How different is your company, and your industry, from five or ten years ago, and why? When you read about trends in your field, do you understand them? Do new people coming into the company seem to have different, or sharper, skills than you do? What do your subordinates think of you? Jack Snader, CEO of a sales-training firm called Systema, observes that the way underlings approach you can be a warning: "If one of my people comes to me and says, 'What am I supposed to be doing, exactly?' then I know from that question that I am just not communicating clearly enough. That is, I should know it if I'm willing to look past my own ego and see that that is what it means."

Ah, the ego thing. One of the hardest, and yet most urgent, tasks for anybody is to try to see ourselves as others see us. Charles Palus, who coaches executives at the Center for Creative Leadership, says the ability to examine where you really stand—undistracted by wishful thinking and other forms of self-delusion—is "postheroic. You have to be willing to give up being a 'hero.' Be willing to eat some dust. Be humble, which is where true knowledge lies." Niccolò Machiavelli, that career strategist par excellence, said it about five hundred years ago in his classic treatise on politics, *The Prince.* "A prince . . . ought to discourage absolutely attempts to advise him unless he asks for it," Machiavelli wrote—but here's the kicker: ". . . but he ought to be a great asker, and a patient hearer of the truth."

Done any asking lately? Done any listening?

The Skills Dilemma:
Jack of All Trades or Master of One?

If you want to start taking a hard look at your own value to your organization—and consequently how far you might expect to go in it—a good place to begin is on the relatively firm ground of those measurable abilities, professional and technical, that are often called "hard" (as opposed to "soft") skills. Look back over the past year or two. What have you been doing to develop your skills? What new ones have you acquired? There are lots of ways to sharpen the tools in your toolbox—or spin stronger strands for your web, if you like that metaphor better.

Luckily, the perennially high cost of turnover means that your employer may well be eager to help you. Companies are beginning to realize that they have to offer more and better opportunities for training and development if they want to hold on to hard-to-replace employees. A recent survey of senior human-resources executives, by the American Management Association, showed that "employability training" and "technical training" took two of the top three slots on a list of factors that encourage employees to stick around. (The third one was "flexible work arrangements.")

The Saratoga Institute, trying to figure out why people change jobs, did another study that turned up a startling result: Of sixty thousand people who quit their jobs in 1998, 41 percent left because the company didn't provide enough training, tuition reimbursement, or other skill-building help. Be assured that the human-resources people in the company you work for, especially if it's a big organization, are well aware of these numbers. If these folks haven't gotten around to keeping you informed about training opportunities that are available, call the HR department or stop by and ask them. You might be surprised at the number of classes, seminars, and other programs that are just waiting for you to sign up.

Of course, you can pursue more training or education on your own, too, and often on the company's nickel. One of the most common questions posed by my readers is: Do I need an MBA to

Q. I work for a large technology company and would like to begin studying full time for an MBA in a year or two. My applications to B-schools would be helped by my supervisor's recommendation, but how can I ask him for it? He has not been happy when other people have left, although they were leaving for other jobs, not school. How should I approach him?

A. The key here is to make it clear that you intend to come back at the end of your studies, and that your intent is not to toot off to a competitor. The fact that you aren't going to start your studies for a year or two is important because it gives you and your supervisor a chance to plan a strategy, that is, which courses should you take in order to contribute the most both to the company and to your own career? And how can your department start preparing for your absence? Don't be afraid to discuss these things with your boss. Part of his job is to realize that they are important questions—not just for your future but for his.

get ahead? It's a tough one, because most of the top B-schools require you to go full time. So, assuming you can get in, you not only have to cough up $70,000 or more in tuition, but forego your salary for up to two years. In this robust job market, a two-year hiatus from the working world could cost you some pretty great opportunities—including, at least hypothetically, the chance to get in on the ground floor of a start-up—that in the long run might well be worth far more than any degree.

You could opt for a not-so-prestigious MBA program and study part time, but it's highly debatable whether a degree from Podunk U. will give you enough of an edge to repay the effort and expense of getting it. "People have rushed into MBA programs because they hear about MBAs getting the big money," David Wilson, CEO of the Graduate Management Admissions Council, told me recently. "But the 'brand name' of the school you choose is immensely important. A part-time MBA, which by definition comes from a school that isn't top-tier, is unlikely to help you make a major career shift or get you a big increase in pay." He adds: "I worry about people who go to B-school thinking it's a silver bullet and end up with an empty Coors can."

One alternative to an MBA is an executive MBA (EMBA), a condensed and intensified version of a traditional MBA that is designed to prepare managers for more and broader responsibilities while they're still doing their jobs. Merle Giles, who directs the EMBA program at the University of Illinois, says the average student is thirty-seven years old and has about fifteen years of work experience, so it's a somewhat older and more seasoned crowd than typical MBA students. EMBAs are getting mighty popular: In 1988, there were only about 55 schools offering them in the United States, but by 2000, the number had jumped to 190. (To find one near you, go to www.emba.org and click on "Member Schools.")

You might also consider getting a graduate business degree online. As of this writing, about a hundred universities offer MBAs over the Internet. The course work is just as demanding as in traditional, show-up-in-person programs, but you do it on a much more flexible schedule. Vicky Phillips, an educational consultant who has studied this phenomenon, says employers value an online degree just as highly as the other kind. Other observers, however (as of this writing), think the jury is still out on it. Mark Smith, a managing director of recruiting powerhouse Korn/Ferry International, observes: "Certainly my clients are intrigued by the idea of on-line education and willing to keep an open mind about it, but they have some concerns—not so much about the content of the course work, which is generally fine, as about the context. With a 'real, live' MBA, especially those that use the case-study method, you get a lot of interaction and exchange of ideas with classmates, including the chance to hone team-building and negotiating skills. There is some skepticism among employers about whether you can get that quality of experience in a virtual envi-

Q. I recently signed up for a six-month management-training course I'll be pursuing in my "spare time." My department head approved it enthusiastically, but the company won't pay for it until after I've completed the work. Is this standard practice?

A. Yes, it is, which is why corporate continuing-education programs are almost always called "tuition reimbursement" plans: You pay now, they reimburse you later if you don't flunk out. This is partly a sneaky way of motivating you to do your best, since your wallet gets slammed if you fail. For college and graduate courses, most companies require you to maintain a certain grade level—usually B or higher—in order to get reimbursed. Make sure you understand up front what your own company's rules are. Ask for a copy, in writing, of the full reimbursement policy— just to avoid any misunderstandings later.

ronment like a chat room." Two other possible drawbacks: An on-line sheepskin generally takes longer to earn and, since you're on your own with no set schedule of classes, you have to be fantastically efficient at organizing your time so as to get all the work done. If you'd like to look into it, a directory of on-line graduate programs is available at www.accredeteddegrees.com.

All well and good, but it helps to choose a destination before you head for the airport. How do you decide which skills to develop? This is obviously a highly individual choice and depends on where you ultimately see your career going. If, for instance, you're now in marketing but suspect you'd do better if you understood a little more about what the finance people are talking about (or vice versa), then it's clear what kind of training you should try to get. And if you'd like to change careers altogether, then of course you need as much exposure as possible to your new chosen field.

Often, though, the question is more amorphous. "I am confused by all the conflicting advice one hears about how to advance in a career," wrote one reader of my column, describing a widespread quandary. "On the one hand, I keep reading that everyone should try to gain a variety of different skills and try to get 'crossfunctional' knowledge and experience. But on the other hand, I look around and notice that the best way to be indispensable in my company is to be the resident expert in one particular—and relatively narrow—area. So which is it?"

The short answer is: both. The best approach I've seen so far—because it works no matter how much or how little your own current employer values versatility— was told to me a few years ago by Dennis Wiater, then a senior consultant at Blessing/White. Says Wiater: "People who want to build really successful careers should follow the same strategy the best companies are using for their own development. That is, focus on core competencies." Wiater contends that you need to spend four hours using and developing your strengths for each hour you spend learning a new skill or correcting a weakness. He calls this the 80/20 Formula: Spend 80 percent of your time getting even better in areas where you already excel.

This may sound counterintuitive, but it's founded in common sense. "To really add value in the long run, you need to play your own game, not somebody else's," explains Wiater. "The 80/20 strategy will continually upgrade your best, most marketable skills." He adds that if you look around, you'll notice that the most effective managers are good at recognizing their own weak spots—and delegating stuff they're not good at (or just not interested in) to people who can take up the slack. Here again, a knack for honest self-assessment comes in handy. What are your strongest and weakest points? What would you delegate if you could? It's worth noting that acknowledging a weakness is important, but obsessing over it is a mistake. "Dwelling on your weaknesses just tends to decrease motivation," says Wiater. And who needs that?

Let's say you're already devoting 80 percent of your skill-development time and attention to getting better at what you

Q. I've heard that volunteer experience looks good on a résumé, but I've never had any. How much time do I need to put in?

A. Oh, dear. Do you mean "How many hours do I have to put in to make it look as if I really cared?" I don't think there's a hard-and-fast answer to that question. But I should warn you that if you're contemplating slogging through some volunteer duty you find tiresome only because you hope it will help you to get a better job, potential employers will sense that—so you may be better off not bothering with it at all.

already do well, and you want to use the remaining 20 percent to branch out into something entirely different. This is never a bad idea, because it will make you more marketable (or promotable) in the long run. But since you're probably already deeply entrenched in one area of the company, how do you get a foot in the door in some other part of it? Many companies are making a real effort to encourage crossfunctionality—again because research shows that it keeps people from getting bored and quitting to find new challenges—but others just aren't there yet. If your employer is in the latter group, don't despair. When I asked readers of my column to describe how they sneaked across departmental boundaries, they sent in some great tales that might give you some useful ideas. Several dozen wrote to say that they accumulated terrific experience—and valuable contacts in unfamiliar parts of their companies—by working on interdisciplinary task forces and offering to help out some other department with a specific short-term project.

Others reported achieving the same thing by doing volunteer work for nonprofit groups in their communities. "Board memberships in local arts organizations taught me grant-proposal writing, financial management, and event planning, among other things," wrote a Minnesota reader named H. M. Wyman. "And volunteering for an AIDS home-care organization taught me crisis management."

It's sometimes possible to start the corporate equivalent of a student exchange program, to trade talents with other departments—but if my correspondents' experience is any guide, don't expect too much to come of it. Wrote a reader named Simeon: "A proposal for sparking a flurry of interdepartmental cooperation will probably be eagerly accepted, except that it will never actually happen. It threatens too many managers who like to maintain control over their own little fiefdoms."

To get around that, he urges "a little clandestine action," or what might be called guerilla self-training: Do some homework on the area you'd like to learn more about. Read some books, take a class or two, talk with people in that department, talk to the competition if you can. "Then, when a project comes up that you think you can contribute to, ask for a piece of it. Work on it at night, work on it during lunch, work on it when you're supposed to be doing something else. The key is to do a good job—and to just do it without making a big deal out of it," Simeon says. If it goes well, he adds, get the boss over there to ask your boss about "borrowing" you again in the future: "Enlisting the help of another manager takes the heat off you. Make it his idea and let him champion you."

Mike Aviles, who was president and CEO of sunglasses maker Foster Grant, wrote to say that he couldn't agree more. "Every company has problems. Know where they are, suggest some solutions, and do the work yourself without waiting for somebody to give you permission. If you voluntarily work on a crossfunctional project on your own time, it shows people that you have the initiative and the willingness to 'get dirty,' so they'll be more inclined to move you into a position where you can really make a difference." Aviles has done this throughout his career, and "it was this experience that positioned me to take on the job of CEO."

The Skills That Really Matter: What's Your E.Q.?

"Dear Annie" goes the letter I receive, in one variation or another, a couple of hundred times a year, "I have excellent skills and many years of successful experience at what I do, but time after time, I see people getting promoted above me who are less qualified than I am. What is really important to the senior managers who are deciding whether to move someone up in the company?" Well, life is unfair, and we've all seen the occasional instance where a stunningly mediocre, or even downright incompetent, performer gets a plum assignment or a big boost up the organization chart—because he or she plays golf with the right people, because he or she is an old college pal, or for some other reason that's annoyingly unrelated to the job at hand. Even so, most of the time, let's face it, it just happens that someone who seems "less qualified" than you are is probably very qualified indeed—but in markedly different ways.

John Rau, a former dean of the school of business at Indiana University, did a study a few years ago of eighty companies and how they chose their senior managers, including CEOs. He found that, without exception, technical skills—a brilliant engineering background, or a stellar sales record—matter far less than more conceptual, "soft" skills, such as the ability to think strategically or a talent for motivating people. "In trying to move from middle management to senior management, you're going to bump up against this very different set of requirements," says Rau.

There's lots of evidence that "soft" skills matter at every level of a company, not just the loftiest. Psychologist Daniel Goleman pioneered the notion of emotional intelligence, as distinct from the kind of intelligence that can be measured in an I.Q. test. "E.Q." is made up of attributes like self-awareness, impulse control, persistence, empathy, and social deftness. In 1998, in a fascinating book called *Working with Emotional Intelligence,* Goleman zeroed in on how these qualities, or the lack of them, can make all the difference.

Goleman based his findings on exhaustive research, including one project where he gathered "competence models"—lists of the most necessary or desired traits—for 181 different jobs in 121 companies worldwide, whose combined workforces number in the millions. "Once we separated out the purely technical skills from the emotional competencies, and compared their relative importance, we found that two out of three of the abilities considered vital for success were 'soft' skills like trustworthiness, adaptability, and a talent for collaboration," Goleman told me. That finding has been supported by other in-depth studies showing that emotional competencies are twice as important to people's success today as book learning or technical know-how.

"The rules for work are changing," Goleman says, "and we're all being judged, whether we know it or not, by a new yardstick—not just how smart we are and what 'hard' skills we have, which employers see as givens, but increasingly by how well we handle ourselves and one another. In times of extremely rapid and unpredictable change,

Q. Recently I was promoted to supervisor in my group of research engineers. Humor (the self-deprecating kind, nothing mean or off-color) has always come naturally to me and people have always responded positively to it. But now that I'm a "boss," could it be seen as frivolous or making light of our jobs? Will senior management see me as a lightweight? Your opinion, please.

A. On the contrary, humor (especially the self-deprecating kind) is a great management tool. It puts people at ease, makes you seem approachable, and is often the best way to make a point. Look, there are consultants who charge thousands of dollars a day to teach managers how to use humor in the workplace, to motivate people and boost morale—which ultimately raises productivity. If you've already got the hang of it for free, don't change a thing. As for senior management, they knew you were funny when they promoted you, right? I'd be willing to bet that figured into their decision.

like right now, emotional intelligence increasingly comes to determine who gets promoted and who gets passed over—or even who gets laid off and who doesn't."

In an era of global competition, a knack for dealing effectively with other people—which begins with a real effort to understand them—is absolutely vital to anyone who hopes to make a splash overseas. Arlene Isaacs, a New York City career coach who specializes in helping people master international assignments, notes that American managers too often suffer from cultural blindness. A typical scenario: You are trying to start up a joint venture with a Japanese firm. To meet with the head honchos of your prospective partner, you go to Tokyo alone. You don't know how to speak a word of Japanese—not even "hello" or "thank you." You don't have a proper business card, and you plop yourself down in any old seat at the conference table. You've just made four major blunders, in Japanese eyes, and while these may seem like petty details to you, before you know it, you're on the plane home and the deal is off. How did you blow it? By not knowing enough—or caring enough—to learn the basics of the culture you were flying into. Sayonara, baby. A marvelous way to avoid a debacle like this: Read a book by Roger Axtell called *Do's and Taboos Around the World*. It's a concise and often hilarious country-by-country guide to such matters as business gift giving, meeting protocol, and what to do with unfamiliar foods like sheep's

Q. After ten years as an emergency-room nurse, I recently completed an executive MBA program and am interviewing for jobs in management. Do you have any tips for me?

A. Yes. Concentrate on the fact that most people have more portable skills than they think they have. You, for instance, have technically never been a manager before. But in interviews, emphasize that you've had lots of practice at functioning well under extreme pressure, working with a diverse team of highly skilled professionals, and dealing effectively with the public under stressful conditions. These are abilities that—believe me—would be highly useful almost anywhere.

eyes and fried scorpions ("Slice them up in tiny pieces and quickly eat them").

Naturally, the ways of exotic cultures take some learning—but even here in the United States, navigating the political waters in the average company (large or small) demands a high E.Q. and a finely tuned sense of what kind of impression your habits and attitudes are making on the people around and above you. "One distinguishing characteristic of a high E.Q. is, how persuasive are you?" Goleman told me. "Can you get 'buy-in' for your ideas from the people around you? To get to a position of leadership now, you need a knack for articulating a goal and knowing how to bring everyone on board to get it accomplished. Can you take the pulse of a group, understand its unspoken currents of thoughts and concerns, and communicate with people in terms they can understand and embrace? That takes huge social intelligence, including a strongly developed sense of empathy." Another sign of high E.Q. is grace under pressure, and the ability to change direction quickly or do several tasks at once without getting frazzled or losing your sense of perspective—or your sense of humor.

Here again, as with the aspects of self-evaluation mentioned earlier, most of us tend to overrate ourselves: None of us likes to think that we are inarticulate, or

Q. For the past nine months I've been part of a team working on a project that will require us to create several new jobs (in a category that hasn't existed until now). I want one of these jobs, and I'm qualified for it. Should I tell my fellow team members now? Should I talk to our team leader or wait?

A. By all means tell your leader now that you have your eye on one of the new jobs. This will give her time to figure out how to replace you. You might also ask for her advice on how soon to mention your interest to your teammates. Maybe one or more of them has already told her they'd like one of the new positions too, in which case no one is likely to be shocked that you're thinking the same thing. Patience is great but, in this situation, delay will probably just hurt your chances.

hard to get along with, or inflexible, or oblivious to our colleagues' concerns or opinions—or if we are sometimes aware of
these flaws in ourselves, we can usually think of a reason or two
why the circumstances warranted what we did or said, or failed
to do or say. But as in the earlier phases of your self-evaluation,
the more unstintingly honest you are, the better. It's impossible
to fix or improve something that you won't allow yourself to
see. For *Fortune,* Goleman devised a somewhat condensed version
of the E.Q. test in his book, and you can take this quiz at
www.sfortune.com.

Here's a suggestion for an intriguing exercise—and maybe a
valuable reality check: Hand copies of the quiz to a few people at
work whose judgment you respect, including perhaps your immediate boss, a couple of peers who are neither your best buddies
nor biased in any other obvious way, and one or two people below
you in the organization who have worked closely with you. Ask
them to rate you according to the quiz questions. You may be surprised by their answers, and by how much the score they give you
varies from the score you give yourself. "You want to be on the
lookout especially for points of agreement, that is, areas where
your boss and your subordinates all see the same shortcomings in
you," says Goleman. "Maybe nobody thinks you listen very
well, or everybody more or less agrees that you have trouble
adapting to change. Whatever the specific problem, that's where you
need to direct your attention."

Boosting your E.Q. is not—repeat not—a matter of changing

Q. I've been offered a better job in another part of the company, with more pay and more opportunity to grow. But my current boss is a personal friend. What do I say to him?

A. If he is a friend, he will understand why you want to make this move. He may wince at first—of course he'll miss working with you (and no doubt vice versa); and maybe there'll be a twinge of envy involved, too—but then he'll congratulate you. Heck, he may even spring for a bottle of champagne. And if he doesn't, then what kind of friend is he, really?

who you are, but rather of acquiring or refining certain skills that can be learned by anyone who wants to learn them. One reader, an accomplished techie who wanted a job one level higher than the one he had, was turned down for it because the position would have involved a lot of interaction with marketing people— and, this reader wrote, "my boss says that I would just alienate them because I come across as reserved, insensitive to other people's feelings, and overly analytical. How can I change my personality?"

You can't, but that's okay. Says Colleen O'Sullivan, an executive coach for training and development behemoth AchieveGlobal: "We [coaches] don't want to stamp out anybody's authentic self, and anyway we probably couldn't do that if we tried. But people can be taught to choose different kinds of behaviors, in particular situations, that will help them get where they want to go." Once you've got a good idea of what's holding you back—either from your own self-assessment or because someone has come right out and told you—then you have a good starting point. Almost all big companies now offer self-assessment exercises, followed by appropriate training (in communications skills, for example), through their human-resources departments. "More and more, in this tight job market, companies are investing in people, especially

Q. Help! I've just been hired as office manager for an Internet start-up, and my boss asked me to research the standard dress code for Silicon Alley companies. How can I find out about this? Should I just call a few of them and ask?

A. You could, but whoever answers the phone would probably just laugh. Says Bruce Bernstein, a former high-tech entrepreneur who now runs the New York Software Industry Association: "Gee, I don't know. I met a [male] programmer the other day who was wearing blond dreadlocks and a kilt." He notes that most people at tech start-ups will "mimic what the owner is wearing. If the boss wears jeans and Grateful Dead T-shirts, then so will the employees." So I'd advise your boss to dress the way he wishes everyone else would, and hope for the best.

management-track people," says O'Sullivan. "It's in your employer's own best interest to help you with this."

At the same time, look around and find someone who seems to have a talent for winning allies and influencing people. Watch how he or she responds to given circumstances, including tone of voice, body language, and length of time spent listening as opposed to talking. Then try to emulate that person's style. To get this far in your career, you've probably already had at least one role model, and perhaps several. Why not choose one more, this time with "soft" skills in mind?

Fairly often lately, I hear from up-and-coming managers whose bosses are packing them off to a kind of coaching that human-resources types half-jokingly refer to as "charm school." This makes them nervous, because the explanations for it (if any) are usually so vague. "Often, a boss can't exactly put his or her finger on precisely what it is you are lacking—or else he or she knows exactly but is afraid of offending you by spelling it out," says Debra Benton, who coaches executives at companies like Mattel, Gillette, PepsiCo, DuPont, Hewlett-Packard, and AT&T. And people generally hesitate to ask for specifics because, says Benton, "they're worried about seeming dumb, or they're afraid that this process is in some way punitive." It isn't: "What it means is that

> **Q.** I'm American but have been working overseas for many years. When my current salary is converted into dollars, it looks very small. Now I'm trying to get a job in the U.S., and I want to be paid according to what I'm worth. In interviews, should I lie about my salary?
>
> **A.** Never, ever lie about your salary (or anything else) in a job interview. Employers understand that pay scales vary widely, as does the cost of living, in different parts of the world, or even in different regions of the United States. They won't hold your low pay against you—but they would certainly be unhappy, and you could be fired, if they discover later that you lied about it.
>
> If it would make you feel better, go ahead and explain that your salary is a good one where you've been living. But this is not likely to strike interviewers as a major news flash.

you're being groomed for a bigger job. So think of it as a compliment."

Benton has done extensive research on what changes superiors most want to see. Among them are "executive maturity," defined as "political savvy and diplomacy"; team leadership; social ability ("You may be either too buttoned-up or not buttoned-up enough"); and "technical orientation," meaning that you tend to "intellectualize facts rather than sell ideas." (In plain English, you're very bright, but you're boring people to tears.) Whatever your shortcomings, any coach worthy of the name will already have discussed them with your boss, and perhaps even a few of your peers and subordinates, so you won't have to guess what you're supposed to be learning.

In addition, Benton says, "I ask my clients to bring a list of areas where they believe they may need improvement." She then compares your list and your boss's list. "There should be some overlap between the two. If not, the problem may be rooted in a general lack of self-awareness." Believe it or not, people who have been to charm school tell me it can be fun—especially if you keep an open mind and leave your ego at the door.

Do You Deserve a Raise?

Odds are that you believe you do: Of 1,383 employees polled by CareerPath.com in early 2000, more than 50 percent said they were underpaid. (Only 2 percent said they were earning more than they were worth, and frankly I'm surprised there were that many.) In this job market, there's no question that employers are flashing some pretty impressive pay packages to retain current stars and entice new ones. This is a rising tide that lifts all boats: The more people change jobs, the more newcomers reap an open-market premium that, however gradually, boosts pay levels for everyone.

Yet one detailed survey of employees in six hundred U.S. companies found that of all employees who had recently asked for a raise, only 52 percent actually got one. If you were in the other 48 percent—or are hoping not to be—read on.

First, a statistical note: If your salary was about 4 percent higher in 2001 than in 2000, then, according to Hewitt Associates' annual survey of U.S. companies, you got an average-sized raise. For the past few years, the only employees whom companies planned to lavish with far bigger base-pay hikes were techies and engineers. Obviously, if you really want (or need) to earn a lot more, you could probably jump ship and sign on with a different company, and plenty of people are going that route. But let's say you'd like to stay in the job you've got for now—if only it paid better. Over the years I've talked with dozens of compensation consultants, executive coaches, and human-resources executives, who collectively have had a ringside seat at many thousands of salary negotiations. And over and over again, they tell me, people make the same mistakes when it comes to asking for more money. So let's start with a look at how *not* to go about it:

•**Don't neglect to analyze your worth to the whole organization, not just your part of it**. "You may be indispensable in your own department," says Michael O'Malley, a Ph.D. in psychology and a principal at William M. Mercer in New York City. He has designed compensation plans for clients like PepsiCo, Fisher-Price, and Aetna. "But is your department essential to producing the company's revenues and profits? Or are you a big frog in a pond nobody really cares about? Especially with so many companies outsourcing staff functions now, you have to look hard at how easily and cheaply your entire area could be replaced." (For a quiz that may help you analyze this, go to www.fortune.com, and search the Careers page for "Do You Deserve a Raise?")

•Don't confuse effort with contribution. "You might be working very hard, putting in lots of twelve-hour days and taking work home on weekends. But does that alone entitle you to more money?" O'Malley asks. "You have to be ruthlessly realistic about what all that effort is adding to the company's bottom line. Is it really measurably productive, or is it mostly just 'face time'?"

•Don't assume that longevity alone should get you a raise. I can't tell you how many letters I get from people who've put in ten, fifteen, or even twenty years of faithful service at some big company and are nonplussed—to put it politely— to find that relative newcomers, including some brand-new college grads, make more money than they do. This is largely because, in the struggle to attract new talent, companies are finding they're obliged to pay an open-market premium. Okay, but that's not the sole reason. Says Jay Schuster, a partner in Los Angeles pay-consulting firm Schuster-Zingheim and Associates: "These days, having a long track record with a company is not enough to justify giving you a raise. Those new people whom you suspect of earning more than you do must be in such demand for some good reason. Do they have skills that you lack?" (They wouldn't by any chance be techies, would they?) Which brings us to our next faux pas . . .

•Don't whine (at least not to your boss) about what other people are making. "I've seen people drive themselves nuts trying to peg their own pay to what somebody else in a similar job, or the same job, was or is making," says Peter LeBlanc, president of the LeBlanc Group, a human-resources research company headquartered in Raleigh, North Carolina. "And by the way, they're always comparing themselves with someone whose pay is higher than theirs. Nobody ever says, 'Gee, maybe what I'm doing isn't really worth that much money.' "

LeBlanc points out that with the advent of the pay structure known as broadbanding, wide disparities in salary among people doing similar jobs—say, a range of $40,000 to $70,000—have become much more common: "Pay today isn't determined by job description or title but by experience, contribution, and special skills."

Besides, notes Robin Ryan, a career coach and author in Renton, Washington, "saying you deserve a raise because someone else got one just infuriates most bosses." Eeek.

•Never say you should get a raise because you need the money. "We had one fairly senior guy try to negotiate a huge bonus because he needed to pay off some gambling debts," the chief of human resources at a large manufacturing company told me recently. (She asked to remain anonymous.) "He doesn't work here anymore." Far more commonly, people will blather on about how they need a raise because they just bought a new house, or had a baby, or have two kids in college at the same time and are subsisting on franks and beans. Says Robin Ryan, "This kind of argument will fall on deaf ears. Your personal finances are your own business." What's worse, if you can't even make your own checkbook balance, what does that say about your business acumen? Nothing you'd want broadcast around the office, that's for sure.

•If you really don't want to quit and go elsewhere for more money, do not bluff. Let's suppose you've got a solid job offer from a competitor—the temptation to use it as a negotiating tool may be hard to resist. Trouble is, that tool is a sledgehammer, and bosses understandably resent it. Often they resent it so much that even if they can ill afford to lose you, they respond by saying, "Sounds like a great opportunity. We'll miss you. And by the way, clean out your desk by four o'clock. Here's somebody from security to escort you."

Oops. Now what?

All right, so how *do* you increase your chances of getting the raise you want? Try these steps:

•**Take an objective look at whether you're really worth more than you're making.** It never hurts to have a clear idea of how your current pay compares with what similar jobs are paying elsewhere. This information isn't hard to get if you're willing to do a bit of discreet scouting around. Look at job postings and chat rooms on the Net, get hold of salary surveys by professional associations in your field. For an excellent look at how your pay compares with the average in your field and at your rank, in your very own zip code, go to www.Salary.com.

However, says Michael O'Malley, "regardless of what is going on in the larger job market, ask

> Q. After two years in my current job, my responsibilities have increased tremendously. Five months ago I requested a raise and was told I was being reviewed for a salary adjustment. But I've heard nothing. How long do you think I should wait for a response? I feel I've been extremely patient.
>
> A. Indeed you have, but come on. *Five months?* There are times in life when silence is a clear answer, and the answer is no. This may just be one of those times. Go back and ask again—and this time be sure to document in detail (and in writing) exactly why you believe you're worth more.

for a raise only if you have produced some tangible improvement since your last pay hike." This could be a slick new-product introduction, a brilliant cost-cutting campaign, or anything else that has contributed some measurable benefit to the company. If you've taken on more responsibility since your last raise, spell out exactly what your added contributions have been. Yes, your boss ought to be well aware of all this already but, notes Steve Gross, Mercer's national practice leader for compensation: "It's frequently the reliable strong performers who are taken for granted. In my seminars, I ask people, 'Who here feels appreciated by their employer?' After the big laugh, only about one-third of the hands in the room go up." Don't be afraid to blow your own horn, as long as you can back up your case with facts.

•If you're nervous, practice your pitch with a friend. Many people are so uncomfortable talking about or asking for money that they freeze up or else go into a stream-of-consciousness ramble that leaves their audience mystified. If this applies to you, coach Robin Ryan recommends that you prepare exactly what you plan to say and how you want to say it, and then do some role-playing with a friend who can pretend to be your boss. Note: This may need to be a very patient friend. "Go over it several times, as many times as you need, until you are comfortable and confident," says Ryan. She also suggests that you try to anticipate what objections your boss may raise, and practice calmly responding to those.

•Don't be angry. Says Steve Gross, "If you really feel underpaid, talk to your boss before you've had a chance to stew about it and get mad, because in anger you may say things you don't mean—and can't take back." Michael

O'Malley agrees: "Lots of people feel awkward about seeming to make demands, so they never mention to their boss
that they think they're underpaid. Then, by the time they
finally get up the nerve to broach the subject, they blow up
and insist on instant results."

A far better approach, O'Malley says, is to have a series of
casual conversations over time, in which you pose a few questions
like "Gee, do you think I'm still in the right pay grade, since I took
on the whole Fantod project?" or "Did you know it's been almost
fourteen months since my last salary review? Time sure flies!"
Explains O'Malley, "You need to prime the pump a little and alert
your boss that you are thinking about this, so that he or she has a
chance to focus on it and do something about it. Never forget that
in most big companies it takes three to six months to get a raise
through the system. Nothing is going to happen by next
Tuesday."

He adds: "One other thing I always tell people is that threats
and ultimatums do not work. A belligerent attitude about money
will do a lot of damage to your career in the long run. You want
your boss to pay you more because she thinks you're worth more,
not just because she wants you to shut up and go away."

•**Pick your moment carefully.** Every compensation guru
I've ever met has emphasized this, so I'd be remiss not to pass
it along: In this, as in so many things, timing is crucial. Let's
say you've tallied up all your accomplishments for the past
year or so, come up with some airtight arguments for why
you're worth more money, and practiced your pitch until you
could recite it in your sleep. You show up in your boss's doorway, all psyched for the Big Talk. But then you realize that he
is deep in a frantic phone call about some corporate calamity

that has just befallen: A major client flew the coop, a huge product shipment went astray somewhere in Nebraska, the chief financial officer has been indicted for securities fraud, or whatever. Here's what you do. You say, "I can see this isn't a good time for us to talk. I'll come back later." Summon up a neutral, reassuring sort of smile, if you can. Then turn around and leave.

"You have to be a little bit patient in choosing the best time to ask for a raise," says Steve Gross. "It may even take you a couple of months to find a moment when your boss is receptive and ready to focus on what you're saying. Don't corner him when he's got half an hour to catch a plane."

Okay, now let's think the unthinkable: You've done everything right, but nevertheless the answer is "no." Stay cool. "No matter how fabulous you are, not every salary request gets approved," observes Robin Ryan. Maybe a raise for you is just not in the budget right now. That doesn't mean it never will be: "Once you've asked, people know what you want. If you continue to be a great performer, you may well be rewarded for it a few months down the road."

That's especially true if you're willing to ask your boss what you need to do in order to get the pay you want. Says Mel Stark, a vice

> **Q.** Can I ask for another raise even though I just got one at my last review three months ago? (It was a very measly raise.) I've gotten a promotion since then, but no extra money.
>
> **A.** You can ask, of course—but I wouldn't. By giving you a better title, the people above you are letting you know that you're valued, meaning that another raise is probably in the offing before too long. If you don't want to wait, sit down with your immediate supervisor and work out some kind of incentive-pay plan entitling you—if you produce results—to a higher salary or a bonus. Tying a bigger paycheck to specific goals achieved always makes it easier for your boss to defend his decision, should anyone challenge him on it.

president at human-resources consulting giant Hay Group: "Why not find out what further value you can add to earn more money? Ask for very specific goals. Then meet or exceed them."

One big trend is in your favor: The Hewitt pay survey shows that U.S. companies, while doling out those measly 4.2 percent average raises, are budgeting a lot more these days for performance-related pay, often called variable or incentive pay, which jumped 16 percent between 1999 and 2000. Bob Gore, a principal at Towers Perrin in Boston, says pay-for-performance has become so popular that "if you ask to be paid more on the basis of results, and then achieve great results, I'd be dumbfounded if any decent employer didn't reward you accordingly."

And if that doesn't work, cheer up. You can always go out in search of your own open-market premium.

Networking for Fun and Profit

I really should reveal a personal bias here: I loathe the word "networking" and wish someone would come up with a snappy synonym for it. (I've tried, but so far inspiration hasn't struck.) For now, the N word is convenient shorthand for the lifelong process of bumping into a large number of people, more or less randomly, who are a step or two outside of your usual workaday sphere and who might be able to do your career some good sometime, or vice versa.

This is a harmless, indeed necessary, thing—and it gets more essential the further you go in your career. Consider: The Bureau of Labor Statistics reports that fewer than 20 percent of all working Americans found their current job through a friend, relative, old school chum, or other personal connection. By contrast, among executives (defined as senior managers earning more than $100,000 a year), 72 percent—well over three times the average—landed in their current position thanks to an acquaintance they had cultivated at some point in the past.

Still, the N word itself has taken on such connotations of calculated, manipulative false friendliness that I cringe whenever I come across it. A few months ago, somebody sent me a self-help videotape about networking that promised to teach the viewer "how to turn contacts into friends and friends into connections." Yuck. I'd like to think that people choose their friends on the basis of how much fun they are or how interesting, or possibly how hilarious—or all three and then some—but not because of the potential for some commercially advantageous "connection." Friendship is worth more than that. I don't mean to suggest, of course, that friends can't do each other the odd business favor, or that people one meets professionally can't turn into real friends over time (sure they can!). But I'd prefer not to have to wonder, every time someone seems to like hanging out with me, what it is they're really after. Wouldn't you?

An even bigger paradox, in any discussion of how best to network, is that there really is not much point in trying to strategize about it, because the most effective networking can't be planned. It's pure serendipity. You know the kind of encounter I mean: Your next-door neighbor has a cousin, to whom you're introduced at a backyard barbecue, who mentions after a couple of beers that if he seems preoccupied, it's because he urgently needs to find an engineer who can write code for a particular kind of software that your brother practically invented—and your brother just told you on the phone a few days ago that he's getting bored with his current job. A couple of phone calls later, presto, your neighbor's cousin is all set to lavish stock options on your brother (hey, doesn't he owe you a finder's fee?) and everybody's happy. This is how it's supposed to work—a sort of efficient-market theory (which assumes a constant free flow of information) operating on

sheer random word of mouth—
and every now and then it's
magic. True networking is a kick
precisely because it's so haphazard. In this sense, it's like love.
You can't go out looking for it
without seeming (or in fact
being) a little bit desperate; but
when you happen to stumble
across it—wow.

Since you rarely know in
advance when an important networking event will occur, the
main thing is to be paying attention when it does. Career coach
Nancy Friedberg says that once
you've reached a point in your
career where you've accomplished a few noteworthy things,
"There are people who are aware
of you and maybe even watching
you, whether you know it or
not—people in your business,
your peers, your boss's peers,

Q. I've been trying to find a
new job, and gave as references several people whom I've
known for years, both from work
and through networking groups.
One of these people, much to my
surprise, has been saying negative
things about me to prospective
employers. How do I handle this?

A. Assuming you know which
reference it is who's bad-
mouthing you, it would be worth
a phone call to that person just to
say that you are wondering why
your own assessment of your past
performance doesn't seem to
mesh with his or hers—and can
he or she suggest some areas for
improvement? If you resist the
urge to get mad about this, you
might learn something valuable.

If you don't know for sure
which reference has been tripping
you up, replace all of them with a
whole set of new ones. This is one
situation where knowing lots and
lots of people can really come in
handy.

your opposite number at one or more competing companies. Take
a few moments to figure out who these people are. Then, when
you happen to run into them, don't talk about the weather."

Instead, Friedberg helps her clients to formulate an eight-word
summary of their best stuff: "This could be a brief description of
your latest successful project, or of what you want to achieve with
your next one." If you can't fit it into eight words, try to keep it
under twenty. Then work it into the conversation, Friedberg says,

"in an elevator, over lunch, at a conference, at a trade association meeting." Why? "Once you have built a reputation for yourself that is distinct from your company's, your company sees you as more valuable. And, in fact, you are."

Luckily for the shy and self-effacing among us, good networking can sometimes be as easy as answering the phone. A question I often get comes from readers who are happy (and busy) in their current jobs, so they decline to talk to executive recruiters who call, for fear of starting a rumor that they're "looking." Still, they can't help but wonder, as one high-tech manager besieged by headhunters put it: "What am I missing by not at least saying 'hi'?" If this applies to you, too, what you are missing is simply this: When you need a good recruiter in your corner—as someday you might—he or she won't be in a big hurry to say "hi" to you either. So by all means do talk with these folks. It doesn't need to take up much of your time, but you can learn an awful lot of useful stuff even in a five-minute chat.

For one thing, if a headhunter is trying to fill a position similar to yours at another, possibly competing, company, you can get some useful insights into how business is going over there by asking what, exactly, the ideal candidate would bring to the job. Is e-commerce experience a must? Are there other areas of expertise that would be helpful? What's the approximate salary range, and is there incentive pay involved? What about stock options?

Why should the recruiter divulge all this to you? Well, because you're going to help out. Since you're not "looking" right now, you're going to think of at least two people who fit the bill and who might be feeling a little restless in their current jobs. You know two people like that, don't you? Heck, you might know ten or twelve: Tell the headhunter you'd like to check with them. Then do it. Hope something sparks, and go on about your business. If even one of your matchmaking suggestions works out, your own career network could grow exponentially. Over the years, people do recall who did them a favor at a crucial moment—or at least who tried.

Recruiters are also a fantastic source of information about pay. If I had a dime for every time somebody wrote to me to ask, "How can I tell if I'm being paid fairly [or competitively, which amounts to the same thing] for what I'm doing?" I'd be writing this on a warm beach somewhere. There are, as mentioned earlier in this chapter, several ways to figure out how your pay stacks up against others'. But it's also hugely helpful to have a couple of savvy recruiters you can call and ask for a candid, knowledge-

Q. What do you think of professional groomers who train or teach you interview skills, etc., and then promote your résumé, promising you a job?

A. You should always beware of anyone who promises to get you a job, because that is a guarantee that no reputable recruiter would make. I suspect these "groomers" you refer to are charging you a fee (or trying to), right? That's another warning sign. Any headhunter you'd care to get mixed up with is being paid by the employer, not the would-be employee. As for paying someone to help you polish your résumé, all good-size bookstores and public libraries stock a dozen or more excellent, easy-to-follow guides to résumé writing. Why not just take a good look at one of those?

able update of what your job is really worth right now. Of course, you're likely to get better information if you're not a stranger calling out of the blue. One good turn does earn another—and that is more true with headhunters than with just about anybody else. After all, their livelihood depends on finding the best person to fill a given job. It might not be you right now, but as Scarlett O'Hara said, tomorrow is another day.

Arguably the most important, and most effective, networking anyone can do is also—at least it seems from where I sit—the most often overlooked and neglected, and that is simply keeping in close touch with your own boss. It's ironic, with all that one hears about the decline of traditional hierarchies and the flattening of organizations into more egalitarian arrangements, that so many people are so intimidated by the people directly above them that they can't bring themselves to initiate a conversation. Are bosses so scary? Why? To paraphrase Shakespeare's Shylock, if you tickle them, do they not laugh? If you prick them, do they not bleed? Well, all right, don't try either of these experiments next time you see your boss, but you get my drift.

I often hear from people who feel that after a few years in the same job, they've hit a dead end where they're no longer learning anything or tackling new challenges but are just going through the same old motions. The question invariably is, "Should I look for a new job outside the company, even though I'd rather stay?" And when I e-mail these folks back and ask, "Have you discussed this with your boss?" the answer is almost always "no."

This reticence is self-defeating. A big part of any manager's job is, or ought to be, keeping an eye on the career development of the people who report to him or her—if only, with employee retention always such a thorny problem, to prevent their best underlings from wandering off to a competitor. Don't be afraid to talk with your boss about where you'd like to see your career go, and how quickly.

It's a subject that should natu-

> **Q.** I am stuck in a dead-end job. It used to be fun, but I'm bored stiff and would like to move to another area of the company. However, I see no current openings, and my boss wants me to keep working for him. He is a "lifer" who thinks that years-of-service is more important than moving up. Should I leave the company?
>
> **A.** Have you really asked around all over the company and found nothing available that you'd like to try? If so, then leave. In the words of the philosopher Nietzsche, "Is life not a hundred times too short for us to bore ourselves?" There has never been a better time than right now to find a new job, so start looking. And try to avoid companies that encourage "lifers." Such places tend to be full of dead ends, and the last thing you want is to get stuck in another one.

rally interest him or her but, in another of the work world's many new paradoxes, you'll probably have to be the first to broach the subject. Says Deborah Bright, president of New York City–based career-counseling firm Bright Enterprises, which numbers among its clients Pfizer, MetLife, the New York Stock Exchange, and the Professional Golfers' Association: "Bear in mind that everyone is so busy these days, and has so much on his plate already, that—if you feel your career has stalled and no one above you cares—it may just be a case of 'out of sight, out of mind.' If you say nothing about your dissatisfaction, people will just assume everything is fine, and you'll stay frustrated—or else you'll get another offer somewhere and quit, leaving everyone scratching their heads over why you left."

As with asking for a raise, lots of people seem to be reluctant to talk frankly because they don't want to seem like complainers. That instinct is sound. "In discussing your career with your boss, it's not so much what you say but how you say it," observes Bright. First, figure out what you'd rather be doing, and how or where in the company you might be able to do it. Bright recommends choosing fast-track areas where you think your skills would allow you to make a real contribution, and where you're pretty sure you won't be as bored as you are now. Then, when you talk with your boss, "the emphasis should be on asking for guidance on how you can contribute more and make a positive difference—not 'I'm bored, I'm overqualified for what I'm doing, I deserve better.' In fact, use the word 'I' as sparingly as possible." Incidentally, this last point is great advice in lots of situations.

The ability to make your thoughts known to the people above you—and get some insight into theirs—is never more essential than during a merger or other change of command at the top, when you may suddenly find yourself reporting to a whole new bunch of senior managers who don't know you from Adam, or vice versa. "In this situation, 90 percent of your colleagues will be hiding in their offices, moaning, groaning, and panicking," says Paul Sniffin, managing partner in executive-coaching firm Oi Partners in Baltimore. "Don't be one of them." Rather, he says, "take the time to see the organization through the new bosses' eyes. What is important to them? You have to be proactive about this. Go and 'interview' the people above you. Listen especially hard for any mention of a problem you might be able to help solve. Then get to work on it."

Sniffin also suggests bringing your résumé up to date—not just in case you end up leaving (voluntarily or not) but because "it will make you focus on what you have accomplished. Reconstruct your history of achievement—you computerized your department, you designed a hot product, or whatever you're most proud of—and then find ways of subtly letting management know what you've done." Many people make the mistake of assuming that a new boss has already heard all about their past glories. Not so.

The tricky part here is to point up what you've contributed with-

---

Q. At my company's annual holiday party a few months ago, I drank a lot more than usual, and late in the evening I was dancing with the wife of a colleague and we got a little carried away. This was a mutual attraction that we acted on in a moment of stupidity, but it is keeping me awake nights, because her husband has just been promoted and is now my boss. What if she told him about "us"? Should I say anything to him? Or just pretend it never happened? Or start updating my résumé?

A. For crying out loud, why say anything? If your boss's wife has kept mum about this, um, incident, you'd be doing no one any favors by bringing it to his attention. You may simply have gotten away with a huge faux pas here. Now let it go, and get back to work.

The whole subject of drinking (or not) comes up in my mail from readers with some regularity, so let me propose a good rule: Drink alcohol only when you are among friends—and corporate politics being what they are, most people have far fewer friends at an office party than they think they do.

out seeming to dwell on the past. "You want to come across as flexible and open to change," says Marie Jennings, a career counselor at Russell, Montgomery & Associates in Nashville. "Shooting down untried ideas—'Oh, that will never work here'—will not make you part of the new team."

Important as it is to communicate upward, be sure you don't forget to network with the people around you who control the day-to-day nuts and bolts of the business. Robert Kelley, a professor at Carnegie Mellon University, has spent years studying how people attain superstar status at topnotch companies like 3M, Hewlett-Packard, and Merck. Among his findings: It does matter who you know—and who knows you—but while average performers aim to get ahead by socializing with the boss, stars forge strong ties to the people Kelley calls "knowledge mavens," those often obscure but powerful people (including certain techies) who can help you figure out faster, better ways of doing critical tasks. All the stars in Kelley's study have made it a habit to identify these folks, get to know them—even if it's just for the odd casual chat in the hallway—and see what develops.

Now, before we leave the topic of the N word (at least for now), a few thoughts about those networking opportunities par excellence: office parties. Despite the fact that these usually present a ready-made chance to meet and greet coworkers whom you may not see very often—or maybe because of that—lots of people detest office parties. (You know who you are. Every year between Thanksgiving and New Year's, I hear from thousands of you.) Maybe it's the weird hybrid atmosphere of forced merriment coupled with covert corporate maneuvering or the fact that you feel obliged to act as if you were having a good time when what you're really doing is—let's face it—working. I don't know anyone who has never dreaded the prospect of an office party (do you?), although most of us manage to grin and bear it, and may even end up glad we went. But apart from the run-of-the-mill apprehension that often precedes these wingdings, there are two intractable reasons why some people will do just about anything to avoid going to one.

The first reason, as you might have guessed, is simple shyness. Some people who are terrific at interacting with their colleagues one-on-one nevertheless come down with a bad case of heebie-jeebies at the thought of mingling in a large group—and maximum mingling is, of course, the whole point here. Part of the trouble is that unlike during the average workday, at a party you're expected to let your real personality show. It's not unlike an actor stepping out of a scripted role and "playing himself," and for some people that can be scary. The great actor Sir Laurence Olivier never suffered from stage fright in his work; but he revealed in his 1982 autobiography, *Confessions of an Actor,* that social gatherings made him so anxious that on more than one occasion he fainted dead away and had to be carried from the room.

Over the years, I've gotten many letters from readers seeking tips on how to overcome their shyness and learn to make small talk with peers, bosses, and customers. The coaches I've asked have all pointed out that small talk is in fact not small at all: It's a vital chance to get to know what's really going on in the organization and to scope out people's real thoughts and concerns, which is especially crucial with customers, both internal and external. The secret is to ask open-ended questions that elicit more than a yes or no answer—"What's new over in marketing?" is always better than "Everything going all right over there?"—and then let the other person do most of the talking. Most people like talking about themselves, and if you listen attentively to what they say, you'll not only lose your own self-consciousness, but you'll get a reputation as a great conversationalist as well.

It might help to bear in mind that nobody is ever totally at ease in these situations, even if they seem to be. Says Deborah Bright, who has helped many an executive client beat the preparty jitters: "Even people who know how to 'work the room' so well that they make it look effortless are very well aware that they are being judged, and so is everyone else there, so that really relaxing—the way you would at home with a loved one and a glass of wine—is out of the question." What's the only real difference between you, O Shy One, and the masters of mingling? They've had more practice. "The more business socializing you make yourself do, the more it will become second nature," Bright says. "And you may even come to enjoy it. But even if you never do, just keep in mind that this is like any other part of your job, whether it's putting together a

> **Q.** My wife and I would like to host a dinner party for the department heads in my division, but we're wondering: Is it all right to ask them not to bring their children? We've been to several quasi-business functions, including office parties, where small children ran rampant. Our house isn't childproof (we collect antique porcelain), so the prospect is making us nervous—yet we don't want to seem "anti-child." Your thoughts?
>
> **A.** It seems to me that you are not at all antichild but simply anti-damage-and-destruction. Your best bet might be to reserve a table at the best restaurant in town and send out invitations to each department head "and guest" (or spouse, if you know his or her name). I'd be surprised if anyone showed up with toddlers in tow—but even if they do, at least your porcelain is safe.

budget for your department or evaluating your employees. You have to do it, it has real value to the company, and being thrilled with it is not—repeat not—a prerequisite for being good at it."

Now, let's suppose the situation is somewhat different. Let's say you're really not shy at all in large gatherings, such as trade association meetings or conferences, but you still loathe going to parties at your own company. The way an organization throws a bash is a pretty good indicator of its overall culture: Is the party buttoned-down or bacchanalian, dry or booze drenched, elegant or rip-roaring? If it's your company's style of party giving that bugs you, if it's just not at all your idea of a good time, think hard about whether you're working in the right place. One manager at a large midwestern manufacturer wrote me to complain that her employer was always throwing "casual but mandatory" parties that ended with "everyone getting drunk and making idiots of themselves." This made her so uncomfortable that she always found herself standing apart from the festivities and, more often than not, finding some excuse to leave early.

Fine—but in some companies "getting drunk and making idiots of themselves" is an important, if silly, bonding ritual, so that being a disapproving wallflower can prove (rightly or wrongly) a real career impediment over time. Based on this manager's distaste for these parties, I predicted that she wouldn't be working there for very long. She wrote me six months later to say that she had a new job in a company whose culture—and more subdued style of partying—suited her much better.

After our original exchange appeared in the column, several readers sent terrific suggestions on how to extract the best possible results from an inherently dumb situation. One clever project manager at a software company reported sipping Snapples all through a beer-soaked company picnic—and then appointing himself the designated driver to give his boss and another senior executive a lift to their respective homes. He used the drive to "tell them my ideas for new products, and the next day, amazingly, they both remembered everything I said. I'm now running the team that is developing two of those ideas."

Now, that's great networking.

The Grass Is Always Greener: Knowing When It's Time to Move On

You've probably seen the statistics. Thanks to a severe shortage of skilled workers, dizzying numbers of Americans are changing jobs. The trend is especially pronounced among the young and restless: The Bureau of Labor Statistics reports that the average worker now goes through nine jobs by age thirty. In high-tech the average job tenure has shrunk to thirteen months (from eighteen months in 1998). A recent study by the Employee Benefit Research Institute says that workers aged twenty-five to thirty-four change jobs about every three years. And wanderlust cuts across generational boundaries. Among workers aged fifty-five to sixty-four, for instance, the average stay in one job has dropped from seventeen years to twelve.

Things have changed quite a bit since the late nineties when unemployment was so low that companies paid juicy premiums to people recruited from outside. In tough economic times, fewer employees change jobs by choice, and layoffs free up lots of formerly scarce talent. Yet there are always fields—sales, for example, and many areas of high-tech that require advanced training and certification—where demand keeps outstripping supply so that job-hopping is as common as it ever was.

It rarely makes sense to quit a job just because everyone else is

Q. Even though I'm only twenty-four, I've already had three jobs. Now, I'm completely dissatisfied where I am, but I'm afraid employers will see me as a "job hopper" if I leave. To make a long story short, I left my last job because of a career change from human resources to Web development—and now am earning half of what comparable "Web dev" jobs pay in my industry, plus getting no support from this unreasonable bureaucracy. I know no job is perfect, but I am so unhappy here that I hate coming to work in the morning. What should I do?

A. Quit. Here are two good reasons: (1) No potential employer is going to hold it against you that you are chucking a job that pays only half the going rate (what kind of chump would stay?); and (2) nobody twenty-four years old should hate going to work in the morning. Someday, due to unfortunate circumstances (a big downturn in the economy, for instance), you may find yourself stuck in a job you dislike with no real way out—although I devoutly hope you won't. Regardless, age twenty-four is decades too soon to start.

doing it. And I hear plenty of laments from readers who changed jobs, sometimes more than once, and now wish they hadn't. Sometimes this is because the switch turned out to be a leap from the frying pan into the fire (from a tyrannical, irrational old boss to a new boss who is even worse, for instance). Occasionally the regrets spring from worries about long-term financial security. A reader named Keith, who is thirty-four and has worked for eight different companies since he graduated from college, notes that although his pay has risen with each jump, he has no pension, "because I never stayed in any one place long enough to get vested. In your twenties, retirement seems so far away, or you think you'll be a dot.com millionaire by then. Now I'm trying to save like crazy to make up for lost time."

Still, if you're really dissatisfied with what you're doing, it can't do any harm to seek something better. But what if you're on the fence, not really thrilled where you are but not having a terrible time either? How can you tell if you'd be better off elsewhere? This question arises most frequently with people whose higher-ups have promised them some sort of career advancement—a bigger project to run, a transfer to a more challenging area—that just hasn't happened yet. Should you keep waiting for the big break? Or make a clean break and move on? Even in this less-than-perfect job market, patience can look like a liability.

Try not to be in too big a hurry. Lois Frankel, president of Corporate Coaching International in Pasadena, California, has done extensive research on the most common career mistakes managers make. One of them is equating delay with defeat. If a promotion or other step forward is in all likelihood coming, but taking longer than you'd like, Frankel suggests making the best possible use of whatever time is left to you in your current position. She has found that many people overlook opportunities to broaden their skills—and hence ultimately make themselves more marketable—right where they are.

"Let's say you've launched a great new product and you're impatient for your next big challenge," she says. "Great! You've proven that you can get something up and running. But keeping it on an even keel and achieving something new in an operation that is already successful requires a whole different set of skills. Why not work on developing those?" The most versatile, well-rounded managers, those who eventually make it to the very top, have had lots of practice at making a good thing even better. "Is there really nothing more you can do, no new heights you can reach, no new records you can set, in the job where you already are?" asks Frankel. "To be honest, that's hard to believe."

William Morin, a longtime luminary in the career-counseling field, was CEO of giant management-development firm Drake Beam Morin for eighteen years before starting his own consulting practice, Manhattan-based WJM Associates. He has coached executives at more than two hundred Fortune 500 companies, including General Motors, Kodak, IBM, and Merrill Lynch. Morin has devised a seven-question quiz to help you decide whether to stay with your current employer (answer "true" or "false"):

•Your boss likes you and is your advocate in the company.

•Your boss is doing well in his or her own career.

•You've been promoted within the past two years.

•You're vested or near vesting, and building the value of your benefits, 401(k), pension plan, etc.

•The company is thriving and has clear growth opportunities.

•You're being fairly paid and given average or better-than-average raises. (Remember, the average white-collar raise these days is about four percent annually.)

•You have had a discussion with your boss within the past year that indicated that you are valued and that he or she sees where you might be headed in the company.

If your answer to all, or almost all, of these statements is "true," Morin advises, then you should stay where you are for now, and keep picking up new skills that will make you an even hotter property later. "It's always best not to get lazy or complacent, of course. Do keep a weather eye on other opportunities as they come along," says he. "But you don't have to be in a big rush. Patience is a virtue, especially when it comes to your career." It's an unfashionable view, for sure, but one well worth pondering.

Tom Jones, principal consultant for a California-based management-development firm called WORx, offers another yardstick that might help you decide whether to seek greener pastures. "When clients ask me if they should stay or go, I tell them to consider whether they already have three things," Jones says. "First, the opportunity to make a positive difference. Second, opportunities to grow and develop both personally and professionally. And third, the chance to do things that others cannot or will not do." If any one of the three is missing, he says, you're probably in the wrong place.

Let's say your current job flunks Morin's test, or Jones's, or both, and you're about to grab what looks like a much juicier offer. Congratulations! Now, I don't want to rain on your picnic (or put a harsh on your mellow; isn't that a great expression?). But once you've had the celebration, please stop for a moment to consider a truly unnerving statistic: About 40 percent of new management hires fail within the first eighteen months. That's according to studies by the Center for Creative Leadership in Greensboro, North Carolina, and by executive search and coaching firm Manchester Inc. Yikes! So, for every five managers who change jobs, two will flop in their new roles and find themselves job hunting again in less than two years—becoming what human-resources people refer to as "revolving door hires." Manchester, in a survey of 826 companies nationwide, defines failure as "being terminated for performance, performing significantly below expectations, or voluntarily resigning from the position"—usually with a not-so-subtle push from above.

Not surprisingly, considering that it costs a company roughly twice a manager's annual pay to replace him or her, hordes of consultants, coaches, and gurus of various stripes have been studying the question of why managers fail. The unanimous conclusion: Personal chemistry and cultural compatibility—that old black magic called "fit," or how well your overall management style meshes with your employer's—are all-important. Asked to identify the reasons why freshly hired managers flame out, the executives in Manchester's survey said that "failure to build good relationships with peers and subordinates" is the culprit an overwhelming 82 percent of the time. The three other big stumbling blocks: confusion or uncertainty about what higher-ups expect (58 percent), a lack of internal political skills (50 percent), and an inability to achieve the two or three most important objectives of their new jobs (47 percent).

Sometimes the fit between a given corporate culture and a new manager is so abysmally bad—often because of unclear or contradictory signals at the outset about just what the new manager is supposed to be accomplishing—that people get sacked for doing exactly what they thought the job was about. Executive coach Bill Morin tells of one company that spent $280,000 finding and hiring a "change agent" and then canned the guy because he wanted to make too many changes.

Then, too, sometimes a management style that works beautifully in one company becomes the kiss of death in a new job. Michael Wakefield, a senior executive trainer at the Center for Creative Leadership, gives the example of a driven, ambitious, take-no-prisoners sort of person who succeeds in one place by pushing others hard—and then goes to another company to find that his style is considered so abrasive that nobody can stand working with him. "The strengths and skills that got you to the dance may not get you danced with once you're there," Wakefield notes. "It's insidious too because, once the source of your old confidence is taken away—that is, when you begin to realize you've stopped succeeding—you start to get very disoriented." You may also get very fired.

How can you avoid this nightmare? People who've analyzed this situation say that most people who fail in a new job have made two big mistakes. First, they've been so bewitched by a great-sounding job offer, especially if it

Q. I was interviewed recently for a job at a consulting firm that traditionally puts candidates through four rounds of interviews. I really believe I have the skills this company wants, and I know I could contribute a great deal. But I just found out I was "screened out" on the second round. Can I reapply to this firm in the future or should I just forget it and move on? I still really want to work there.

A. This may sound corny but it's true: Persistence does often win out, and sometimes there is nothing more powerful than desire. You have nothing to lose, and maybe a lot to gain, by writing a letter that reiterates in precise, but not overwhelming, detail just why you would like a chance to try one more time. Put particular emphasis on how you believe the company could benefit from hiring you. Ask for a brief meeting in the near future. This kind of don't-count-me-out initiative has been known to move mountains, even if not overnight. If you give up now, however, you'll never know. I have a quote from General George Patton taped to my office wall. It says: "You are not beaten until you admit it. Hence don't."

pays heaps of money, that they haven't stopped to examine (or admit) what they really want out of the new position, whether it's balancing family and career, or developing new areas of expertise, or generally achieving whatever made changing jobs seem attractive in the first place. "It's so easy to get seduced by a terrific offer," says Lois Frankel at Corporate Coaching International. "But how do you know if a new job will meet your expectations—and hence whether you're likely to succeed in it—if you don't know what your expectations are?"

The second big blunder, the experts say, is not doing enough homework, including not asking enough hard questions in job interviews. In a typical one-hour interview, you should be asking between ten and twenty questions. What kind of questions should these be? Luckily the Manchester survey gives some specific clues to what will help you identify the best fit. Among the hiring managers polled, 76 percent urge you to find out what specific results will be expected of you in your first year in the new job, and 64 percent recommend that you ask for a detailed timetable of what is supposed to happen when. Finding out how often the people above you want progress reports and provide feedback (45 percent) also couldn't hurt. Will you be monitored weekly, monthly, quarterly, annually? Are you okay with that?

While you're at it, pay close attention to the ambience of the place. Says Bob Lee, a cofounder of executive recruiters Lee Hecht Harrison and former president of the Center for Creative Leadership, "Take a look around at the physical signs. For example, is the company set up with a lot of small offices, closed doors, walls, and barriers? Are there meeting rooms and common areas or are people not expected to get together often in small groups? Do people stop to talk to each other in the hallways or is there an unnatural hush?" To put it simply, are you comfortable with the atmosphere, or does it seem either too stifled or too much of a free-for-all? One thing's for sure: If you can't picture yourself feeling at ease day-to-day in whatever the environment is, you're unlikely to do well there.

You can ask questions about culture, too. Human-resources consultant Phil Cooke suggests that you try to "learn how values are reflected in the company. What issues keep managers awake at night? How does the company celebrate success? Does it reward risk? How?" It's fashionable these days for companies to tell you that they value open communication. But, he says, "dig deeper. Ask for examples of how this is actually demonstrated." Cooke also suggests that if you have to cool your heels in a reception area before a job interview, use the time to chat with the receptionist or with an assistant sent to escort you. Ask why he or she came to work for the company and what makes it a good place to work. If you get a blank stare or an evasive answer, well, that tells you something, doesn't it?

Randy Harris, senior vice president of human resources at Nextel Communications in Reston, Virginia, has changed jobs successfully several times. "A crucial question is, am I going to have the resources to do what I'm expected to do here, including the time it will take to do it?" Harris says. "The kind of disconnect that causes failure is, your new boss is expecting a certain result within three months, but you suspect it will take a year. If you're trying so hard to make a good impression that you neglect to hammer out a workable plan right at the outset, you've already doomed yourself."

Before you sign on anywhere, gather as much hard information as you can get your hands on. Read the company's annual reports for the past couple of years. Scrutinize its Web site. Hunt down press clippings and securities analysts' reports. If possible, talk with some current and former employees. The more diligent your research—and the more alert and open-minded you're willing to be—the less likely you are to encounter nasty surprises later.

Your best protection against washing out: Make very sure you understand what Ray Harrison calls the CFOs (critical few objectives). One of Manchester's cofounders, Harrison is now president of a firm called Executive TransforMetrics, based in Princeton, New Jersey, that helps companies—and senior managers—define and achieve their goals. He says: "Any management job has 101 responsibilities, but there are usually only two or three that

Q. Is it acceptable to call a company before a job interview and inquire about the dress code? I've been on too many job interviews where I was overdressed in a suit and tie or (worse) too "casual."

A. It's fine to call and ask. So many companies have gone "casual" five days a week now, and there is so much confusion about what "casual" actually means, that interviewers will certainly understand why you need at least a hint about what to put on in the morning. They'd proba bly appreciate one themselves.

you absolutely must excel at. We often see people go into a new job with an amazingly vague and foggy idea of just what those really are." Most managers who make up the aforementioned 40 percent failure rate start to go off the rails in their very first few weeks in the new job. How? By not asking enough questions of the bosses, peers, and underlings who know what the CFOs are— or by not really listening very carefully to the answers. Explains Harrison, "Many successful people, unfortunately, think they already know everything. This is where failure begins." Gulp.

One further word about making the leap to a new job: Try not to burn bridges behind you, especially if you're going to a dot.com. Plenty of people have made that move, of course. Not so long ago, the daily business press was full of senior managers bailing out of big established Old Economy companies to take a shot at Internet fame and glory. The Association of Executive Search Consultants reported in March 2000 that executive searches to fill dot.com positions (including on-line media, e-business, and Internet jobs) soared 739 percent in just one year, with no slowdown in sight.

Still, here's a countertrend you may not have heard quite so much about: Even before the Internet bubble burst, the washout rate in Dot.com Land was even higher than the 40 percent average for all industries, and an as-yet-uncounted number of managers were quietly heading back where they came from. As one of them wrote me in 1999: "After eleven months of fifteen-hour days, terrible, erratic, unprofessional top management, and no sense that anybody is accountable for anything, I'm feeling 'homesick' for good ol' corporate America. I want my old job [at a Fortune 500 company] back, or something like it. But won't I look wimpy if I go crawling back and say, 'I made a mistake, please rehire me'?"

This may be hard on your pride, in the short run anyway, but it's not a disaster. You can go home again. Jeffrey Heath, president of The Landstone Group, a New York City recruiting firm, says that regardless of the economic climate, new hires who already know a company's business and culture—because they've worked there before—are so welcome that they're often called alumni rather than ex-employees. Among his clients, Heath has seen many cases where managers who had quit and spent a year or two somewhere else were rehired by their former employers at much higher levels than they'd probably have reached by staying. "But you absolutely must leave on good terms," he says. "People will always remember how you behaved at the end, and it will color their impression of your entire time there, and even their recollection of whether you were any good at your job." Gloating about the tons of stock options you're getting at your next place of employment is, by these lights, not at all wise.

Even if you expect never to return, it pays to make a graceful exit. Give plenty of notice—more than the standard two to four weeks, if at all possible—and do what you can to help find and train your replacement. Live up to all your contractual obligations. If, for instance, you signed an (increasingly common) agreement to repay the recruiters' fees your company spent to find you in the event that you stayed for less than a year, and you are in fact leaving within the year, here's a tip: Get out your checkbook. I mention this because I've gotten letters from people who are looking for a way out of paying. That's understandable—the fees are sometimes quite steep—but shortsighted. As Marshall Loeb, a former managing editor of *Fortune,* used to say, "It's a long career and a small community." Money is just money, but your good name is priceless. You'll soon be making a lot more dough—isn't that, at least in part, why you're moving on?—but your reputation can't be replaced.

Besides, in such a fluid work world, it's more important than ever to avoid making enemies, because who knows? Someone at the company where you work today could be your boss somewhere else tomorrow—and wouldn't it be nice if that came as a pleasant surprise?

CHAPTER THREE

Difficult Bosses, Toxic Coworkers, and Other Irritants

If two people agree on everything, you may be sure that one of them is doing all the thinking.

—LYNDON JOHNSON

Anyone can become angry. That is easy. But to be angry with the right person, to the right degree, at the right time, for the right purpose and in the right way—that is not easy.

—ARISTOTLE

Mostly, we get along pretty well with the people around us at work or at least, that's what the available research shows. In mid-2000, Atlanta-based consultants Randstad North America released the results of a nation-wide survey of 6,357 employees at U.S. companies of all sizes. An intriguing (and oddly cheering, I think) finding:

Among people who said they feel loyal to their employers and are planning to stay put for a while, the largest number—71 percent—said that's because they like the people with whom they work. By contrast, 65 percent gave "challenging work" as the biggest kick they get out of their jobs; 54 percent cited "flexible work hours."

Other studies echo this theme. According to one poll, conducted jointly by Rutgers University and the Center for Survey Research and Analysis at the University of Connecticut, 59 percent of Americans are "very satisfied" with their current jobs overall. Many more than that—74 percent—are "very satisfied" with their relationships with coworkers. Another 20 percent reported being "somewhat satisfied." So an overwhelming 94 percent majority of us are either downright pleased to be working together or can at least tolerate each other's foibles, day in and day out, with a minimum of friction.

There is even anecdotal evidence that we don't just like each other, we actually need other people around us in order to be at our most productive and do our best work. An example: The atmosphere in the accounting department at the British Broadcasting Corporation's London headquarters used to be so hushed that workers there spoke to each other in (infrequent) whispers.

Q. I work on a team with other managers who arrive late to meetings, without even calling me back until I've made several attempts to find out whether they're coming. I see this behavior as rude and unprofessional, but my boss says I need to be more flexible. Am I wrong to expect people to be courteous?

A. No, but it seems likely that you are holding too many meetings that your colleagues just don't think are as important as the work that is detaining them elsewhere. Does everyone really need to be at every single meeting, or can you run these confabs on a "need to know" basis? And must you keep calling people on the phone to see whether they're coming? How irritating. Start the meetings on time, and let latecomers gather information catch-as-catch-can. Otherwise you risk becoming the office pest, which will make people go out of their way to avoid you.

When the accountants showed signs of stress and loneliness, consultants were brought in to study the problem. They diagnosed a severe case of a debilitating silence called pin drop syndrome. The cure? The company installed a "mutter machine" that emitted indecipherable human chatter, a companionable form of white noise that wasn't loud enough to be distracting but that nonetheless lightened the formerly tomblike ambience. The number-crunchers' malaise disappeared, and productivity soared.

Of course, a plain old radio or television can act as a "mutter machine," too. Every writer I know who works at home alone for long stretches of time admits to sometimes leaving a TV on all day in another room, tuned to CNN—not because he or she is particularly riveted by the day's news, but just for the calm, continuous, reassuring burble of human voices.

And yet . . .

Like and need each other though we might, there are times when our colleagues drive us crazy. These are the moments when people write to me.

Interestingly, I don't get many gripes about bosses. This leads me to believe that *Fortune* readers either understand and respect their higher-ups much more than you might suspect, or if not they just don't bother to complain. Still, when someone does write to describe a problem with a boss, it tends to fall into one of

Q. Last year, when my boss and I discussed the possibility of my being promoted, he said I should "trust him" for seven months. It's now been eleven months and counting. Recently two jobs opened up at the level where I feel I should be, and he said, "I'm not prepared to promote you right now. I have other things I need to do." Also, he seems to be avoiding me lately. I've had other good job offers. Should I keep on being patient here or go elsewhere?

A. Hmm, let's see. Your boss broke his word to you about the seven months, and now is reluctant to look you in the eye. This doesn't sound promising. If I were you, I'd take one of the other offers. Something tells me he won't be surprised when you hand in your notice. Do leave on friendly terms, though. There's never any sense in burning bridges.

Q. What should you do if you get along well with the person your boss reports to, but not with your boss? Can I tell my boss's boss just what is wrong with the way things are going?

A. You certainly could, but you'd probably regret it. Every coach, counselor, or consultant I've ever approached with any variation of this question has *always* said, "Yikes." The temptation to go over a bad boss's head may at times be overwhelming, but resist it. Two reasons: (1) Anything you say is virtually sure to get back to your boss, and (2) you will more than likely earn a companywide reputation as an untrustworthy little political weasel. These are not good things. If you can't speak with your boss directly (and are you really sure about that?), then zip your lip.

three categories: (1) bosses who throw temper tantrums (almost always characterized by my correspondents as "irrational," although that might be open to debate), usually over some minor mishap or other; (2) bosses who hire other people to throw fits for them, so they themselves can continue to be liked (this might be called the Good Cop, Bad Cop School of Management); or (3) bosses who just have weird, though relatively harmless, quirks that get on everybody else's nerves in a big way—but since the boss is, after all, the boss, no one wants to say anything about it to his or her face, so what's an underling to do?

"Help! I Think My Boss May Be Losing His Mind"

"Totally irrational." "Utterly unpredictable—calm in real crises but likely to blow up over trivial little errors or delays." "Disarmingly pleasant one minute, then ranting and raving and cursing his subordinates the next." These are some of the phrases that crop up, over and over again, in letters about Bosses from Hell. "I know my immediate supervisor is under a lot of pressure, but his tantrums are terrible for morale," wrote one miserable information-systems manager in a large manufacturing company. "I'm spending too much time trying to shield the people under me from his fits of anger."

Often, people mired in this unenviable middle ground just quit and move on, and consultants who have studied employee turnover say that frustration with bosses who can't control their tempers is a big reason why people leave high-tech companies in particular. Dr. Richard Hagberg—whose firm, Hagberg Consulting Group, counsels troubled executives—says that many senior managers now are "technical wizards" who are also, alas, "pessimistic, irritable loners, inflexible and lacking social skills." He's basing these remarks on his huge study of 2,000 executives who were assessed by more than 25,000 peers and subordinates over a period of 14 years. "We frequently get called in to try to help managers who fit the same profile," says Hagberg. "Their technical knowledge and talent drives their career paths upward—until they reach a point where 'people skills' become essential to success. Then they flame out." And the people under them get burned, or flee.

If you're working for someone like this, and the situation has really become intolerable, you might consider going over his or her head and suggesting to an even bigger boss that this person needs some kind of professional help. That's always a risky move, notes human-resources expert William Yeomans. "First, try discussing the problem with your boss directly," he says. "The key is to be very nonconfrontational and take the burden onto yourself, by saying something like

Q. I work for a manager who is encouraging during our one-on-one sessions. Yet people tell me that when my name is mentioned for bigger opportunities, he always says negative things about me. It's very confusing. How do I handle this? Should I confront him, or just go to work for someone else?

A. A direct confrontation, in which you essentially accuse your boss of disgraceful backstabbing behavior, is probably not a good idea. Instead, ask for a formal performance evaluation from him; and *get it in writing*. That way, the next time someone tells you he's been bad-mouthing you again, you can produce hard evidence that he's contradicting himself (if in fact he is). If that doesn't work, by all means find a new boss. Life is way too short for this kind of nonsense.

'I'm wondering whether I'm unintentionally causing some kind of problem, because sometimes we get along so well and other times you seem so annoyed. Can we work this out?' You have very little to lose from this approach, and you may gain something."

Patricia Addesso, an organizational psychologist who has seen many of these cases, agrees—and she has a question for you that echoes an old song: How long has this been going on? "If your boss has spent his whole career ranting and raving at the people under him, he is doing it because it has always worked for him. It makes people scurry around." Or did the problem just start recently? Another test: Are the temper tantrums aimed only at subordinates or occasionally at peers and higher-ups, too? If your boss has always carried on this way, and only at people who can't talk back without risking their jobs, then this is truly a toxic boss, and you'll either outlast him or her or else move on. If the behavior is recent and seems out of character, says Addesso, "You owe both him and yourself the favor of talking about it."

I often get the feeling, reading between the lines in letters I receive about out-of-control bosses, that their unhappy subordinates are genuinely concerned about them. "So go to him in private and say, 'Are you okay?'" suggests Addesso. "Be as specific as you can." Don't say, "I think you're losing your grip." Do say, "Last Tuesday in that department meeting you were so hard on Joe

Q. How do you deal with a boss who is overcontrolling? For example, my boss asked me to fill out a form in pencil, and I walked into her office an hour later to see her writing over my work in pen. I did not say anything. Should I have?

A. Maybe she thought she was doing you a favor by going over it in ink (after presumably realizing she should have asked for ink in the first place), rather than bringing it back to you to do over. Why do you see this as "overcontrolling"? If this is a good example of how she usually is, I'd say her tendency to micromanage is mild at best, and harmless. Ignore it. As a general rule, in fact, the more of your co-workers' little quirks you can overlook, the happier and healthier you will be.

when he brought up the Salmagundi thing, and that was so unlike you, I was just wondering if you're all right." Perhaps because she is a shrink, and thus fully mindful of the fact that your boss may indeed be headed round the twist, Addesso adds a bit of advice that sounds eerily like FBI hostage-negotiation tactics: "Never approach someone in this situation with anything that sounds like 'You're screwing up.' Instead, the tone to take is, 'I'm puzzled by this. Can you explain it? And what can I do to help?' "

One further reality check: Do other people have the same problems with this person, or is he blowing his stack only when you're around? Could it be, for example, that his mood swings really were a not-so-irrational response to something you did or failed to do? I don't mean to suggest that screaming at people is ever a great way to handle a snafu: It isn't. But there have been times when—after I've asked for a few more details about what led up to the latest fireworks display— readers have recounted some truly staggering mistakes on their own part, to which the boss was "overreacting." Hmmm. Here as in so many situations (see Chapter 2), the ability to step back and take a dispassionate look at one's own performance could prevent all kinds of headaches.

What if the person doing all the yelling is not the boss, but someone to whom the boss has

Q. Can you give me any tips on how to deal with the fact that although my boss and I are like two peas in a pod, I really don't like (or get along with) the person my boss reports to? I'm asking because I'm soon going to be reporting to this person myself. He's a bad apple, and no one here can stand him. Any advice?

A. You don't have to like someone to make a good impression on him or her. Keep your own career goals front-and-center in your mind, and try not to let personality conflicts distract you. Make sure at all times that you do your job really, really well—and that Mr. Popularity knows it. And cheer up: The latest statistics show that the average senior manager will only stay in his or her current job for about two years. So you probably won't have to grit your teeth and put up with this "bad apple" for very long anyway.

delegated it? "Our company's CEO has an absolutely horrid assistant, who has angered and alienated everyone from senior executives to mail clerks," wrote one reader, who signed himself "Seeing Red." (Clearly, anger is contagious.) "Sometimes she actually screams insults at people who are trying to get in to see the CEO, and she has been known to throw things. Once she hurled a bronze paperweight at someone. Many of us have complained to the CEO about this, but nothing has been done. Considering that I have to see him regularly, she is making my job a nightmare."

Ah. Well, if the CEO knows this person is offending everyone and he hasn't done anything about it, that speaks volumes. "This is not at all unusual. We see it all the time," says consultant Tom Jones, who specializes in helping to fix dysfunctional workplaces. "I've heard executives defend assistants who throw things, or worse. The boss will say something like 'So—apart from that, what's the problem?' " In other words, hostile assistants are just doing what they—and their bosses—see as their job: keeping people, by whatever means necessary, from barging in to the Big Guy's office.

Jones observes that in making peace with such a person, a little empathy usually goes a long way. "This is the gatekeeper, and so naturally you focus your frustrations on her. She's standing"—or

> **Q.** I am quite miserable in my job with [a giant petrochemical company] and find it hard to acquire new skills, since my boss keeps giving me strange, meaningless jobs to do and never has time to listen to my side of the story. My motivation is at an all-time low, and I am afraid that all this negative feeling on my part is making my relationship with my boss even worse. How can I communicate my frustration in an effective way?
>
> **A.** In the Appendix you will find many books by truly brilliant and learned students of the whole, incredibly complex subject of how to communicate with people who don't really want to speak with you. But useful as those are, it sounds as if your best bet would be to start updating your résumé. A boss who consistently gives you "strange, meaningless" assignments is trying to tell you something.

sitting and pitching things—"between you and what you want," he says. "But imagine for a minute what her life must be like, with this constant bombardment of demands that she's been told to deny. Typically, gatekeepers feel very left out. They've been put in an adversarial position with everyone in the company who has knowledge of what's going on." He adds: "Whenever someone tells me that someone else has to change, I always reply that I believe people will not change unless they are first accepted for who they are now."

Fine and dandy, but how does that help here? Jones suggests trying to have a calm talk with the gatekeeper. Explain that you do understand that her job is to protect the boss from distractions and interruptions, and you respect that. But, assuming you really do have solid business reasons for needing a bit of his time, spell out exactly why it will be bad for the business if you don't get in to see him. Be specific. Give numbers, not attitude, and facts, not feelings. Enlist this person in a mutual project: How can we both get what we need? "If you take an objective approach, you may be surprised at the change in the other person's attitude," says Jones. "That's because suddenly, instead of being treated as an enemy, she's being enlisted as an ally. And, instead of being seen as a problem, she's participating in a solution."

It's possible, of course, that no amount of friendly persuasion will get you past a true pit bull of an assistant. In that case, thank heavens for e-mail. If you really need to get information to the Head Honcho, a technological end run is sometimes the quickest (and, unless you're prepared to dodge flying objects, the safest) way to do it.

Bosses Are People, Too (Which Is Why They Act So Strange)

Hey, we all have our little peculiarities. Why should the people we work for be any different? Frequently, as with anyone else (a family member or a friend), the choice is clear: Either politely ask the person to please stop doing whatever it is that's so irksome, or else hush up and learn to ignore it. One woman wrote me that her immediate supervisor taps his pencil on the table in meetings "in a rapid syncopated rhythm, over and over again for an hour at a time, until I think I'll go out of my mind—although in every other respect, he's a great guy and has been a wonderful mentor to me in the company." So, a little pencil tapping is so terrible? Why not ask to borrow the pencil (since he obviously doesn't need it to write with), hand it back at the end of the meeting—and just hope he hasn't brought a spare? As a rule, any idiosyncrasy that doesn't interfere with getting the work done is worth overlooking. Among those that do get in the way of business, the most widespread seem to involve talking. If

> **Q.** I realize this is a trivial question, or might seem so, but here goes. I hate, hate, hate having my picture taken. While it is easy to duck away or say "no" when friends or family pick up a camera, how do I stop my boss? He recently insisted on taking my picture at a vendors' meeting (it was later posted on the company Web site), and I was trapped by the furniture and could not escape. I think it is abusive to photograph anyone against their will. How can I handle this next time?
>
> **A.** First of all, there is nothing trivial about anything that clearly makes you this unhappy. Have you spoken with your boss, in private, about this? If not, do. Ian Gillies, a Toronto career coach who has considerable experience with sticky wickets like this one, suggests you go to your boss's office, state your case very simply—"Please don't keep taking my picture. I really don't like it"—and then leave (smiling if possible). Don't justify or explain. Says Gillies, "You need to make your wishes clear, but no one needs to hear your life story, and you shouldn't feel pressed to explain." Just say "no."

you have a boss who either never talks to you at all or, conversely, talks constantly until you can't hear yourself think, you're not alone.

Silent types tend to be overly dependent on e-mail—sometimes to absurd extremes. "I was fired via e-mail," wrote a reader named Jeff not long ago, "and the stupidest part was that the guy who fired me was sitting six feet away. When I asked him to explain, he made some lame excuse and scrurried away." Not all e-mail addicts are as bad as that—although, to judge from my mail, lots of them come close. Asks a reader named Susan, "What can you do with a project manager who relies on e-mail for every trivial little exchange of information? I and the other one hundred or so people who work for this woman get a little weirded out when she insists on e-mailing us instead of talking to us, even though our cubicles are in most cases only a few feet or yards away from hers. Once the hard drive on her notepad crashed and, after she got a new hard drive, it took twenty-three hours to replicate her e-mail database because she had over six thousand posts. She's not a nasty person or anything—we think she's just very shy—but this constant e-mailing is driving us nuts. Any thoughts?"

Brian Stern, a managing director at management consulting firm Savile & Holdsworth, spe-

Q. My boss takes an hourlong nap every afternoon. I don't know what to say to people who call or stop by and ask to speak with him, and I'm getting tired of inventing stories about where he went. How can I handle this?

A. Why do you have to invent stories? Simply tell the truth—"He's not available right now"—and take a message. It's only an hour, after all, and it is a truly sad day when colleagues can't back off and mind their own business (they do have some, don't they?) for sixty minutes in a row. Consider this: Albert Einstein, Winston Churchill, Thomas Edison, and Franklin Delano Roosevelt—not to mention Silicon Valley start-ups like Sybase, which maintains a nap room for all employees—have done pretty well for themselves with a little snooze in the afternoon. Your boss may be on to something.

cializes in teaching people in companies how to communicate better. "We know from studying team performance that 'water-cooler'—or capuccino machine—conversations are extremely valuable. A great deal of useful information is exchanged informally. But if the boss won't chat, or even say hello, it tends to inhibit everybody else," he says. With that in mind, Stern recommends that you and a group of co-workers get together and propose a meeting with your project manager. Then start the discussion, not by saying, "We think it's strange that you won't talk to us," but rather, "We think we could be a more productive team if we all talked more instead of relying on e-mail." The three essential components of trying to manage any boss, Stern notes, are information (does she know there is a problem?), support (suggest ways to fix it and then follow through with your end of the bargain), and motivation (give her lots of pats on the back for even trying).

Be patient, because change, if any, will be gradual. After the meeting, the next time your boss e-mails you to ask something— "What's the file number on the Robinson account?"—just get up out of your chair, walk over to his or her desk and, with a pleasant smile, say quietly, "The file number on the Robinson account is 10987." If you and your colleagues keep this up, it will lead to longer and longer conversa-

---

Q. How can a boss expect his employees to work to their full potential if he doesn't? I mean he doesn't keep to the schedule that he posts and he never has staff meetings. We haven't had a staff meeting since October of last year, even though many have been scheduled.

A. What on earth do you want a staff meeting for? The rest of us are trying to get out of as many as we can. Well, okay, I'm kidding (I think). But it does sound to me as if meetings are not your main concern. If you feel you don't get to see enough of him, go to him and say so. Then explain why. If your real beef is that you believe you're working harder and smarter than he is, you're probably working for the wrong boss. In that case, do yourself a favor and make a move before you've had too much time to stew about it.

tions until—who knows?—your boss might even chat with you around the watercooler someday.

At the other extreme from e-mail addicts are nonstop talkers whose hapless underlings are hard-pressed to get a moment's peace. These are essentially likable people; they're just, um, overly sociable, so that asking them to please pipe down would probably make you seem, and feel, churlish. Someone who signed him- or herself "Quiet Please" describes a typical hypertalkative boss: "I work for a guy who is twenty-eight years old, very enthusiastic, and he can't seem to stop yakking. Unfortunately, we share an office, and he carries on a running monologue all day, demanding answers to questions like 'How much do you think this chair cost?' Yesterday I had to take a report out to my car in order to finish it on time. Help!"

A quirk that keeps you from doing your job—or forces you to take work out to the parking lot—has got to be stopped. In this instance, the direct approach is best. Barbara Hannah, an executive coach in Atlanta, points out that since he is your boss, he has a vested interest in making sure you get your work done; so don't be shy about saying so. "Next time he interrupts you with this stream-of-consciousness chatter, put your work down, look him in the eye, and say very calmly, 'Jim, you're the boss, so it's your choice. Do you want me to keep stopping what I'm doing to talk with you, or do you want me to get these reports finished on time'—and don't end with a question mark," says Hannah.

An excessively gabby boss may not put a cork in it on the first request. "He is obviously trying to get some personal need met by talking so much," Hannah says. But keep repeating your little speech, word for word, until the message sinks in. Or you can do what another exasperated reader did under similar conditions: Invest in a pair of ear plugs, and think about looking for another job.

Q. I work in a five-person office of a small company that has several employees who work from home. They all live much farther from the office than I do. I want to ask for permission to telecommute also because—although I do believe I would be more productive at home—the real reason is that I can't stand being around the people here. They are ethically and morally challenged and waste a lot of time talking loudly about very personal matters. If my boss asks me why I want to work from home, should I tell her about my distaste for these colleagues?

A. No. Why open that can of worms? Maybe she likes these people. Just tell her you think you would get more and better work done at home. Give an example: You could concentrate more intently on certain projects without the distraction of noise from adjoining cubicles. Numerous studies have shown that telecommuters are indeed more efficient than their office-bound peers, if only because they spend so much less time sitting in traffic jams. You don't need to put down your coworkers to make this point; and the fact that your company already has some telecommuters is certainly in your favor.

Always keep one thing in mind: Nobody's perfect, but everybody can teach you something. As Geraldine Laybourne, chairman of Oxygen Media, once told *The New York Times:* "When people complain to me about their horrible bosses, I say, 'Aren't you lucky,' because the more examples of bad management you see, the more you'll learn. I learned more from my worst boss than I did from my best. I took notes on how I would not manage." Smart.

"If Your Hair Isn't on Fire, Go Away"

That is what's written on a sign a reader named Peter hangs on his office door when he doesn't want to be disturbed. "People laugh when they see it, but they get the point," he writes.

I bet you know what he means. Among the most common complaints I hear is from folks whose colleagues are always dropping by to chat—which is nice, except that, as a correspondent named Michelle put it, "I've got a lot of deadlines to meet, and having to stop and hear all about what somebody did over the weekend doesn't exactly get the work done on time." We've all been there: You're feverishly working away on something, your concentration is total, you're really on a roll—and here comes that one coworker (every office has at least one; most have several) who will now want to spend ten or twenty minutes schmoozing, after which it will take you at least that long to get back on your train of thought. You don't want to hurt anyone's feelings—especially if the intruder is someone you genuinely like (just not right now)—but you really need to keep right on working.

You can. In fact, you owe it to yourself. If you're lucky enough to have an office door with a lock on it, use it. Otherwise, adopt some not-so-subtle body language. A friend of mine who once worked for then-TV producer Andrew Heyward recalls that Heyward had cultivated what staffers came to call his "death stare." "When you appeared in his office doorway, you could tell instantly whether or not you were welcome. If he wanted you to go away and come back later, just one look would curl your toenails." This may sound harsh, but consider what controlling interruptions did for Heyward's career: He's now president of CBS News.

Not everyone can master the art of the death stare. If you can't, says Ian Gillies, a career coach in Toronto, try this: "As soon as you see the person com-

Q. I have a coworker who spends about five hours a day making and receiving long-distance personal telephone calls, surfing the Net, and playing computer games. I've reported it to our boss, but he is too busy to notice that this jerk is still at it and is neglecting his job. Any suggestions?

A. Five hours a day? Really? Well, if his goofing off is directly affecting your ability to get your own work done, you'd be justified in telling the boss about it again. If not, just mind your own business. People who waste this much time at work eventually sabotage their own careers with no help from colleagues.

ing, stand up and move toward him or her." That is, do not let yourself be trapped behind your desk. If the offender doesn't take the hint, you can always keep on walking. Or, as a reader named Chris from Chicago suggested, you might "turn your back and get suddenly too busy to hear what the other person is saying. Computer screens are handy for this. This method has saved me a lot of wasted time. I used to worry about seeming rude, but with some people, being just a little bit rude is the only way to make your point." Alas, yes.

The problem of privacy is particularly acute for people who work in doorless cubicles. A couple of years ago a reader named Denise wrote to say that she and her colleagues had resolved this: "Around here, a little orange cone, the kind available at a sporting goods or toy store, is placed at the entrance to the cube when the person inside doesn't want to be disturbed." In 1999, a company called Protocol Office Systems in Washington, D.C., came out with a product that serves the same purpose a little more elaborately. It's a set of three foam-rubber blocks, called Protoblocs, in red, yellow, and green—which, as anyone with a driver's license can probably guess, indicate "Stop or else: This means you" (red), "Disturb only if really necessary" (yellow), or "Come on in and set a spell" (green). Employees at America Online, Freddie Mac, and the World Bank have taken to perching these atop their cubicle walls. Brian Dean, AOL's manager of facilities planning, told *Fortune* he wants employees there to make the color-coded signals "a part of their everyday routine." Here's hoping it catches on.

As cubicle dwellers everywhere can attest, the design of the darn things—whose flimsy, far-from-soundproof walls usually don't reach all the way to the ceiling—practically guarantees distractions even when you're sitting alone at your desk. This raises some new questions of etiquette. "In our cube farm, you can hear every word that coworkers say within fifty feet or so," wrote a reader who signed him- or herself "Big Ears." So, "When is it okay to respond to a question or remark I overhear? Some comments seem to be directed at no one in particular. For instance, 'Who brought the cookies?' When colleagues talk or joke across walls, is it okay to join in? Or would it be more polite to pretend I don't hear them?"

If this applies to you, one course of action would be to adopt what Judith "Miss Manners" Martin calls Polite Fiction: Pretend you overhear nothing, ever, in a cubicle or anywhere else. "The strange thing," Martin says, "is that people who suffer from the symptoms of Polite Fiction—temporary deafness, blindness, and amnesia—tend to be especially beloved for their disabilities."

Q. One of my coworkers is always making remarks about his sex life. The latest example among many: I had to call him at home one evening to let him know I'd be late for a meeting the next morning. When I got to work, he said, "Your phone call interrupted my foreplay." Is this sexual harassment or what?

A. Of course it isn't. If all he's doing is making dumb remarks, he's perfectly within his legal rights. No one has yet managed to outlaw bad taste, which may be lucky for us all at one time or another. However, you might suggest that he get himself a wonderful invention called an answering machine. And the next time you need to contact him after hours, try e-mail.

The real problem here has less to do with politeness than with productivity: A constant stream of crosscubicle palaver makes it difficult for chronic chatterers' neighbors to concentrate on the task at hand. Marjorie Brody, an executive coach who heads Brody Communications in Jenkintown, Pennsylvania, suggests holding a meeting wherein everyone on the cube farm agrees not to talk through walls. She proposes another rule: No playing back voice-mail messages on speakerphones, which, especially when several people are doing it at once, can turn a quiet cubicle maze into the Tower of Babel. If that doesn't work, says Brody, just tune out. "Unless a question or comment is addressed to you personally, don't respond. Otherwise, you're only encouraging this inconsiderate, unprofessional behavior."

Must Office Politics Be Poisonous?

"Politics are almost as exciting as war, and quite as dangerous," Winston Churchill once remarked. "In war you can be killed only once, in politics many times." If you've ever found yourself on the losing side of a corporate power struggle—especially one in which the winners used nasty, underhanded tactics to get their way—you know what he meant. Yet politics has also been called the "art of the possible"—and, in any case, a certain amount of political maneuvering is inevitable in any environment where money and influence are at stake, so you might as well accept it. "Every office has politics," notes Michael Frisch, an organizational psychologist who is a consultant at Minneapolis-based Personnel Decisions International. Frisch often gets called in to settle ugly internecine intrigues at huge, otherwise quite respectable companies. "Politics is a fact of life, like the weather. And, like the weather, politics can be good or bad."

For those to whom the phrase "good politics" sounds like the ultimate oxymoron, let's quickly define it. In a healthy political environment, people naturally have differing priorities and opinions, but everyone feels free to express his or her concerns openly and to work toward compromise solutions to common problems. In this scenario, politics is quite simply a highly efficient, if informal, part of the overall decision-making process. People advance their own points of view without tearing down anyone else's. They also gain credibility and foster a spirit of teamwork by sharing credit where it's due and acknowledging other people's contributions to their ideas or achievements. If a serious conflict arises between two employees, they discuss it directly with each other and refrain from stabbing each other in the back.

Now, by contrast, let's talk about your company. Ha ha! Only kidding! It is a little shocking, though, how vicious some corporate cultures are—and, judging from my mail over the past couple of years, many are becoming more so. A political environment that resembles a piranha tank is doubly troubling to someone who has been thrown into it unexpectedly. With all the job changing that goes on these days, unpleasant surprises abound. No one interviewing you for a new job is going to say, "Welcome aboard and, oh, by the way, here's your company-issued stiletto. It works best with a quick thrust between the second and third ribs. . . ."

If you're hoping to fix a really poisonous culture all by yourself, you will probably be disappointed. The more likely outcome is that it will change you—unless you have the good sense to leave before that happens. However, particularly if you're a manager or a team leader with some small bit of influence over other people's careers, there are

Q. Is it ever appropriate to put on makeup, such as lipstick, powder, etc., during a business meal?

A. Since you signed your letter "Ted," I assume you're not asking on your own behalf, but are hoping to wave this page in front of someone's face, perhaps the moment she whips out her lipstick at the table. That would be quite rude of you. Anyway, I called Alan R. Schonberg, founder of Management Recruiters International, and posed your question. "Have you ever noticed how few women actually do that makeup-at-the-table thing anymore?" he asks. It is indeed very Joan Crawford. "The few who do really stick out like sore thumbs. It may seem trivial but, as a boss or a prospective employer, I have to say it would cause me to wonder about this person's judgment generally." The same applies, by the way, to other kinds of carelessness Schonberg has witnessed at business meals in restaurants. He offers these tips: Don't bring your cell phone. Don't complain about the food. And never, ever talk down to waitpersons.

certainly things you can do to keep the ambient nastiness from getting out of hand. "What is interesting about sneaky, cruel behavior," says Michael Frisch, "is that it tends to become the norm in organizations that are averse to conflict." That might sound illogical, but it isn't: "When there is no way to publicly and routinely air differences and express dissent and disagreement, it all gets pushed down 'underground,' beneath the surface of daily interactions. And that is where the trouble starts."

If that's the case where you work, then the solution is clear: Start, or persuade your boss to start, getting people to talk openly to each other. Frisch and many other experts recommend holding regular staff meetings where everyone is allowed— encouraged, even—to discuss their differences face-to-face.

Since this will take some getting used to, if you take on the role of moderator, be as calm and objective as you can be. "So, Jack," you might say, "I understand you had a little problem with the way we handled that last widget project. Would you like to tell the rest of us about it, so we can do better next time?" Then Jack, who spent half an hour last

---

Q. I was being considered for a promotion, and had to go through a series of "interviews" at a higher level of the company. The senior guy in charge of this process said he would get back to me "soon." That was over a month ago, and still nothing. When I called to follow up (I also sent two e-mails), his assistant said he was out of the office. Isn't it just common decency to answer a person one way or the other? I'm tempted to let him know what I think of his rudeness. What would you do?

A. Nothing. Just let it go. For one thing, if he's giving you the brushoff, you haven't lost much. (Would you really want to work for someone who left you hanging like that?) And for another, you haven't got nearly enough information to start spouting off about his rudeness. "Out of the office" can mean almost anything. Stuff happens. Suppose he's recovering from a quadruple bypass or coping with a death in the family or sitting on a sequestered jury somewhere— and you send him a snarky letter berating him for not getting back to you promptly. Now who looks rude?

Tuesday ranting to you about how Sally screwed it up (when Sally was not there to defend herself), gets a chance to vent. And make sure that he speaks to Sally, who should then have a few moments to explain why Carlos, also present at this confab, could have gotten his part (on which her part depended) done a little faster. These problem-solving meetings work best when they operate on three ground rules: (1) Nobody comes to blows, and personal insults are not permitted; (2) nobody leaves the room until solutions (even if only tentative ones) have been agreed on; and (3) each meeting ends with setting a date for the next one.

Once the communications ball has begun rolling, accept no substitutes. "When someone comes to your office to tear down someone else, you should be too busy to listen—as you no doubt truly are anyway," says Frisch. "Say, 'Have you told So-and-So what you just told me?' If the answer is no, make it clear that you won't listen to any complaint until it has been expressed to the other party involved." Period, end of discussion, throw the bum out. As Frisch puts it, "You can't allow yourself to become the repository of negative gossip, or you've lost any hope of creating a better situation." Never sink to the level of any behavior you would like to see changed.

Frisch doesn't guarantee that taking the high road will get you where you want to go. The effort of encouraging people to treat each other decently—even if only by setting a good example—may eventually just wear you down. Or, in the immortal words of a reader named Ray (who lived, no kidding, on Pork Point Road somewhere in Maine), "Never try to teach a pig to sing. It wastes your time and irritates the pig." Still, you might feel better for having tried. The worst that can happen is that if you give up and move on, at least you can truthfully tell your next employer that you tried to be part of a solution, not part of the problem.

But what if, as sometimes happens, your company's culture is generally open and aboveboard, with a minimum of backstabbing and strife, except for one person who seems to have made it his or her mission in life to undermine you? Consider a fairly typical lament, from a reader named Lily: "Lately I've been having trouble accessing our company's mainframe from my home PC. My network LAN/WAN manager keeps telling our superiors that I am doing things to the computer, such as adding unauthorized software, and that is why it doesn't work—even though he and I both know I've made no changes except those he specifically instructed me to make. How does one deal with a coworker who tells lies about what one is or is not doing?"

Sheila Ruth, a professor emerita at Southern Illinois University who runs workshops at companies across the country on how to deal with toxic colleagues, says that this LAN/WAN manager fits the classic definition of toxicity: He blames people around him for everything that goes wrong, even (or perhaps especially) when it is clearly his own fault, and yet somehow contrives to make higher-ups think he is wonderful. Remember the obnoxious kid in grade school who was sweet as pie around adults and beat you up when the grown-ups' backs were turned—but nobody believed you? "By adulthood, toxic people have had years and years of practice at this kind of behavior. They are master manipulators," says Ruth.

What's maddening, of course, is that such folks have usually been careful to cultivate a network of friends in high places. You go over their heads at your own peril: "If you complain to his boss, this person will turn it back on you. He'll make you look like a whiner or worse." If you can possibly stand it, Ruth says that your best bet in such a situation is to wait the other person out: "Sooner or later he will pick the wrong target and get fired—or he'll get promoted so high up in the organization that you'll no longer have to work with him. He'll be someone else's problem."

If you really can't take another day of a toxic colleague's dirty tricks, however, there is another option, but be warned: It requires some humility (or false humility; for this purpose, either will do). Says Savile & Holdsworth managing director Brian Usher: "Try to make this person your ally before he does real damage to your career. And you need to do it publicly and in a nonthreatening way." In Lily's case, Usher suggests posting an e-mail on the companywide intranet requesting a uniform set of guidelines for home PCs: what software is to be used, correct log-on procedures, and so on. And, gee, since So-and-So (Mr. Toxic) is the real expert on all this, wouldn't it be great if he could help out the rest of us dummies by heading up the team that writes the guidelines?

In other words, appeal to his ego, which, judging from his behavior, is a pathetically fragile thing that needs constant stroking. "Here is a guy with a lot of technical expertise who may feel that no one appreciates it," says Usher. "If you enlist a small group of allies to say, 'Would you help us learn this stuff?' and make him feel valued, you may be surprised at how his atti-

Q. What's the best way to deal with bullies in the workplace? Not bosses, but colleagues who seem to make your workday more difficult on purpose?

A. Funny you should ask. A couple of global studies by the United Nations recently reported that intentional meanness in the workplace is becoming a more common (or at least more commonly reported) problem in many parts of the world. This worries employers too, partly because it damages productivity but also, at least in the United States, because of the risk of lawsuits. Unfortunately, anyone who behaves in a bullying way is probably not going to be easy to reason with. But you must try. Explain that certain actions really make it hard for you to do your job. If that conversation goes nowhere, as it well might, then do not hesitate to go to your boss and describe the problem. Be specific. You need to cite examples of particular incidents and/or verbal exchanges, rather than making general statements like "So-and-So is making my life a living hell." This may be true but it isn't useful. If your boss can't or won't help you, look for another job.

tude—and consequently what he says about you behind your back—will change."

A toxic coworker will often hide his or her true colors (none too pretty) until the pressure is on—for example, until he or she is competing with you for the same promotion. Then the gloves come off. Over the years, I've heard from quite a few beleaguered readers who had thought that a particular colleague was a friend, or at least not an enemy, and were then shocked to find themselves slandered (subtly or not) when some corporate prize was at stake. One unhappy correspondent wrote me that his rival for a great new job was "sending a number of poison-pen e-mails to upper management, criticizing my every move and saying all kinds of disparaging things about me."

In some companies, of course, a certain amount of vicious underhanded behavior is actually expected or even encouraged by the people at the top, who, far from recognizing it as the destructive nonsense that it is, see meanness—however counterproductive and pointless it may be—as a sign of "toughness." In those instances, I've advised victims to let the other guy have the promotion (or whatever the prize happened to be) and start job hunting, because who wants to work in a place like that anyway?

On the other hand, let's suppose someone is flaming you without any encouragement from above, and you just want it to stop. Annette Simmons, a consultant at Group Process Consulting in Greensboro, North Carolina, wrote a fascinating book called *Territorial Games: Understanding and Ending Turf Wars at Work*. Says she: "People don't egg houses in broad daylight, so find a way to shine a spotlight on what your attacker is doing. A private, unemotional discussion can often turn a bully into a coward. Or you might consider joking about the whole situation in a public forum—a staff meeting, for instance—which works to dispel the power that secrecy gives gossip."

Don't be defensive, which only makes you look guilty—and never, ever respond in kind by launching a smear campaign of your own. "No one escapes snipers in his or her rise to the top. There are always people who fight dirty," Simmons says. "In the end, your best protection is a good track record, good relationships—and enough good sense to keep inching out the rope to these people until they either hang themselves with it, or else have trouble hiding all that rope."

There Is (Alas) No "I" in "Teamwork"

Hypercompetitive teammates who try to grab all the glory. Senior managers who, individually, take full credit for a whole team's output. Team members who try to get out of doing their share of the work. Companies that expect you to train coworkers on your team, but don't reward you for doing so. These are just a few of the most common complaints I get about that marvelous—and terribly trendy—thing called teams. Most U.S. companies now are, or claim to be, organized into these small, fraternal work units. But one recent national survey of Fortune 1000 and dot.com managers said the respondents expect teamwork to increase by 44 percent between 2000 and 2005, so anyone who isn't yet a member of a team soon will be.

In many respects, teams are great, at least in theory. They unite people around specific common goals and can be the most efficient way of allocating tasks so that projects get done quickly and well. Because teams encourage—indeed, require—rapid, constant communication, everyone knows what he or she is supposed to do and how each piece contributes to the success of the whole. Ideally, a team that has been together for a while is a close-knit group, all for one and one for all, that works as swiftly and seamlessly as a Swiss watch.

There's just one catch: Teams are made up of people, and people are odd. They are also, by nature, fundamentally self-interested, often insecure, and frequently stubborn. If you're a member of a team that doesn't exactly run like a well-oiled machine, you've got plenty of company.

Most of the time, disagreements about who's supposed to do what can be settled simply by talking it all out. "I love being the leader of a [twelve person] team because—unlike in my last management job, where I was supposed to be overseeing eighty people's work—I can keep in close touch with everyone 'under' me and solve problems before they get big enough to cause real trouble," wrote a reader named Sal. Still, Sal wanted advice about what to do about two team members who seemed to be trying to undercut one another's efforts. (Does this sound familiar?) According to Lynda McDermott, president of EquiPro International—a New York consulting firm that has helped hammer out team problems at Pfizer, Hewlett-Packard, Bankers Trust, and Mobil Oil, among others—hypercompetitiveness among teammates is a sign that a team has temporarily lost its focus.

"Usually, people will unite behind a common cause, some compelling objective that everyone can buy into. When that happens, individual differences tend to fade into the background," says McDermott. "But without a clear goal, people start trying to undercut each other because they're afraid that their individual contributions will get lost in the shuffle." Smart teams regularly sit down together and talk out who's doing what, who might need help from a teammate and—most important—try to keep sight of why the team exists in the first place. They reinforce their common interests and reiterate what the ultimate point is. If you belong to a team that isn't doing that, it's time you started. Without a crystal-clear agenda that the whole group shares, individual agendas naturally sprout like weeds.

Loyalty to the common good does not mean, however, that you shouldn't stand up for yourself, especially if teammates seem to be exploiting your good nature—and, oh boy, do I get lots of letters about this. "Once again it is 7:30 P.M. on the evening before a big deadline, and once again I am alone in the office finishing up the work of an eight-person team, because everyone else—three men, four women—had to relieve the babysitter, go to a school play, pick up a child from soccer practice, etc., etc.," wrote a reader who signed herself "Doormat." "Seven times in the past year, the whole team has taken kudos for projects that would not have been finished on time if I hadn't stayed and done the work myself."

Q. I get along really well with my team, and we've done some great work that has advanced all of our careers. Just one problem: I have one teammate who keeps falling asleep in important meetings. What would be the best way to handle this without embarrassing him?

A. Falling asleep during the day can be a sign of a serious medical disorder (such as narcolepsy or sleep apnea, to name two). Take your colleague aside and say that you are concerned about his napping habits and you think he should see a doctor and get a complete physical as soon as possible. If he has any sense at all, he'll thank you. If not, from now on, sit as far away from him in meetings as you possibly can.

Well, for Pete's sake. One of the make-or-break challenges facing any team is how to make sure the work—and the credit—gets divided fairly among the members, and this cause is not served by anyone's meekly agreeing to shoulder so much of the load. Why not sit everyone down and say, "Hey, I know you have personal commitments to attend to, and that's fine, but here's a news flash: Next time, anyone who doesn't stay until the project is finished should not be surprised if his or her name is not on the final version." Then stick to your guns. In the immortal words of Ann Landers: "No one can take advantage of you without your permission." So stop giving it.

Q. I was recently pleasantly surprised to see my name published in a professional journal as one of the contributors to a project at my company that turned out exceptionally well. I only worked on this "with my left hand," so to speak, for a short time, and I really don't even know the team leader who wrote up the results. Should I send him a note expressing my appreciation? If so, what should it say?

A. "Thank you."

Assuming that all of a given team's work gets done without any real hitch, the question of who gets recognized for it can be a sticky one. Apparently, there are legions of senior executives (including CEOs) out there who see nothing wrong with "writing" technical papers and learned speeches—based entirely on the hard labor of a lowly team of, say, engineers—and then presenting these gems in public as their own work. "Isn't this plagiarism?" asked an outraged reader signed "Steamed," whose team worked nights and gave up vacations for nine months, only to have a higher-up swipe all the credit for the outcome without so much as a nod of acknowledgment.

Technically, it isn't plagiarism, but it is pretty rotten—and yet "Steamed" and his teammates were reluctant to vent their spleen at the offending executive, who could have responded by firing them all. If this sort of theft has befallen you too, it would be a mistake to let the injustice of it discourage you from doing your best on future team projects. Instead, consultants Jacalyn Sherriton and James Stern, who have helped teamwork run smoothly for clients like IBM, Bristol-Myers Squibb, and Panasonic, offer a couple of suggestions.

First, says Sherriton, bear in mind that there are various ways to make sure that credit is distributed fairly. Some companies list all team members alphabetically on the final reports and records of a given project, while others divide the team into "core" and "contributing" members, to distinguish those who did most of the heavy lifting from those who were less involved. The important thing is to try to establish a uniform companywide standard. If your company doesn't have a formal suggestion system, write a memo to whichever higher-up you think is most genuinely interested in seeing teams succeed. (There is such a person upstairs somewhere, isn't there? If not, no wonder you're having trouble.) Without pointing fingers, or letting on that you are "steamed", suggest that—in the interest of accuracy and fairness—each team begin reporting who did what in exactly the same way on each project. If you can make this happen, a project report signed by only two people, when there were in fact eight team members, will be rare enough to raise eyebrows.

If you can't manage to get any uniform standard in place, Sherriton and Stern urge you to do the next best thing: Next time you join a team, propose to the whole group that you all decide in advance how credit will be spread around at the end—and get that agreement in writing, ideally with everybody's signature at the bottom. The advantage here is obvious: If any one person tries to hog the glory, you have black-and-white proof that he or she is out of line.

But when it comes to presenting some outstanding achievement to the world at large, Sherriton notes that bosses often grab the spotlight because, quite simply, team members who did the actual work are too slow off the mark. "Some people who are new to the team approach are just not accustomed yet to being 'empowered,' " Sherriton observes. "The next time you write all or most of a project report, why don't *you* volunteer to have it published in a trade journal or offer to present it at an industry conference? Why wait for someone else to do it?" Of course, assuming you do present this baby to the world, it goes without saying that you will remember to acknowledge and thank every single person who ever had a hand in it—won't you?

The widespread hoo-ha over who gets the credit for a team's work would not be so venomous if not for the fact that so many senior managers—including unfortunately many who set pay policies for their companies—aren't really accustomed to teamwork yet, either. They tend, alas, to pay lip service to the idea of teams, and claim to value team players, while still rewarding individual stars with raises and promotions—which naturally throws a wrench into any real esprit de corps. This is why I get so many questions from people who would like to help out less experienced colleagues by sharing information and advice—or who are required to train new people and pass along their timeless wisdom to wet-behind-the-ears teammates—but who fear that by so doing they'll lose their own cherished top-dog status. "I feel I'm giving up my competitive edge if I help out coworkers who have less knowledge than I do. But I don't feel right about refusing, either," wrote a correspondent who signed himself "Hans Solo." "Do you see any way out of this dilemma?"

Yes. At the risk of sounding like the world's oldest Girl Scout, here's what I think you should do in this situation: Help everybody who asks you for help. Why? Because in the long run, it's the best thing you can do for your own career. Brian Ashley, a career coach in Los Angeles who specializes in counseling people who are striving to be the best at what they do, points out that if you try to protect your own advantage now, "you are building a little box

---

Q. As a nonsmoker, it seems to me that I am always working—and often covering for absent colleagues—while my addicted coworkers are outside taking a "cigarette break." Sometimes these "breaks" can run to ten or twelve per day, at an average of fifteen minutes each. How can I get compensated for the extra work I am doing?

A. Well, if you go and ask for smoke-break compensation, you are going to look pretty silly, so forget about that. Instead, just think; you'll probably outlive those smokin' delinquents by a decade or two, and enjoy a healthy, active retirement while they're wheezing away (or worse). Isn't that compensation enough?

for yourself. Sure, you'll probably shine in your current position—but what about your next job, and the one after that? Always remember that you are playing in a bigger arena than just your present job. Careers these days do not start and end with just one company. As you help others to learn and grow, you build a reputation for yourself that will extend over a whole network of future acquaintances and connections." By these lights, refusing to help the less-proficient is not just unkind, it's self-defeating.

Ashley knows what he's talking about. Before he took up coaching, he spent twenty-seven years in middle and upper management at several Fortune 500 companies. During that time he acted as mentor, teacher, coach, and cheerleader for dozens of peers and subordinates who years later have made good elsewhere. "They've all become president of this or national sales director of that," he says. "These are not bad people to have in your corner. And make no mistake, people do remember that you were there for them when they needed you. If all it costs you today is ten minutes of your time, why not make that investment?" The smart money says you won't regret it.

Who's the Difficult Colleague in Your Office? (Any Chance It Might Be You?)

I don't mean to keep harping on the idea of trying to evaluate your own performance as objectively as you can, but I'd be remiss not to bring it up just once more, this time in the context of interpersonal relations at work. There's something I'd like to get off my chest, and it's this: About 50 percent of the time, people who write me to complain about an uncooperative (or hostile or otherwise bothersome) coworker sound as if they are no bargain themselves. To judge from how they describe the situation and their own role in it, it often seems to me that if I had to work with this person, I'd be pretty prickly, too. Although it's hard to answer such people tactfully, from time to time I do ask, "Have you tried putting yourself in the other person's place for a minute and asking yourself how you'd like a taste of your own medicine?" Still, I suspect my suggestions, and those of experts I consult, are falling on deaf ears.

Want an example? Okay, here's one at random. "Dear Annie," wrote someone who signed herself "Glorified Gofer," "I'm an executive assistant to a very forward-thinking chief operating officer in a 'blue collar' industry. My boss wants people to perceive me as part of the management team. The problem is that some of his employees and other managers here have really bad time-management habits, but they won't listen to my suggestions for changing this, because they still think of me as a 'gofer' (stopping me in the hallway for cab requests, giving me food orders for lunch meetings, etc.). How can I get them to listen to me?"

Hmmm. Well, respect is a funny thing. It has to be earned by dint of actual accomplishments that are at least equal to those of the people from whom you're seeking it. If you want to start criticizing people and bossing them around, you first have to prove to them that you know something they don't. What's not at all clear here is what exactly qualifies an executive assistant as a time-management expert. Is anyone (except obviously the letter writer herself) honestly surprised that managers and employees don't welcome "sugges-

---

Q. I'm in my early thirties and have a B.A. in business administration and an M.A. in organizational management. I am so burned out on the business world that I'm seriously considering going back to school for a Ph.D. in psychology. Is it too late for this kind of change? Am I insane for wanting to do it?

A. For heaven's sake, of course you are not insane. With your present background plus a doctorate in psychology, you could find whole new worlds of opportunity opening up before you in business, where shrinks are quite busy these days—for reasons that I think are already obvious to you. Go for it! Good luck!

tions" about their "really bad" work habits from the boss's secretary?

As a practical matter, if the chief operating officer is serious about wanting "Glorified Gofer" to be part of the management team, he needs to give her some real management-level responsibilities, so she can show the people around her that she can produce results. After a couple of years of solid accomplishment, perhaps a few very gentle suggestions about others' ways of doing things would get a fair hearing. Until then, however, who can blame her colleagues for resenting her presumption? To be blunt, just who does she think she is?

More to the point: Who do any of us think we are? On what precisely are we basing our opinion? And are we really sure that others see us as we see ourselves?

It's not at all unusual for people to overrate their own wonderfulness, of course. And therein lies a rueful irony. In mid-2000, the *Journal of Personality and Social Psychology* published a fascinating study by David Dunning and Justin Kruger, both Ph.D.s who teach psychology at Cornell University. Their research showed that when people are lacking in basic cognitive skills, including the ability to reason logically and to imagine or anticipate other people's reactions to their own behavior, these shortcomings—like a blind spot in a car mirror—also prevent them from recognizing what it is they're doing wrong. What it boils down to is: The more incompetent you are, the smarter you believe yourself to be.

Maybe you're alienating everyone around you without even realizing you are doing it, let alone having any clue as to why or how. People who fit this profile "will miss out on opportunities that could make their lives better," says Dunning. "They'll often forego training that they need. They will not seek out second opinions that could correct basic mistakes. So they may not rise in an organization. They may even get fired"—and never figure out what went wrong.

The only way to avert this dismal fate? "People should strive to improve their objective abilities," Dunning told *Psychology Today* magazine. "They should ask themselves about reasons their decisions might be wrong. It prevents them from being overconfident."

Don't overdo it. Too much doubt and hesitation can lead to paralysis by analysis. However, it never hurts to practice asking yourself whether you've really thought through whatever it is you're doing, including your approach to the people around you. Practice seeing things through their eyes, to the extent that you can. Question your own motives and methods once in a while. Be at least as critical of yourself as you are of anyone else. It could save your career.

One other mental habit worth cultivating: relax. Sometimes it may actually happen that you are right and everyone else is wrong. But how you react is crucial, not least because your physical health may depend on it. The human body is not designed to tolerate long periods of futile rage. While you're watching your cholesterol, keep an eye on your mood, too. In his book *Anger Kills: Seventeen Strategies for Controlling the Anger That Can Harm Your Health,* Duke University psychiatrist Redford Williams describes in truly chilling detail how being angry all the time can eventually shut you down altogether. Many other medical studies back up his findings. For example, Robert Kerns, who teaches psychology and neurology at Yale University, has done research proving that wallowing in negativity aggravates chronic physical pain such as headaches and backaches. Other studies suggest that anger also suppresses the immune system, leaving you open to a wide variety of physical ills, including cancer.

Hey, no job in the world is worth that kind of risk. So, how do you mellow out when someone at work is getting on your last nerve? Jim Paisley, a clinical psychologist and executive coach at Leathers Milligan & Associates in Phoenix, Arizona, offers this suggestion: Every time you start to stress out, stop for a moment and analyze the actual importance of the event in question—someone went out of his way to show you up in a meeting, or a colleague ignored a deadline—and assign the incident a score, on a scale of 1 to 10. A 1 will be completely forgotten a week from now; a 10 is the end of the world as you know it. "Most of the everyday b.s. that annoys people is really maybe a 2, or at most a 3," says Paisley. "If you treat everything like a 10, you're headed for a heart attack."

Here's something else that may help you keep cool the next time you're peeved at the office pest: If this person is really obnoxious, then the odds are that over the course of your career, you'll make a lot more money than he or she will. A couple of years ago, executive recruiters Ray & Berndtson set out to study the relationship, if any, between personality types and pay levels. Do nice guys really finish last?

Apparently not. The researchers discovered an interesting correlation. Belonging to a personality type called "neurotic"—which is "marked by displays of anxiety, insecurity, and hostility"—is expensive. "Neurotic" managers in the study earned at least $16,000 per year below average for their peer group. You might think of this as a premium you're earning for the hassle of putting up with your wacky colleague.

Every once in a great while, life does turn out to be (sort of) fair after all.

CHAPTER FOUR

Nobody Ever Told You It Was Going to Be This Complicated

Failure is only the opportunity to begin again more intelligently.
—HENRY FORD

Life is what happens while you're making other plans.
—JOHN LENNON

So here we are, tumbling along over the rocks and bubbles of the New Economy like so many ducks on a rain-swollen creek. The rules are new (no more promise, explicit or implied, of lifelong employment at any one company). The assumptions are different (risk is good, failure is chic, multimillion-dollar companies are founded on thin air, and people over fifty are hopelessly behind the curve—until their skills become so outdated as to be in desperately short supply:

Then they're as cool as Tony Bennett). This could all change—again—tomorrow. It probably will.

Inconveniently, we are still located on the same old planet, where a few constants remain. There are still only twenty-four hours in a day, seven days in a week, and a finite number of years in any given lifetime. Having a family, or any other passionate personal pursuit, still demands a certain irreducible amount of time, care, and attention. And, despite technology that keeps us in touch with each other more quickly and easily than could have been imagined less than a generation ago, no one has yet perfected a way of being in two places at one time.

Moreover, human beings are still the same old model, only subjected to more and different kinds of pressures than in the Old Economy. The same old troubles are still with us, only maybe more so. (It looks that way from where I sit, at any rate.) People make mistakes, sometimes disastrous ones. They fail at work—or, if they succeed there, they worry they may be failing at other things, and wonder what is going to matter more in the end. People get laid off. They get fired. Sometimes they sabotage their own careers and self-destruct, for reasons even they (let alone anyone around them) can't comprehend. Private pains and weaknesses, including the long-term ravages of too much stress, can derail even—or especially—a fast-track career.

A business world increasingly built for speed has little patience for anyone who can't keep up, or who just isn't entirely convinced that the game is worth the prize. Now more than ever, it's possible to run faster and faster without achieving any appreciable forward motion. This makes lots of people feel like failures if they haven't become, say, stock-market millionaires or dot.com start-up CEOs by age thirty. On top of the demands heaped on us by the actual work we do, many of us have become adept at setting standards for ourselves that practically guarantee a constant sense of falling behind, particularly if we take time out to raise families or simply to regroup our forces and rethink where we're trying to go. It's easier, and often seems safer in the short term, just to keep running. I hear from many, many managers who fit novelist and playwright William Saroyan's definition of a fanatic: "A man who redoubles his efforts after he has forgotten his aim." Living this way is a real high-wire act. It's easy to fall off. And, trust me, if you've ever taken a long tumble without a net to catch you, you're far from alone.

Some days, my mail reminds me of a homespun meditation on the human condition from a novel by Fannie Flagg called *Welcome to the World, Baby Girl!* (Flagg is better known as the author of *Fried Green Tomatoes at the Whistle Stop Cafe.*) In it, a character named Aunt Elner muses: "Poor little old human beings—they're jerked into this world without having any idea where they came from or what it is they're supposed to do, or how long they have to do it in. Or where they're gonna wind up after that. But bless their hearts, most of them wake up every morning and keep on trying to make some sense out of it. Why, you can't help but love them, can you? I just wonder why more of them aren't as crazy as betsy bugs."

The perils and complexities of trying to succeed now (or of even trying to define what success really is)—and a few thoughts on how to deal with some of the things that can go very, very wrong—are what this chapter is about. If you're one of the lucky ones who has never suffered a moment of self-doubt, let alone endured a trip to Career Hell that you couldn't seem to find your way back from, then congratulations and long may you prosper.

Now, all the rest of us . . . let's talk.

The Great American Stress-Out (or, Are You Sure You Have Time to Read This?)

Are you overworked? Because we're each unique, it's hard to generalize about what "overwork" really means. This is one place where the old saying "One man's meat is another's poison" is the plain truth. Your idea of an exhilaratingly full schedule might be my notion of an intolerable grind, or vice versa. The only sure rule is this: If your job is so relentlessly demanding that it makes you miserable—even when you're not working—then you're working too hard. Unfortunately, and perhaps counterintuitively, this can eventually wreck your career. It can also kill you, which you might think of as the ultimate career-buster.

It's no news flash that years of layoffs, restructurings, and other wide-ranging changes in how companies run things have heaped heavier workloads on vast numbers of people. Economists who study shifts in work patterns over time have been debating for about a decade now whether Americans are actually working longer hours than ever, or whether they just feel as if they are and thus exaggerate their real work hours when responding to surveys. Yet some reasonably reliable statistics overwhelmingly suggest that one paradoxical price of robust productivity is the van-

> **Q.** I'm an information-technology contractor, placed by an agency that retains me as a salaried employee. My current position has taken a turn for the worse, since my project no longer exists and I spend my days literally doing nothing. I have a few months left on this contract, but I will go insane if I stay here. Would it be bad form to ask my agency to place me somewhere else?
>
> **A.** As a rule, any job that makes you feel you will go insane is a job you should quit as soon as possible. It's hard to see how requesting a more challenging assignment could make you look bad—and there is such a dire shortage of people like you right now (as the chronically understaffed and overworked can testify) that letting you sit idle is scandalous. So by all means do ask for a new post, and good luck with it.

ishing of enough time off in which to savor the rising prosperity that comes with it. As one reader wrote me recently: "I'm seriously considering a career change, from running a futures-trading desk at [a major Wall Street firm] to teaching elementary school. Why? I've already made more money than I'll ever have time to spend, at this rate. I never see my kids and I just realized the other day that I haven't had a real vacation (sans laptop and cell phone) in six and a half years. I'll be forty in a few months, and I feel as if I'm missing my life."

An extreme case, that one, but I've no doubt that plenty of other folks know this tune. Consider: Data released in mid-1999 from the Census Bureau and the Bureau of Labor Statistics showed that the number of hours worked by members of the average middle-class American household shot up by almost 20 percent between 1979 and 1998. According to a nonprofit research group called the Economic Policy Institute, parents in two-income families put in a combined 3,335 hours at work in 1998, up from 3,200 in 1979—an increase of eight weeks of work per year. This trend runs counter to what's been happening in other parts of the world. The International Labor Organization reports that a typical American works 1,966 hours per year, sur-passing the Japanese by about 70 hours annually, and the Europeans by 350 hours, or almost nine full work weeks.

Of course, as anyone with a home computer, a home fax machine, a cell phone, a beeper, or any combination of these can attest, it's getting harder to know exactly when work stops and free time begins. You can't go to a ballet or a ballgame without seeing at least a smattering of people in the audience or the stands muttering into their little phones or peering at their Palm Pilots. Maybe you are one of them. And be honest: Even on an evening or a weekend when you are supposed to be relaxing (assuming you do get one of those now and then), have you never decided to check the office voice mail and e-mail "just in case"—and have you never consequently discovered some urgent (or simply intriguing) situation that sucked you straight back into work mode?

For many of us, letting go of work takes a conscious effort of will, and even then it has a way of creeping back in, especially for so-called knowledge workers who carry their best equipment between their ears and so can never really put it down anywhere. I've constructed some of my favorite columns, in my head, while making a peach pie or weeding a flower bed. I bet some of your best ideas have struck you when you've been physically out of the office, too—on a plane, in a restaurant, waiting in line at the Motor Vehicle Department. That's great, but it also means that the work switch is never set on OFF, because what if you miss something? What if the solution to a work problem is just waiting there in your brain, and you miss it because you're distracted by— oh, I don't know, anything. Life, for instance.

Here's a recipe for eventual burnout: Start with a genuine interest in what you're doing, add a big dollop of superquick communications technology, and then stir in one more ingredient, hypercompetitiveness. Everyone is feverishly vying to come up with the next Big Idea or win the next political skirmish. Never taking a break becomes, or at least comes to seem like, a matter of survival. In some organizations, anything short of obsessive dedication looks like slacking off. At General

---

Q. I've been working incredibly long hours at a start-up for the past four years, and I'm beginning to hate my job. Now the company is announcing all kinds of changes, which are supposed to be exciting, but how can I get psyched up for change when I am already at the breaking point?

A. It is going to be next to impossible to get excited about further demands from a job you already can't stand. I think it sounds as if you should take some time to figure out what you would rather be doing. Then go do it. Change is a constant everywhere now, but misery doesn't have to be.

Electric, for example, people joke that "a half-day means leaving at five"—and you get the distinct impression that although they're laughing they're not kidding. Even on vacation, plenty of hard-chargers seem loath to step out of the loop for long. A survey of five thousand managers, by Management Recruiters International, found that 82 percent reported taking work along on their most recent leisure trip, while 28 percent said they also kept in touch with coworkers by phone, 13 percent kept an eye on their office e-mail, and another 13 percent have cut short a vacation to return to the office.

Once upon a time, the most stressed-out workers were the ones whose daily labors routinely put them in touch with obvious physical danger. These employees were steelworkers, coal miners, dock workers, textile millhands. The danger came from molten steel, toxic chemicals, falling beams, lung-clogging dust. Of course, many people still work under that kind of direct physical risk. In the New Economy, where millions of workers toil in rela-tively clean, quiet, well-lit places, the health hazards are, weirdly, almost as gruesome. They're just invisible to the naked eye, and may take longer to produce dire symptoms. Bureau of Labor Statistics research says that in 1997 (the latest year for which fig-ures are available), white-collar occupations showed a higher inci-dence rate of stress-related disability than blue-collar jobs. Among the industries with the most stress: services, retail, finance, insur-ance, and real estate. In all, the National Institute for Occupational Safety and Health reports, a quarter of all American employees describe their jobs as "highly stressful."

So what? Well, first of all, working too hard for too long can actually do your career more harm than good. Ever been so fraz-zled by trying to keep track of a dozen things at once that you began to forget important details, like a lunch date with your boss or a report that was due a week ago? Ever notice that the longer

Q. I'm thinking of looking for a new job, but I just found out I'm pregnant. Should I postpone my search until after I've had the baby?

A. Absolutely. Although it is illegal for employers to discriminate against pregnant women, they often do it anyway (but good luck proving it in court); and simply not revealing that you're expecting could lead to some very hard feelings when the truth does out. However, the biggest reason to hold off until after the baby comes is that the combination of a new job and a new baby would be incredibly stressful. Unless you really have to change jobs now, you'd be far better off tackling one major life challenge at a time.

the hours you put in, the fewer really good, fresh ideas you seem to have? Hey, you're human. When Homo sapiens's brain is strained, it produces a hormone called cortisol. According to a fascinating study in the *Archives of General Psychiatry* (June 1999), researchers who injected volunteers with cortisol discovered that those who received the highest doses for the longest time had the most trouble remembering a story they had just been told. And that forgetful group had been getting the injections for only four days, so imagine what months or years of elevated cortisol levels might do. (The experiment had a happy ending, by the way: When the volunteers were tested again, a week after the shots stopped, their memories had reverted to preinjection sharpness.)

In Silicon Valley, where workaholism is endemic, tech companies have become so concerned over the effects of constant stress that they've spawned a whole new mini-industry of psychologists, gurus, and even yoga instructors—sometimes referred to collectively as "get-a-life consultants"—to help employees cope. The rest of corporate America may be quickly following suit, since costly absenteeism and turnover are on the rise everywhere, and there's considerable evidence that these problems are often stress-related. One 1998 nationwide survey showed that, overall, employers had seen a startling 180 percent leap in stress-induced absences in the space of just one year.

Clearly, losing one's mental edge, or sometimes just not showing up for work at all, or trying to flee excess pressure by constantly changing jobs, is not likely to do anybody's career any good in the long run. That's hardly the worst of it. Medical research is turning up new information all the time that directly links stress to heart disease, strokes, and suppressed immune-system functioning. The biological mechanisms involved are complex and still not completely understood, but there's little doubt that constantly feeling rushed, anxious, and exhausted causes the human body to produce high levels of toxic chemicals, including homocysteine, an amino acid that triggers heart attacks. In Japan in the eighties, when the Japanese economy was as turbocharged as ours in the United States is now, dropping dead from a heart attack at work was so commonplace that there is a word for it— *karoshi*, or death by overwork. "*Karoshi* widows," who had lost their spouses this way, mounted the Japanese equivalent of a class-action suit, seeking damages from employers.

A totally stress-free life probably has never existed and never will (and, even if it did, wouldn't it be awfully dull?). But now more than ever, protecting both your career and your health—and avoiding the calamities that can come from sacrificing either one on the altar of the other—requires keeping stress under control. A few employers are making real efforts to help. Ernst & Young, for instance, started a pilot program in 1999 that expressly encourages employees to ignore their e-mail and voice mail during weekends and vacations, while "utilization committees" keep an eye on workloads, redistributing assignments when anyone consistently racks up more than fifty-five hours a week. Still, managing your own stress level is largely up to you, and there are as many ways to do it as there are people: I might find that listening to jazz for half an hour relaxes me, while you'd rather pop down to the gym. The first step, though, is to give yourself permission to step away from work—and that can be the hardest part.

"Successful people get to the point where they don't feel valuable unless they're leaping tall buildings in a single bound," observes Ann McGee-Cooper, a Dallas consultant who wrote a book on how to beat job stress called *You Don't Have to Go Home from Work Exhausted!* "Most managers think they can't enjoy anything until after all their work is done. The trouble is, these days their work is *never* really done. So, without any fun in their lives, they go into a state of exhaustion and depression"—and, presto, career burnout soon follows. McGee-Cooper suggests taking short "joy breaks"—calling a loved one on the phone, doing a few stretching exercises, going out for a short walk, whatever would refresh you—several times a day. "Fun is necessary," she notes. "It changes your neurochemistry. It's good for you."

Fun may take some getting used to, at least initially, because in these often strangely puritanical times, relaxation is both desired and frowned upon. Funny, isn't it? The same computer technology that was supposed to make life easier (and in many ways does) may be causing us to think of ourselves, consciously or not, as more and more machinelike. The advertising industry, for one, encourages this tendency in subtle, pervasive ways. Just one example: A series of print ads for Hewlett-Packard that has appeared in *Fortune* and elsewhere, poses the question "You don't take breaks, why should your computer?"

Now, obviously this is a clever ad, because it caught my eye

> **Q.** After twelve years with this company, during which I've had to lay people off and do the work of several managers who left, I just found out that a whole new restructuring is going to start next month. I really am fed up, so much so that I'm depressed all the time. It's taking a toll on my marriage. I'd like to go back to school to learn a new career, but would such a radical move be a big mistake?
>
> **A.** At this juncture, a radical move might be the best kind you could make. No job is worth being depressed over, but what really alarms me here is that your marriage is suffering. Good jobs are a dime a dozen these days, but a good spouse is hard to find.

and held it, which is Madison Avenue's answer to the Holy Grail. In fact, the message ensnared my attention so thoroughly that I stared at the page for quite a while before I figured out why it bugged me. The reason was simply this: Leaving aside my computer's maddening habit of taking lots of unanticipated breaks (but that's another story), I am not a computer myself. Neither is anyone else. So why compare the behavior of computers and people, as if we had somehow merged into one species? Talk about a dangerous habit. Any human being who allows him- or herself scarcely more downtime than one would expect from, say, an Intel Pentium processor, has got a major systems crash coming—and probably at the worst possible moment, if actual computer behavior is any guide.

> **Q.** As a young female professional nearing thirty, I'm starting to consider having a family, and lately I've been thinking about how to make the best use of my time before I do so. I keep getting the feeling that I have to work twice as hard as my male colleagues in order to make up for the time (maternity leave, etc.) that I am going to lose later on. Is it unrealistic to think I can plan my career this way?
>
> **A.** Not at all. It may not seem fair, but you'd be wise to establish yourself as a "star" before you take time off to have kids. Otherwise, you're likely to find that reentry, even after a brief spell away, will be difficult and—depending on the pace of change where you work—could leave you far behind your peers. I'm not sure you need to work "twice as hard," though: Just focus all your energies on making a visible, measurable difference. And make sure that the people above you recognize what you are contributing.

Here's a tip. When you begin to feel overloaded, say no to something. This might be an extra assignment that popped up at the last minute (which someone else could probably handle as readily as you can, or more so); or a meeting at 6:30 P.M. that might just as effectively be scheduled for the following morning; or a short-notice business trip that would make you miss your

Q. I hope you don't think this is a silly question, but I'm curious: Is there any truth to the idea that having a pet can help reduce stress? (I want to buy my workaholic husband a dog.)

A. Good idea. Researchers at the State University of New York at Buffalo found in 1999 that the company of a dog or cat can indeed cut stress-related increases in blood pressure. The study, which tracked forty-eight stockbrokers already taking medication for high blood pressure, showed that those who spent time each day with four-legged pals experienced big drops in blood-pressure increases that had been brought on by job stress. "The ones with pets had a 50 percent drop in stress responses," said researcher Karen Allen, who owns a Border collie. Beyond that, dogs can be hilarious (mine are)—and laughter is one of the best stress-relievers going.

child's Little League game tonight, but could really be put off until tomorrow or the next day with no appreciable harm done to the business. Just say "no," either politely or, if necessary, not.

Many people who've been high achievers all their lives fall victim to something I call "A-Student Syndrome," a constant striving for perfection that becomes so ingrained and so excessive over the course of a lifetime that it transmogrifies into a full-blown neurosis. But the truth is, you can have a successful career and a fulfilling life without making A's in absolutely everything. And the chances are excellent that no one expects you to keep up a perpetual 4.0 average anyway (after all, who's perfect?)—no one, that is, except that nasty nagging little voice inside your own harried head.

In mid-2000, a reader of my Web column, who was under intense pressure in a sales job at a high-tech company, wrote that he feared he was headed for a bad case of burnout. He asked for suggestions from others who had been in his shoes on how they had avoided, or recovered from, a near-collapse brought on by overwork. The comments that poured in were fascinating—and, without exception, wise.

A typical tale, from a reader named Sandy Main: "I'm in sales and have been for most of my career life. Six years into it, I learned I had high blood pressure (at the ripe age of thirty!). When I took a good look at my career, I realized that I had put most of that pressure on myself, and I had to come up with a way to control it instead of it controlling me.... [Now] I just take one day at a time, and do the best that I can do without driving myself crazy. If the deal goes through, then great. If it doesn't, I did everything I could do to make it happen. I just move on to the next one.... Burnout is created by you. Calm down and stop killing yourself. Work smarter, not harder! If you're putting in twelve-hour days, shame on you!"

The point about letting go and moving on is well taken. Too often we let ourselves wallow in what didn't go right (a classic A-Student Syndrome symptom), instead of simply realizing that you can't win 'em all and letting the past be past. A bit of sage counsel on beating this kind of utterly futile stress comes from, of all people, the poet and essayist Ralph Waldo Emerson (1803–1882): "Finish every day and be done with it. You have done what you could; some blunders and absurdities crept in— forget them as soon as you can."

And for heaven's sake, put your vacation time—all of it—to good, lazy, leisurely use. You're entitled to a guiltless, hassle-free break. (Repeat after me: "I am not a computer.") It might prolong your life. In March 2000, the American Psychosomatic Society, which studies the connections between mental well-being and physical health, announced some intriguing research findings. A detailed sixteen-year project tracking 12,338 men aged thirty-five to fifty-seven found that, with other factors (diet, smoking, exercise) having been controlled, the men who took annual vacations where they actually relaxed were 21 percent less likely to get sick and die during the almost-two-decades-long study period than

Q. For the past four years I've moved several times to follow my wife as she pursued a master's, and then a doctoral, degree. How do I indicate to a prospective employer that I'm ready to settle down now?

A. Well, there is no substitute for saying so. Most employers these days are accustomed to the compromises that dual-career couples often make, so you needn't be shy about explaining exactly why you've moved so much. In any job interview, the main emphasis is on the future, anyway. If you go in there ready to present a clear and persuasive case for why you'd be great at the job you're applying for now, your hopscotch history should be no obstacle.

men who took no real vacations. The regular-vacationers' chances of dying of heart disease in particular were 32 percent lower.

If you are lucky enough to have a family, either nuclear or extended or both, and if you are so blessed as to have kept up close friendships over years or decades, make time to cherish them no matter what. Increasingly, employers who are worried about keeping their best people from jumping ship are making real efforts to help employees strike a healthy balance between their professional and personal lives. One example: On-site, employer-sponsored day care, once shunned as an expensive liability, is finally on the rise (and not a moment too soon). According to one estimate, about 8,000 major U.S. employers now offer this perk, up from a measly 204 in 1982. At the same time, some companies are scrambling to help employees manage their time by providing everything from banking to dry cleaning to take-home dinners right on the corporate premises.

According to much current research, there's every reason to believe that employers will be doing more of this sort of thing, since more employees and prospective hires are demanding it. This is partly because an ever-growing proportion of managers are women, and women are still the ones who most often take the main responsibility for making sure the kids are okay. An extensive survey of female executives, by the Chicago-based recruiting giant Spencer Stuart, shows that 75 percent of those polled are "actively trying to improve the balance between work and other elements of their life"—and, as is becoming ever more clear to smart employers, any company that wants to keep these women had better be willing to lend a hand, or at least stay out of the way. But getting a life is far from just a "women's issue." A Harvard University think tank called the Radcliffe Public Policy Center published a study in mid-2000 of 1,008 men and women nation-wide that showed a historic shift: Fully 82 percent of men aged twenty to thirty-nine ranked a "family friendly" work schedule as their most important criterion in choosing a job, ahead of money, power, and prestige.

Let's say you work for a company that hasn't yet gotten a clue about any of this. You owe it to yourself to insist on safeguarding your own sanity, even if you have to swim against the tide to do it. As my *Fortune* colleague Stanley Bing once wrote: "The people you love should be around long after you decide to hang it up and move to St. John"; and ensuring that they'll still be speaking to you by then "means pushing back respectfully every time people with no life try to steal yours from you."

You might even be pleasantly surprised at how accepting your colleagues are of your priorities. (Hey, even at GE, somebody must occasionally harbor a secret wish to go home and plant a rosebush or talk to a child or call a friend or something.) There may never be a better moment than now, in this talent-starved job market, to give it a try. Many bosses, anxious to avoid the costs and hazards of replacing you, are willing to be more accommodating than you might think.

Some of them even have real lives themselves. Shelly Lazarus, CEO of giant ad agency Ogilvy & Mather Worldwide, encourages all of the company's employees to get a life apart from work,

Q. I had a job with a Fortune 500 company but left to join a firm that offered me an opportunity (I thought) in e-commerce. Now, after four months, it's clear to me that the job has nothing at all to do with e-commerce. I'd like to leave, since I'm still getting other offers, but won't it look odd if I bail out after such a short time? How can I explain this to future employers?

A. I'll tell you what looks odd to me: I've gotten dozens of letters lately from readers complaining that they were promised one job but given another. This is a bizarre effect of the current recruiting crisis. Apparently some companies are so desperate for new talent that they will tell outright lies to get it. But you should never criticize a previous employer to a current or prospective one, so when you're asked why you're leaving this job so soon, just say, "I really want to work in e-commerce." That is, after all, the simple truth.

because she sees outside interests and commitments as a sine qua non of O & M's chief asset: creativity. Lazarus practices what she preaches. She once skipped a meeting with the firm's board of directors, in Paris, to go on a ski trip with her family. Horrors! But happily, the earth is still spinning on its axis. And Lazarus still runs O & M.

"You must keep a sense of perspective," she explained afterward to consultant and author Robert Rosen. "It's only business."

"I've Been Laid Off! Now What?"

In a work world ever more fraught with thorny contradictions, here's a big one: Survey after survey report that employers' number one worry is attracting and retaining enough skilled people. At conferences of human-resources managers, "the retention crisis" is always at the top of the agenda. Yet, at the same time, American companies are handing out more pink slips than at any time in over a decade. That is, they are eliminating vast numbers of jobs that are simply no longer seen as essential—not because the people doing those jobs have screwed up in any way, but because they happen to be in the wrong place at the wrong time.

What gives?

Certainly, some big staff cuts are going on in Old Economy industries that haven't benefited much, if at all, from cybermania. In early 2000, for instance, Bethlehem Steel Corporation announced that it would cut 15 percent of its salaried workforce, following a $183 million net loss in 1999, brought on partly by ferocious competition from overseas rivals; and J. C. Penney, struggling with some of the same profit pressures that have always beset traditional retailers, said it planned to close about three hundred department and drug stores, eliminating thousands of jobs. Then, too, mergers and acquisitions often create overlaps and duplications that lead to layoffs. After the merger of Exxon and Mobil, top officials of the new combined company revealed they would need sixteen thousand fewer employees, about two thousand of whom were laid off right away.

Still, what's truly new is that a lot of downsizing is happening because—although employers are indeed desperate to recruit and hang on to people with skills—the skills that are needed, as businesses change and shift direction, keep changing, too. The practice of hiring and firing large numbers of people at exactly the same time, but in different parts of the company and for completely unrelated reasons, is so

Q. When I joined this small but growing software company a year ago, I was told I'd be receiving an evaluation and a "bump up" in pay after nine months. In the meantime, my company was acquired by a larger one, and I haven't gotten the review or the raise. I like it here, but I feel I'm being unfairly ignored. What should I do?

A. Any merger does tend to distract managers—who are often busy trying to figure out what the consequences will be for their own careers—but there is no harm in trying a gentle reminder: "I know everyone's busy with the merger, but I was wondering about that review I was supposed to get...." Be aware, however, that the holdup may be due to some kind of restructuring that is in the works, so you may have to be patient. Since mergers so often bring layoffs, one word of warning: If your boss is suddenly reluctant to discuss your future with the company, it may mean that you don't have one.

widespread now that it has acquired a nickname: "churning." A June 1999 study of two thousand U.S. companies, by the American Management Association, found that 36 percent are creating large numbers of new jobs while cutting out existing ones, up from 27 percent one year earlier. By mid-2000, the steady drumbeat of news about layoffs had become so commonplace that it gave rise to some grim humor in the press. *The New Yorker* reprinted a headline (with an obvious typographical error in it) from *The Wall Street Journal:* CHESAPEAKE TO TRIM 205% OF ITS PAY-ROLL, TAKE A CHARGE. Quipped the magazine: "Will the last one out the door please fire himself again?"

For people who find themselves churned right out of their jobs, yet another trend adds injury to insult: less severance pay than in the past—sometimes a lot less. Outplacement behemoth Challenger Gray & Christmas reported in May 2000 that the median average length of severance pay had fallen to seventeen weeks, down 30 percent from twenty-four weeks in the same period the year before. Keen on keeping costs low—since, after all, no one can predict when an economic slowdown will end—companies are inclined to pay less and less to the folks they no longer need. The implication for you, if you work in a company or an industry where layoffs are widespread, is clear: To be on the safe side, pay off your credit cards and try to build up, or at least hold on to, your savings. Come up with a realistic financial plan for tiding you over in the event (no matter how unlikely it may seem right now) that the next batch of pink slips includes one with your name on it.

As you might expect, I hear from lots of people who fear they are about to be churned. "I work for a telecommunications company in the Midwest that is merging with a former competitor," went one typical letter. "Headhunters are calling me, and I'm wondering if I should leave while I have the chance. I like my job, but I'm worried that if I stay I'll get cut loose anyway. Upper management is saying nothing about layoffs, so what signs should I look for?" Foretelling a wave of job cuts is hardly an exact science but for some of the telltale signs, see a quiz entitled "How Safe Is Your Job?" at www.fortune.com.

George Bailey, a partner in PricewaterhouseCoopers in San Francisco whose title is chief innovation zealot, has noticed in his work with mergers-and-acquisitions clients that there are at least three ways to predict whether you'll survive a merger. First, have senior managers stopped talking about "a combination of equals", if indeed they ever started? If your company turns out to be a less than equal party, or has in fact been bought, "start calling those headhunters back," says Bailey. Second, do Wall Street analysts— or even newspaper and magazine reporters—suddenly seem to know more than you do about the company's plans? Not a good sign: "If the people above you intended to keep you onboard, you'd be getting regular updates on merger-related changes, including estimates of how many layoffs are expected and how soon." And third: "Start job hunting if your counterpart in the other organization plays golf with the CEO."

When I asked readers who had been laid off to write and tell me how they knew before any official announcement that the end was nigh, I got hundreds of interesting answers (some of which echo the tips in Chapter 2 on how to tell when you're being nudged toward the door), including:

•Marilyn: "If your supervisor or others above you begin to avoid you, or hem and haw when you ask for a long-term assignment, that's a tipoff."

•Samantha: "Watch out when your boss assures you nothing will change, yet hush-hush meetings with the 'three piece suits' are going on left and right."

•Tucker: "If your performance review is delayed indefinitely, or is unusually vague about future assignments, get your résumé out. Another warning is if travel authorizations, credit cards, or new business cards suddenly become hard to get."

•Neia: "We knew the company would start letting people go when the leasing company sent a 'repo man' to pick up the keys to the corporate cars. The company then threw a lavish Christmas party—and laid off two-thirds of the staff a week later."

•Douglas: "As a rule, I've noticed that those furthest out from the center of any circle or team usually get axed first. So, to decrease the odds, stay in close touch with managers and team leaders. Be where the action is. I call this 'the zebra rule.' It's the zebra at the edge of the herd that gets singled out by the lion."

Q. My last place of employment was so horrible that everyone except the boss dreaded coming to work each day. I finally got sick of it and quit on the spot, without notice. What should I say on my résumé about my abrupt departure?

A. Nothing. "I am continually astounded by the self-incriminating things people put on their résumés," says Robin Ryan, a career coach in Renton, Washington. "Put nothing on there except the dates of your employment, what your job was, and which valuable skills you gained from it."

What if you end up as lion bait? First, resist the urge to blame yourself (or, for that matter, anyone else). Being laid off is often just as big a blow—psychological, emotional, and financial—as being fired for cause. But even though you know in your rational mind that you're now out of a job through no fault of your own, and that a layoff really says nothing at all about your performance or capabilities, it's com-

mon to feel as if you should have done something to prevent it—
and to wonder whether prospective employers won't think the
same thing.

This is a misplaced worry. Job interviewers these days are well
aware that constant, unpredictable restructurings—which any
individual employee is powerless to prevent (and which any given
interviewer may be facing, too, especially in increasingly out-
sourced human-resources departments)—are just like the weather:
It affects nearly everybody one way or another, but what can anyone do?

Here's something else you should resist: any suggestion by your
current employer that you submit a letter of resignation instead
of, or in advance of, allowing yourself to be let go. About every
three months, I receive a wave of letters from readers whose
bosses are encouraging them to quit rather than be laid off, and
many of the soon-to-be-unemployed want to know the pros and
cons of signing a resignation letter. Well, the pros are stunningly
simple: There aren't any. I've asked several attorneys around the
United States, who noted that in most states a letter of resignation—while it may be a short-term balm to your pride—usually
disqualifies you for unemployment benefits, which could replace
from 40 percent to 60 percent of your current income for up to
six months. Says Gerald Maatman, partner in charge of employment law at Baker & MacKenzie in Chicago: "By resigning in the
face of an impending layoff, you'd just be kissing away thousands
and thousands of dollars." Ouch.

Plenty of people bounce back from a layoff without too much
trouble. After all, in this job market, if one company no longer has
a use for your talents (at the moment, anyway), the odds are good
that another one will. Every time the topic of layoffs comes up in
my column, I hear from any number of folks who have been laid
off more than once in the past several years—including one in-

trepid marketing manager who has been churned five times since 1990—and who have managed each time to hop into a better job before their severance pay was even spent. It's not an unusual pattern. A survey by Louis Harris & Associates of laid-off managers, showed that 82 percent believe they are better off in their new jobs than they've ever been before.

Unhappily, however, not everybody is so lucky—or so resilient. What if being downsized knocks you for such a loop that you just can't seem to get back on your feet? "After twelve years of working seventy-hour weeks in a senior position at a Fortune 500 company, I got laid off. This came as an enormous shock because, although I knew there was a restructuring in the works (in fact I helped plan it), I didn't expect to be one of its casualties," wrote someone who signed himself "Spinning My Wheels." The result: "I've been going on lots of job interviews, but I can't seem to get motivated, and I guess interviewers must sense that. I feel so disillusioned that if I were a few years older, I'd retire now and say the hell with it. How can I end this slump?"

Anyone who's put in years of grueling hours, only to get the big surprise kiss-off, is in dire need of a break. If this applies to you, stop going on job interviews. Take a vacation. Play golf, or go rock climbing, or tour with a bluegrass band, or whatever floats your boat. "Too many people's first impulse is to go from

Q. A couple of months ago I was laid off from a job I had held for eight years and, after the initial shock and dismay, I was surprised to find that my main feeling was one of relief. This makes me think I need to switch into a totally different career field, where maybe I'll actually find something satisfying to do, but I need help in positioning myself and figuring out how to transfer my skills. What should I do?

A. At this point it would be worth your while to invest in a few sessions with a professional career coach, who can help you figure out how to get there from here. To get in touch with one near you, go to www.coach-federation.com and click on the "Find a Coach" icon. And best of luck to you in your new career!

high gear to high gear. They rush out and try to get the same kind of job they just lost," says Dave Corbett, founder and CEO of Boston-based New Directions, which specializes in helping managers redesign their careers after a layoff or firing. "What you need is to get into neutral for a while. For high-achieving people especially, there is a lot of guilt around the idea of taking time off. But it's okay. In fact, you have to do it. Stop and think about how you really want to spend the next twenty or thirty years." This may be the first real chance you have ever had to make some thoughtful, informed choices. Take advantage of it.

A bad case of the blues after any career debacle is perfectly understandable. But Corbett says, "That loss of confidence and purpose has got to be addressed before you can move forward." How do you do that? While you are taking a nice breather from the job hunt, Corbett suggests doing three things. First, build a support system of people who care about you: "Involve your family. Sit down with your spouse and find out what his or her aspirations are, and what kind of life you might be able to redesign together. Spend time with friends you may not have seen for a while." The point is to strengthen your sense of yourself as a whole human being—not just, or even primarily, as an unemployment statistic.

Toward the same end, review in detail all your life accomplishments so far: "Go all the way back to high school or even earlier. What achievements have given you the most pleasure? Include everything in this inventory, whether it's a winning touchdown pass you threw in college or a poetry prize you won in the eighth grade. Who are you? What do you excel at? Where are your strengths? What have you loved doing?" Adds Corbett: "We counsel a lot of former pro athletes, and they're good at this process because they know their stats. What are yours?"

From there, the goal is to get back into the working world in a way that reflects your—pardon the consultantese—core competencies. What you end up doing may surprise you. One of Corbett's clients, the former head of a consulting firm, "thought he wanted to take charge of a company again right away. But after some real introspection, he realized that he didn't want that at all." The man now spends about one-third of his time consulting, another third running a mentoring program for inner-city kids, and much of the rest fly-fishing with his twenty-seven-year-old son, whom he'd hardly seen in his years as a corporate hotshot.

Of course, not everyone reshuffles his or her priorities so drastically, but even if you decide you really do want the same kind of job you had before, at least now you'll know why. And one tip from Corbett for your next job hunt: "Focus on each interview as if it were the only one. High achievers tend to be two steps ahead of themselves at every turn. But you can't run a marathon in one twenty-six-mile leap. You run it one telephone pole at a time."

This all sounds great, but does it work? Judging from the mail I got after Corbett's advice appeared in the magazine column, it does indeed. "I got laid off from my seventeen-year corporate job two years ago and . . . took time off to explore my life," wrote Nancy Hendriks from Ajax, Ontario, Canada. She rediscovered a childhood love of writing fiction, "learned how to run a business from end to end as an entrepreneur (never had that chance before) . . . and made a lot of new friends along the way." She then observed: "It is interesting that when we are in the flow of an aggressive corporation, life seems to stop, or at the very least we develop blinders. . . . I'm ready to go back to work [for a big company], mostly for financial reasons, but not in the blindly ambitious way I was two years ago. . . . If someone were to ask me if I wanted to go back to my old job, my old life, the answer would be a resounding NO!"

Added a reader signed "Older and Wiser": "One thing that

being laid off taught me is that while I'll always want to work hard and contribute as much as I can, I'll never again let any job or company become so all-consuming that losing my place in it would devastate me. I am a lot more than just what I do for a living." Another reader named Peter agreed: "If I've learned anything at all in the nineties, it's that *all* jobs are one whim away from a downsizing." Or, as they used to say on Wall Street, when thousands of hard-charging workaholics got laid off after the stock-market crash of 1987: "Never love a corporation, because a corporation cannot love you back."

Okay, So You Failed—but You're Not a Failure

Wouldn't it be terrific if we could all see our failures as Thomas Edison saw his? "I haven't failed," he once said. "I've just tried 1,001 experiments that didn't work." Alas, most of us are far harder on ourselves than that—even though we know in moments of lucidity that beating ourselves up over What Went Wrong will only make it harder to scrape up the enthusiasm, and the courage, to take on a fresh challenge or to regain lost ground. From where I sit, it seems that when people talk about major career mistakes, they're describing three basic situations: debacles that, while they're embarrassing and perhaps costly, leave you still hanging on to your job (but wondering how to get your reputation back); those that result in your getting sacked; and those that seem to recur over and over again, throughout years or even decades, without your understanding why.

The great thing is that none of these—repeat, none of them, nor any of their almost infinite permutations and variations— need be fatal or even permanently harmful to your career. Failure isn't fun, but it is often a far better teacher than success. As an added bonus, it can make you more compassionate toward others'

Q. I just suffered a major set-back at work, and I'm try-ing to look on the bright side, but I just don't see how anything good can come out of this. Any suggestions on how to keep a positive attitude (even though I'm really disappointed in myself)?

A. Try making a list of every-thing you would do differ-ently if the same situation that led to your setback were ever to arise again. And bear in mind that real wisdom comes from accepting that you're not perfect (nor is anyone else). As James Thurber once said, "It is better to know some of the questions than all of the answers."

occasional stumbles, and more willing to see what can be learned from those, too.

"Dear Annie," wrote a reader signed "What Now?" whose trou-bles came from the first, and arguably mildest, of the three types. "Can you offer any thoughts on how to come back from a fail-ure? I was running an important project and—through a combina-tion of mistakes on my part, misunderstandings (bad commu-nication), and some old enmities (certain people wanted me to fail)—it went very wrong. I won-der if I can recover from this, or whether I should just leave [the company]."

Let's say you're in this situation, too. As tough as things look right now, don't succumb to the debilitating notion that failure is somehow your personal cross to bear. Everybody fails sometime. In my own life, it has seemed to me that the people I like the best are those who admit that every now and then something impor-tant to them has not worked out, and that has stung. Sure, there will always be the oblivious souls who have never taken a false step (or who, if they have, won't admit it even to themselves). But these are not people you would want to know. Or work for. Or be. And let's not even get started on the nearly endless lists of great achievers who have suffered setbacks and were none the worse for it in the long run. Think of Babe Ruth. He hit more home runs than anybody in his day. He also struck out a record 1,330 times.

Of course, what complicates life is that some employers send mixed messages. "Lots of organizations pretend to encourage risk taking," says Richard A. Moran, a partner at Accenture (formerly Andersen Consulting) in San Francisco. "But everybody's still terrified. They know better than to believe this 'go ahead and fail' stuff, because they know it can carry a heavy price."

How heavy depends on several factors. For one, how good are your people skills? Andrew Sherwood, chairman of New York City consulting firm Goodrich & Sherwood, suggests that you contemplate how some politicians survive one snafu after another: "A lot of it has to do with how you interact with your critics. Ronald Reagan came back from several major scandals by drawing on a certain warmth, an earnestness that people trusted, and, most important, a keen sense of humor."

Beyond that, how fully you can bounce back may depend largely on how good your reputation was in the halcyon days of yore. If the people above you always used to trust your judgment and admire your performance, you can probably clamber back into their good graces. Do not, Sherwood advises, simply say, "I'm sorry." Do say you're sorry, but then spell out just why you thought your approach to the project would work, and

Q. I was recently fired from a position I had held for the past two years. When I took the job, I signed an agreement that provided for me to receive a bonus if certain criteria were met. This was in lieu of salary increases. After about a year, the company policy changed to eliminate this kind of bonus and put everyone on commissions instead. I did get commissions, which were less than the bonus would have been. But is my original agreement still binding?

A. You need to have a lawyer review your contract and advise you on whether it is binding or not. To find an attorney near you who can do this, go to Martindale-Hubbell's Web site, www.lawyers.com, enter your city and state, and type "employment" or "contract" in the search field labeled "Practice Area." If you do end up getting your bonus, of course, you'll have to give back the commissions. That plus the price of legal help may add up to more expense and bother than it's worth.

describe in some detail how you'd fix it if you had it to do over again. Don't mention old grudges or political minefields, even if they contributed directly to your downfall. The people involved probably know all about that stuff, and you don't want to seem to be whining or trying to shift blame. You also don't want to dignify malice by acknowledging it.

If you know that you failed, and are willing to admit it and frankly examine the reasons for the failure, you're already ahead of the game. Says Rich Moran, "You'd be surprised how many people sit around deluding themselves that everything is fine"—which only makes higher-ups think that you lack a grip on reality. However, Moran adds, you are the only one who knows for sure whether you have the energy and confidence to get back in there, try again, and win. "If you truly don't believe you can get back in the game, by all means go somewhere else and start fresh."

There's no shame in doing that. One of the most felicitous features of the New Economy is that—strange but true—falling on your face is increasingly becoming socially acceptable, even downright fashionable. It's seen as evidence that you stepped out of the predictable and, like Thomas Edison, tried an experiment that didn't pan out, whether it was a new product that flopped or a whole start-up that went under. "Failure is a badge," Irv Grousebeck, an entrepreneurship professor at Stanford University's

Q. What should you say if a job interviewer asks why you were fired from your last job? I work in a very gossipy industry where everyone knows everyone else's business, and word got around that I got sacked after a fight with my boss (which is true, though very oversimplified). I'm pretty sure I'll get a new job soon, but I just don't know what to say about what happened.

A. If you're pressed, give an explanation, but keep it brief. What were you and your boss arguing about? If it was a difference of opinion over company strategy, for example, then say so. But don't put your old boss down—there is always the outside chance that he or she was right—and avoid lengthy self-justifications that will make you seem like a whiner.

graduate business school, told *The New York Times* not long ago. "It is not just that these people had guts enough to take risks," but that employers from Internet boutiques to the Fortune 500 assume that "[people who have failed at something] learned under the whip of urgency." The economy's backflips have also made job interviewers more forgiving than in times past. "We need people with experience," says Jim Wall, head of human resources at Deloitte & Touche. "And, hey, if you're out there competing in the world, life happens."

No one keeps statistical track of how many people have been using a setback as a springboard to greater heights. But I keep coming across anecdotal evidence that, in these topsy-turvy times, failure is no obstacle. In May 2000, a reader of my Web column wrote to say that he had started a business right out of college that went bankrupt after four years, and he was nervous about how prospective employers might view that. Should he hide it and pretend to have been doing something else during that time? A much better approach, I told him, would be to mention that he had run his own business and to talk about all the many things that experience had taught him. He tried it and, a few weeks later, he wrote me that interviewers were so impressed by his initiative, and his candor, that he got a whole string of job offers, each more lucrative than the last. Now his biggest problem was choosing among them—a very nice problem to have.

Let's say that, unlike the reader signed "What Now?" you have no choice about whether to go to a different company and start anew. To be blunt about it, you've been canned. Consider this letter, from a reader signed "Sitting on the Sidelines": "I was fired about four months ago for performance reasons, and I'm not disputing that I probably deserved to be. To make a long story extremely short, after six years with the company and two previous promotions, I think I was promoted the third time to a position that was more than I could handle, and I messed up a couple of big projects. . . . Now I'm trying to get my career back on track and while I have no trouble getting interviews, I've yet to receive a single offer. (I have good references, from former bosses and colleagues from before my Waterloo, so I know that isn't the problem.) What am I doing wrong?"

Without being a fly on the wall in those job interviews, I have no way of guessing what "S.O.S." might be doing wrong; but here are a few thoughts for anyone who shares his dilemma. First, don't go into an interview with a hangdog look about you—that is, with an attitude that broadcasts your belief that you deserved to be fired. Clearly you made some mistakes. Who hasn't? Whatever they were, you are unlikely to repeat them. And if, like "S.O.S.," you were promoted frequently at your old company, you must have been doing something—probably a great many things— right. To get your confidence back, concentrate on those accomplishments. Which ones are you proudest of? Which were most profitable for the company, or had the biggest effect on overall strategy, or both? What skills did you develop in your old job that might be particularly useful to your next employer? What are you hoping to achieve?

It's not easy to accentuate the positive when you're feeling so low you could shimmy under a snake's belly without taking your hat off, as they say in the Carolina Low Country. But try. If, like "S.O.S.," you have solid references, focus your thoughts on those. One mistake, or even a series of them, does not cancel out years of success, although it may feel that way right now. Bear in mind that job interviewers, who don't know you—and are thus sublimely detached from your recent troubles—will take their cue from the signals you send. If you seem sure of your skills and ready to draw valuable lessons from what hasn't gone so well lately, they'll willingly share your view of yourself as a talented person with the flexibility to move forward into the future.

And the future, after all, is what job interviews are about. The most frequent questions I get from readers revolve around worries about past tribulations: a boss who despised them, a rival colleague who went out of his or her way to make them look like a buffoon, even a pending lawsuit against a former employer. Apart from the cardinal rule that one should never, ever, under any circumstances, bad-mouth one's old company, remember this: Job interviewers really do not much care what happened last month, or last year, or three years ago. When you get right down to it, what they are paid to care about—and they do care a great deal—is what you can bring to the party next month, next year, and on into the indefinite future. Wow 'em with your ideas about that, and you'll more than likely be back on top before long.

I'd be remiss to leave the topic of failure without a few words about what I see as Type Three: a pattern of self-defeating behav-

Q. I'm a senior manager with a strong track record, but I recently made a terrible mistake. At an outing with my boss, I drank too much and made a scene. I was "allowed to resign," rather than being fired. Word gets around fast in this business. Is my career over?

A. Says Laura Berman Fortgang, president of InterCoach Inc. in Montclair, New Jersey: "The thing about being drunk is that you are telling the truth, albeit in a distorted or exaggerated way. So think hard about what you said. What was the kernel of truth in it?" Fortgang suggests that this might be a good moment for you to think about a total change of career. Why? "Because a 'scene' dire enough to cost you your job is a symptom of some kind of deep unhappiness that has been building up for a very, very long time. Ask yourself what it was that you were so upset about— and how can you fix it, either in this industry or somewhere else? Try to see this as an opportunity to rethink what you really want to do with your life." Even if your career is indeed over in your current business, that doesn't mean you can't start fresh in a different one. "When you look back on this years from now," Fortgang adds, "you may see it as either the worst or the best thing that has ever happened to you." Here's hoping it's the latter.

ior wherein, over and over again, you find yourself messing up whenever things start to go well for you. This is far from rare, and we've all seen cases of it in corporate life: the talented person, with everything going for him or her, who seems to be his or her own worst enemy, self-destructing for no reason that anyone can fathom. Sometimes self-sabotage takes spectacular forms, and occurs just when the person in question is on the brink of a major triumph. Robert Meuleman, chairman and CEO of Amcore Financial in Rockford, Illinois, once told me about a bright young banker who used to work for him. This fellow had a solid marriage and a shining future—until shortly after his promotion to the presidency of a division. Then he embarked on a flagrant affair with one of his subordinates, whom he proceeded to knock down a flight of stairs. "We don't know to this day why he destroyed his own life that way," said Meuleman, who fired him. "His career has never recovered."

You'd never be so reckless, you say? Probably not. But hold on. Most often, being your own worst enemy is a far more subtle thing. Let's say you're in line for a promotion you've worked hard toward for years, and you suddenly find that you can't seem to get to work on time. Or you start losing your temper in meetings with higher-ups where cool is the rule. Or you somehow misplace all the data for a client presentation that could make or break your team. Or maybe you haven't made any obvious blunders, but you haven't been doing your best work for quite a while now, and you don't know why.

Any of these examples, and then some, may share a common cause: fear of success. It's strange to think that fear of succeeding could be much of an issue or do much damage. But it is, and does. "Fear of success is a terrible problem in this culture," says Brian Schwartz, a psychologist and consultant who has counseled many underperforming executives. "The vast majority of clients I see are afflicted with it." What is so treacherous about this anxiety is that people who suffer from it most acutely are usually not even aware they have it.

The dread of doing well in life is rooted deep in the unconscious. Nobody deliberately sets out to wreck his or her own career. And people are so adept at rationalizing their own mistakes, or misinterpreting those of others, that fear of success can be hard to distinguish from, oh, incompetence, arrogance, inattention, burnout, or any of the 101 other gremlins that can send a career into a tailspin. Often fear of success shows up in the exceptionally talented as a long pattern of underachievement, of schlubbing along in the same old rut. "People who have an unconscious fear of success won't set ambitious goals for themselves, so they achieve far less than they're capable of," says psychologist James O'Connell. "And this is the tragedy of it, because ultimately it stops people from getting what they really want, or even from asking for help."

If this is an unconscious fear, how can you tell if you've got it? Shrinks have been studying the problem since 1915, when Sigmund Freud wrote an essay called "Those Wrecked by Success." He noted the "surprising and bewil-

Q. For the past year or so I've been seeing a therapist once a week, to deal with some issues in my life that I think were having a damaging effect on my career. Recently someone in my office found out that I'm in counseling and, since this person is a close friend of my boss and will probably mention it to him, I'm concerned that I'll be perceived as weak. Am I worrying over nothing?

A. I really hope so—not only for your sake but for that of everyone else working there, your boss included. Anyone who would see you as "weak" for getting professional help has got a few issues of his own to work out. (Would anyone think you were "weak" for going to a dentist if you had a toothache?) But I suspect that you are, to use a bit of shrinkspeak, projecting. The truth about what most of us are doing in our off hours—whether it's therapy, needlepoint, or competitive mud-wrestling—is that no one at the office is likely to be giving it any thought at all.

dering" tendency of some people to fall apart "precisely when a deeply-rooted and long-cherished wish has come to fulfillment . . . as though they were not able to tolerate happiness." As with the Illinois banker, a spate of self-destructive behavior—often involving drinking, drugs, sex, or all three—immediately before or after a major career victory is a dead giveaway. Says Elissa Sklaroff, a therapist in Philadelphia who treats success-fearing executives: "Being on the brink of success brings a crisis, and all of our neuroses pop right up to the surface. On some level, success-fearing people are running from change—especially from having to change their secret self-image as an unsuccessful or undeserving person."

At one time or another, of course, most of us have had occasion to ask, What was I thinking? Maybe you've procrastinated until a crucial deadline has sailed by (I know I have), or inserted foot firmly in mouth at the most awkward possible moment, or had one cocktail (or was it six?) too many at the office Christmas party, or showed up inexcusably late for a big job interview. Over time, too many of these kinds of missteps should be telling you something. "Self-defeating behavior feels, to the person doing it, like an accident or like bad luck. And of course there are such things," says Lenora Yuen, a therapist in Palo Alto who specializes in helping the chronically self-sabotaged. "But after a while, you may start to notice a whole series of 'accidents,' a whole long run of 'bad luck.' " Warning lights should flash.

At the risk of sounding too unduly Californian, the core of the problem of fear of success is a lack of self-esteem, usually caused by bad stuff that happened to you as a child or adolescent and battered your sense of how worthy you are. Says Brian Schwartz, "People will only allow themselves to achieve the level of success that their image of themselves can absorb." Long ago, if someone important to you—a parent, a teacher, a sibling, a bullying teammate—convinced you that you weren't very smart, or very likable, or that nothing you did was ever quite good enough, you will have the devil's own time believing that you're capable of doing well in life or that you deserve to. Because it requires digging into a lot of painful ancient history, overcoming fear of success is not easy. The first step is just accepting that you have it, and that it needs to be dealt with before it does you any more harm. For a quiz designed to diagnose fear of success, go to www.fortune.com.

Is there a cure? Apart from professional therapy, psychologists recommend trying a couple of other strategies. Jim O'Connell urges you to make a conscious effort to guard against negative thoughts ("I'm not as good as people think I am," "I'm not going to get what I want" . . .). The more you pummel yourself, the worse things are likely to get. Self flagellation, O'Connell says, "feeds directly into the unconscious, and there is no filter there to stop it." Corny or not, positive thinking does have power. Remember Henry Ford's dictum: "If you think you can't, you're right. If you think you can, you're right."

Try to get help from a trusted colleague (even a boss) who will warn you when you seem ripe to repeat a self-destructive habit at work. Says Lenora Yuen: "Sometimes just interrupting the behavior will stop it. It ceases to be an automatic routine." Mentoring, in vogue at lots of big companies now, serves at least two vital functions for the success-phobic: It provides this kind of benevolent lookout, and it offers people a dose of the support and encouragement they never got as kids. In some careers, that can make all the difference. Yours may be one of them.

Nothing as complex as fear of success can be beaten without a fight. But the shrinks are unanimous on one point: Among business people, who as a group tend to be, in Elissa Sklaroff's words, "smart, pragmatic, and determined," the long-term recovery rate is quite high.

Whatever the proximate cause of career meltdown in any particular instance—an error in judgment, a personality clash with a boss, fear of success, or simply being in the wrong job at the wrong time—I believe, based on two decades of close observation of the business scene, that there is nothing you can't come back from. And I do mean nothing. In this, as in so much else in life, the key is persistence—coupled with a healthy belief in your own abilities that nonetheless doesn't stop you from asking for help from others when you need it.

Want proof? Look at Ellen Hancock. A twenty-nine-year-veteran senior executive at IBM, Hancock was fired by IBM chief Lou Gerstner. She went to Apple and when Steve Jobs took over, he gave her the boot, too. Gray-haired and unemployed at fifty-four, Hancock hired an outplacement counselor to help her plot her next move. What's she doing now? Well, she's president and CEO of Exodus Communications, which runs the back-office computer systems that power Web sites like Yahoo and eBay. She's also become a multibillionaire, richer as of this writing than Gerstner and Jobs put together. I interviewed Hancock some years ago, for an article in *Fortune* about women executives, and what struck me about her at the time was how smart she was. Now it's clear she's smart enough not to let anything keep her down for long.

Granted, not everybody who washes out of a job—much less two big jobs in a row—ends up a multibillionaire CEO. But think about it. Maybe the most successful business people get where they are, at least in part, because they never give up trying. Or, as some wise person once put it, "It doesn't matter how many times you slip and fall. What matters is how many times you get up again."

Pardon Me, but Is That a Skeleton in Your Closet?

Careers, like any other human endeavor, don't take place in a vacuum. We're all subject to the unruly influences of illness, happenstance, and individual quirks; and life's complications do have an unfortunate way of spilling over into the office, often at the most inopportune times. If a personal problem from your past has ever threatened to come back and haunt you—particularly during a job search—let me tell you, you've got plenty of company. In fact, with so many people changing jobs so frequently these days, it often seems to me that job interviewers must be fairly deafened by the rattling of old bones, whose owners are given to writing me in a panic about how to keep the noise down.

The essential question in nearly every case is whether to bring up an old bugaboo and talk openly about it, or keep mum and hope that prospective employers either won't discover it or won't hold it against you if they do. There are no hard-and-fast rules about this, but experts I've spoken with have generally recommended complete honesty, on both ethical and practical grounds (with one interesting exception, which we'll get to shortly). Sometimes, patching up the past may even require you to go back to a former employer for a heart-to-heart talk about what happened and why.

Consider this letter, from a reader signed "Fully Recovered": "Eight years ago I suffered from a medical condition that obliged me to take medication that made me so temperamental and irascible that nobody could stand to work with me. So my contract with my then-employer was not renewed, even though my boss had always raved about how great my work was before I became ill. Now I'm completely well, off the medication, and back in the job market. Interviewers admire my credentials, but after they've asked for a reference and I give them my old boss's name, I never hear from them again. Has my old illness doomed me?"

The first thing to understand is that plenty of people—including many in a position to do some serious hiring and firing—have been through some kind of personal hell themselves; and nobody comes back from that journey empty-handed. No interviewer at any company you'd want to work for is going to think less of you for having been ill. Rather, the problem here stems from a recent rash of big nasty lawsuits against ex-employers who allegedly gave out false or otherwise flawed data about employees who had left. Many companies are now so leery of being sued (again) that they hesitate to reveal anything at all about anybody. So prospective employers are extremely limited in what they can find out about you from your old boss. Just about the only two questions that won't get anyone in legal hot water are "Was this person in your employ?" along with a few factual details like the dates you worked there and what your title was, and "Would you rehire this person if you had the chance?"

If you've ever left a job under some kind of thundercloud (medication-induced or not), it's the second question that is likely to cause trouble. Says Jim Hunt, president of Atlanta executive-coaching firm eChange2: "A potential employer who asks if your old boss would rehire you and hears 'no'—with, remember, no specific details available about why not—will tend to imagine the worst: Were you incompetent, dishonest, a sexual harasser, or what? They're going to be thinking, 'Do I want to take the

Q. About seventeen years ago, when I was nineteen, I was arrested for possession of marijuana, pled guilty, and spent six months on probation. (It was a first offense and I've never had any contact with the criminal-justice system since then.) Now I want to change careers but I hesitate even to apply for any job where they might do a criminal-background check. Any thoughts?

A. Go ahead and apply for any job you want. It's highly unlikely that this old offense will turn up in a background check, and even if it does, surely any job interviewer with any sense knows that nineteen-year-olds are apt to do dumb things. If you've been successful in the intervening years, this just isn't going to matter—nor should it.

chance?' " So unless you turn that "no" into a "yes," or even a "maybe," you might as well unplug the phone.

"The only way to approach this is head-on," says Hunt. "Go back to your old boss and make an appointment to sit down and talk." Explain exactly what your problem was, in the bad old days, and tell how it's been fixed. It also couldn't hurt to drop a few subtle reminders into the conversation about how much he used to like your work before your trouble set in and spoiled things. Show him, in other words, that you're fully operational, and reference-worthy, now. Who knows? In this job market, he might even rehire you.

Let's suppose it wasn't a health problem that derailed you but a financial one. After a decade of skyrocketing personal bankruptcies (which peaked at 1.3 million in 1998 and declined somewhat, to 1.2 million, the following year), it's no surprise that I hear from so many people who fear that a lousy credit history will wreck their chances of getting a job they want. If this worries you too, cheer up: Only about 25 percent of all U.S. employers routinely seek information about job candidates' personal credit, and most of those are in the retailing and finance industries. What's that you say? You're looking for a job as a department-store buyer? Or a bank branch manager? Oh.

At least no company can peer into your dark past without warning you first. The Federal Fair Credit Reporting Act requires that employers obtain a form, signed by you, authorizing them to poke around. Let's suppose that, like one reader signed "Former Deadbeat," you ran up an unmanageable bunch of bills some years ago and have been slowly digging yourself out ever since. Says Amy Kohn, an employment attorney who now works as a consultant at Hewitt Associates: "Do sign the authorization form if you are asked to." Now, here comes the exception to the total-honesty policy that I mentioned a few paragraphs back. Adds Kohn, "But if the employer doesn't bring up the subject, neither should you." In other words, if nobody asks you to sign the authorization, it probably means that the job you're applying for—even if it is in retailing or finance—doesn't demand a stellar credit history anyway.

Moreover, for jobs that do require it, even a truly grim pile of bad debts doesn't necessarily mean that you won't get hired. A lot depends on how you got in so deep. "Generally, if your credit problems arose from causes beyond your control—say, a layoff followed by a big bunch of medical bills—most employers won't hold it against you," says Kohn. "Describe the circumstances that created the problem, and emphasize your progress in getting out of debt." If, on the other hand, your credit crisis came from having gone hog-wild while shopping on the Internet—"which could lead a potential employer to question your overall judgment," Kohn notes—you might want to postpone your search for a new job until your old lapses get expunged from your credit record. That takes seven and a half years.

If most employers can overlook the effects of an illness (provided they know that's what it was) and couldn't care less about your credit history, then what kinds of things do they try to find out about you? A fascinating poll of 2,640 U.S. companies, by the Society for Human Resource Management (SHRM), shows that routine background checks mostly uncover strictly business-related facts: 81 percent of the companies surveyed say they verify that you have worked where you say you have, and 57 percent seek confirmation that your title in your last job was what you say it was. Fair enough. Fewer than half (44 percent) check—or, more commonly, hire professional investigators to do it—to see if you have a criminal record.

Do driving mishaps count? More than 1.4 million Americans are arrested every year for driving while impaired, so I hear lots of fretting about this. "About three years ago I was on my way home from a friend's wedding reception when I got stopped on suspicion of driving under the influence," wrote one reader signed "On Pins & Needles," who had just finished a round of interviews for a management job at a Fortune 500 company. "I sort of panicked and refused to take a Breathalyzer test (big mistake), which resulted in an automatic suspension of my driver's license for ninety days. At the hearing, the judge gave me a year of supervised probation, which I completed without incident. (I've never been in any other trouble with the law.) Is this likely to surface in a background check? If so, will it take me out of the running for this highly desirable job?"

There is certainly no guarantee that a three-year-old DUI will surface in a background check unless you're applying for a job as, say, an airline pilot. The SHRM study says that 28 percent of corporate human-resources departments "regularly" dig into job candidates' driving records, while another 24 percent "never" do. Intrigued by this, I did my own informal survey of half a dozen executive recruiters and hiring managers, who all said the same thing: If you're otherwise highly qualified for the job you're seeking, your run-in with the law (particularly since it was a one-time incident) is very likely to be forgiven and forgotten. Nonetheless, several of these experts urge you to think about revealing it before the company's gumshoes have a chance to find it.

Says one human resources honcho, who asked to remain nameless here, "People who do high-level hiring are well aware that people make mistakes, and they can usually disregard anything that doesn't seem related to your ability to do the job. But what will make them uneasy is any sense they get that you are trying to hide something. You're far better off coming forward and saying, 'Look, here's what happened' and being very aboveboard about it. In fact, taking this direct approach may well get you admired for your integrity." And that is never a bad thing.

CHAPTER FIVE

Now That You're the Boss . . .

The little people will get even, which is one of a thousand reasons why they are not little people at all. If you're a jerk as a leader, you will be torpedoed. And usually it won't be by your vice presidents; it will be on the loading dock at 3 A.M. when no supervisors are around.

—TOM PETERS

You do not lead by hitting people over the head—that's assault, not leadership.

—DWIGHT D. EISENHOWER

A leader is a dealer in hope.

—NAPOLEON

Congratulations! You've worked hard to get here, and it must feel terrific finally to lay claim to the window office (farewell to the cube farm!), along with—I hope—a nice bundle of stock options or maybe a juicy incentive-pay package. Once the fizz has gone out of the celebratory champagne and the novelty has worn off the view, though, it would be entirely natural to start feeling a little . . . nervous. After all, the People Upstairs are expecting fantastic things from you. And you have, of course, been smart enough to find out in detail exactly what those things are.

Haven't you? I don't mean to rattle you, but let's briefly recall that scarifying statistic from Manchester Inc., cited back in Chapter 2: Roughly 40 percent of freshly hired or promoted managers fail at their new jobs within the first year. Since about half—47 percent—of those flameouts come from not achieving the "CFOs," or critical few objectives, of the position, 76 percent of the human-resources honchos and hiring managers in the Manchester survey urge you to make sure that you grasp what specific results you're supposed to produce in your first twelve months. "Specific" is the operative word here. Ask for numbers, deadlines, and details. This is no time to be shy or to pretend you already know the answers. It also couldn't hurt to keep asking the people above and around you how you're doing every year—or every quarter, or maybe every few weeks—from now on. Objectives can change with stunning rapidity, and sometimes the people moving the targets forget to call and tell you about it.

Any management job comes packed with 101 responsibilities, some of which may seem to be maddeningly contradictory. For instance: Keep costs low, but keep your best people happy so they won't leave. What if satisfying your stars entails offering them stuff that costs money? Ask someone above you how you're supposed to resolve this and, alas, you may just get a gimlet-eyed stare that means: "Hey, you figure it out, pal. You wanted this job, didn't you?" This kind of thing helps explain why the consulting industry, which at its best is skilled at plucking managers off the horns of dilemmas, grew 20 percent a year between 1990 and

2001, about five times the annual growth rate of the U.S. economy overall.

Whatever the critical few objectives of your job right now, it seems to me that there are three things that managers, new or not, would be wise to keep in mind. The first one is, try to be the kind of boss you'd want to work for. It might just keep your best people from quitting. Second, always remember that whatever gets rewarded will get done. The converse is equally true. Being essentially self-interested, people won't do much of anything that doesn't have some kind of a pay-off—and money is not always what they're after. And third: Watch out for the lawyers.

"I'm Really Not Even Sure I Want This Job . . ."

The job of manager—or team leader, or project facilitator, or whatever your company calls it these days—has become so complex, so loaded with stress, and so dispiritingly thankless that large numbers of people are deciding it's a losing proposition. I regularly hear from folks who want advice on how to turn down a promotion without incurring grave political fallout, or how to engineer a graceful step down from a management

Q. Since my promotion to project manager two months ago, I'm having trouble getting my new subordinates (former peers, some of whom are personal friends) to follow my instructions. I want to stay friendly, but I also need people to meet their deadlines and do things correctly. How can I get them to treat me as they would any other boss?

A. You are going to have to set clear goals for your team and put them in writing, so that everyone knows what his or her responsibilities are. Then hold them to it. Of course you can still be friendly—but your team must learn to accept that you are in charge now. It might help to hold an all-staff meeting where you explain what your (and your department's) goals are, and ask for suggestions on how to meet those targets. This way, you aren't being Mr. Autocrat, but you are still holding people responsible for results. Above all, don't get discouraged. This adjustment will take some time and patience but, if you are firm, it will happen.

job that just isn't as enjoyable or influential—and, in some cases, turns out not even to pay as well—as what they were doing before.

Statistics on how many bosses voluntarily bail out are hard to come by. But it does sometimes look as if there are as many people yearning to flee the management ranks of big companies as there are underlings aspiring to join them.

The reasons for managers' malaise are nearly universal: too many meetings, too much conflicting pressure from above and below, too little psychic reward for too much effort, and too little appreciation (or promise of a future) in a world that values people who produce things, not people who manage the producers. "I got 'promoted' from systems engineering to management, and, boy, do I hate it," wrote a Silicon Valley dweller who signed himself "Demote Me Anytime." Part of what galled him was "having to hand out 15 percent raises to techies who used to be peers but who work for me now, while my own raise was barely 4 percent, although I work twice as hard."

Q. My company has adopted a casual dress code, which is fine, but it's gone too far. Recently a longtime colleague died, and some people who work for me attended the funeral (in a church) in what I would call minimum casual dress. They were a disgrace. How can I communicate to them that there are times when only a suit is acceptable?

A. Since you are the boss, why not stop fuming about this and write a memo outlining some exceptions to the casual-dress code? You could say something like: "Henceforth, whenever any one of us dies, the rest of us will be expected to put on a jacket and tie (or a skirt and so on)." Include a few pointers on other situations where casual dress won't do—for example, any event for which the invitation has the words "black tie" printed on it. Think of this as a public service. Down the road, you could save your clueless underlings some genuine embarrassment. At the same time, though, why not lighten up a little? Imagine that when your own funeral rolls around, an office buddy of yours shows up in khakis and a Hawaiian shirt. Are you likely to mind? We are, after all, talking about the one and only social occasion where it is impossible to offend the guest of honor.

He wrote again, four months later, to tell me he had quit that job to follow his wife around the world while she pursued a career in international banking. The last I heard, he was living in Hong Kong.

Let's suppose you're among the legions of the discontented. You're not going to give up without a fight, are you? There are at least two good reasons not to. First, consider that managing—like anything else worth doing well—takes practice. Sometimes a belief that you just aren't cut out for it is nothing more than a prolonged case of opening-night jitters. "I had a terrific career going as a salesperson in a fast-growing company—loved my clients, made lots of money, and was a 'star,'" wrote a reader signed "Panic Mode." Six months into a new job as sales manager, however, "it has been terrible. We're not meeting our targets, our clients are drifting away, and I don't think I'm connecting with the staff. How can I tell my boss that I just can't do this job?"

Whoa.

If you're in a similar spot, consider these words from Mary Dee Hicks, longtime executive coach: "For now, your goal is learning. Leave your ego at the door. This is no time to try to be omniscient, or to try to prove you can do it on your own. Other people around you have been in this position before you. Get support from them. They have information you can use." That means admitting that you haven't got all the answers—often hard for an erstwhile star to do. Hicks suggests finding another newly minted manager in your company, or ideally several, and seeing what you can learn from each other. You might also ask your own boss—who must be a fan or you wouldn't have been given this chance—to steer you into some formal training.

Adds New York City career counselor Deborah Bright: "If you'd really be happier in your old role, you may indeed end up going back to it. It's no disgrace. Some of my most successful clients spend their whole careers switching back and forth from a technical specialty into management and back again, as the need arises or as opportunities change. But you don't want to give up on yourself as a manager before you've had a chance to gain the skills and training you may need to be a star at this, too." After all, the more experience you've had at more than one level of your current company, the more marketable you'll be in the future— and marketability, as I've noted elsewhere in this book, is the only form of job security anybody's really got these days.

The second reason to hang in there is pretty obvious: It's still the only way to get to the top of the company, if not this company, then some other one. Even, or perhaps especially, if your ultimate goal is to start your own business, making you in effect an instant CEO, you're far more likely to succeed if you've already had some exposure to the slings and arrows that all bosses have to face. Let's say you eventually hope to launch an Internet company. There is not a venture capitalist on the planet who will even consider tossing a dime at your enterprise unless you can show a pretty impressive track record as a manager—or unless you can shell out some dough (including, usually, a significant chunk of equity) to someone who can. So you might think of your current position, and what you can bring to it and build it into, as an investment.

Just don't be too surprised if it turns out to be an adventure, too.

"I've Got to Turn This Department Around— but My Subordinates Won't Budge"

What's that you say? Your company's undergoing its third restructuring in eight years and everything's about to change—again? Now you're in charge of transforming your little corner of the enterprise, but everyone who works for you is so sick and tired of continual upheaval that they don't seem to hear a word you say? It's cold comfort, I know, but you are in a typical New Economy bind: A radical overhaul of how things are done won't happen unless everyone pitches in with some (preferably much) enthusiasm. Yet enthusiasm gets more and more difficult to muster as time goes on.

It's particularly tricky to get the troops fired up when they aren't even convinced that you ought to be their boss. "Four months ago I started a new job as a production manager at a consumer-goods company, after about a year in a supervisory position elsewhere. The people who work for me have all been in this business much longer than I have, so when I first came I was quite easygoing and didn't make any changes," wrote a reader signed "2 EZ." "Now I seem to have no control at all and feel I get very little respect and some resentment for being in charge with less experience. We are under pressure from top management to operate a lot more efficiently. But how can I gain authority and make people work harder?"

If this is your problem too, take a deep breath and relax. It's not going to be so bad. Lee

Q. I work for a small business that has only two managers, the owner and the accountant. These two place responsibility on others, but they will not give those few—of whom I am one—any title such as office manager, marketing manager, or what have you. Without a title, how do I handle my fellow employees?

A. Says Dan Gruber, a senior partner at Deloitte & Touche Consulting, "Surely good judgment, experience, and expertise are more important than a title. If you think you need a title to be respected, you've got bigger problems." Gruber likes to tell his clients that leaders are nominated from above, but they're elected from below: "If the others in your office—that is, the employees you're trying to 'handle'—don't defer to your authority, they must have a reason. Your number one priority should be to find out what that reason is, and then fix it." He adds, "If you haven't earned the respect of the people around you and under you, you could have the title King of the World and it wouldn't make any difference."

Innocenti, a training consultant at Performance Strategies Ltd., notes that the combination of whirlwind job hopping and ceaseless restructurings makes this dilemma more widespread than you might suppose. Parachuting in from outside, you at least have one advantage: You were never a peer or a personal friend of any of the folks who now believe (rightly or wrongly) that they are better qualified for your job. So they are no doubt mercifully unaware of any of your past foibles, which should make it much easier for them to start taking you seriously. But you'll have to take them and their ideas seriously first. "Being easygoing at the outset is the right approach," says Innocenti. "However, you need to gather information at the same time."

First, meet with your subordinates individually and find out in detail how they view the job, the department, and the other departments with which yours interacts. What is helpful to them in getting the work done? What gets in the way? How could things be improved? Take notes. Next, talk to people in other areas of the company whose work directly affects yours or vice versa. What do they wish your people would do differently and why? Meanwhile, you need to come up with statistical measures of productivity and efficiency, to use as baselines for measuring future progress. "Your company's MIS staff has all kinds of numbers you can use to gauge your department's output," Innocenti says. "You need reasonable and objective standards." Then set a specific goal, or several, that you think your crew can meet within six months or a year.

Once you've got all that, hold a big meeting with all of your subordinates together. Tell them, in essence: "Here's what you've told me needs to change around here, and here's what others in the company need from us. Here's where we are right now, and here's where we should be in six months' (or a year's) time." Lay it all out as clearly as you can. Ask for comments and suggestions, and make note of the ones you think would work as integral parts of a new plan of action. Be sure and let people know how progress will be measured, and at what intervals (weekly? monthly?). Innocenti suggests holding all-staff meetings often after that, to give everyone a chance to ask questions and iron out problems.

This kind of participative management has been trendy for a while now, but for a boss with less experience than his or her underlings, it may also be the only method that stands a chance. "You need to use dialogue to move people toward change," says Innocenti. "If you try to assert your authority without it, you'll just invite more resentment"—including the kind of subtle sabotage that can really mess things up.

What if you not only have less experience than the people who work for you, but you're also young enough to be their child? The Labor Department reported in early 2000 that the number of managers aged twenty to thirty-four had climbed from 4.8 million to 5.2 million between 1994 and 1999. That trend shows no sign of abating. Here in the New Economy, youth is king. It connotes—accurately or not—energy, optimism, a penchant for innovation, an intimate familiarity with

Q. It's annual employee evaluation time again. The people who report to me are decent and hardworking but basically average performers. If I say that in their evaluations, however, their careers may be doomed, because my company has been trying to weed out anybody who doesn't show fast-track potential. How can I do honest evaluations?

A. You are indeed in a terrible spot. At many companies now (including yours), "average" is just not good enough, and many people cannot understand why not. Your job is to explain it to them in terms that they can grasp, and tell them just what they need to do to develop their "fast-track potential." Start helping them to get new skills and sharpen the ones they already have. Then you can truthfully say, in their evaluations this year, that they are working on improving their performance—and, by next year at this time, you may have remarkable progress to report.

new technology. Youth is also, usually, relatively cheap, which makes it irresistible to cash-strapped start-ups and cost-conscious corporations alike.

But talk about a credibility gap. "A few years ago, at age twenty-three, I was a marketing supervisor at a ski resort. One of my employees was a sixty-five-year-old man recently retired from the local police force and, although he was always polite, he made it clear he would be taking no orders from me," a reader named Meaghan wrote, in a discussion on my Web site about young bosses and older subordinates. "I would ask him to do something and he would nod and go back to his crossword puzzle."

As it says in *The New York Times*'s in-house style book, nothing is unprecedented (which is why you never see the word "unprecedented" in that newspaper). Lois Juliber, chief operating officer at Colgate-Palmolive, once told me: "A first reaction of anger, jealousy, or even fear from people who have been around longer, and have 'paid their dues' as they see it, is natural and may be unavoidable." She was speaking from experience. Juliber is now in her forties, but at age twenty-nine she took charge of a ten-person team whose much more seasoned members regarded her as a brash, underqualified kid. How did she turn that around? "The most important thing is to find some common ground. What do we want to achieve together as a team? What are our goals and how can we help each other get there? If you can sit down and have that honest conversation, a lot of resentment will dissipate"—and, mercifully, you can direct your already overstretched energies to getting on with the job at hand.

A twenty-four-year-old entrepreneur, who had started his own company with two partners right out of college, asked me how best to motivate "talented oldies." By oldies, he meant people "twice my age," which I have to admit made me feel fairly creaky. I talked with David Peterson, a Ph.D. in organizational psychology who is a senior vice president at Personnel Decisions International, about this, and his insights seem sound for managers of any age. Everyone, Peterson observes, is already motivated by something, and your task as a boss is to figure out what that is. "When people ask me, 'How can I motivate this person?' what they really mean is, 'How can I get this person to do what I want?' " he says. "Meanwhile, that person is trying to figure out how to 'motivate' you. The biggest mistake I see is that managers try to guess what drives their employees, while employees try to guess what the boss really wants."

This exercise in mutual mind reading almost never works. Instead, Peterson recommends asking each subordinate what it is that makes work great in his or her eyes. Is it money, recognition, feeling like part of a team, or what? What kind of boss have they done their best work for? Why? "People also have demotivators—boring work, wildly unreasonable hours, a patronizing boss," says Peterson. "With each person, try to find out what those are, too." He cautions against accepting pat answers like " 'I want a bigger challenge.' Yes, okay, but what kind of a challenge? Why? Get down to the basics of what gets this person out of bed in the morning."

Peterson suggests that bosses who are much younger than their employees try to put aside what he calls "the power differential": "You probably aren't accustomed to working with older people as peers—as opposed to, say, teachers or parents. But while you may have more energy and perhaps more of certain technical skills, they undoubtedly have other abilities, born of experience, that you haven't had time to develop yet. So work out some trades. Offer to help them sharpen up their technical acumen, for instance, in exchange for their expertise at dealing with customers. It's about how to work together so everyone benefits, not how to 'manage' them."

Touchy-feely as this sounds, it's based on a couple of home truths. For one, people who can't get what they want by doing things your way will get it by doing things their own way, so you might as well find out up front what it is that makes them tick. And second, over the next ten years—critical ones for any growing business—about seventy-six million "talented oldies" will start thinking about retiring, and taking a lot of accumulated knowledge right out the door with them. Some of this will be knowledge upon which you will have come to depend. In the not-too-distant future, then, you may find that you need them more than they need you. Do you really want to alienate them now?

"When I was twenty-three, I was put in charge of six people who were twice my age," wrote a reader named Carole, during the Web site discussion about age differences between bosses and subordinates. "At first, I tried to be the smartest in the group. That lasted about three weeks. Then I realized the job of a manager is not to tell everyone what to do, because they knew that better than I did. My job was to make sure they had the resources they needed to get the work done. What most managers of any age don't realize is that age has nothing to do with it." Hear, hear. Or, as another reader named Cliff

---

Q. Help! I'm about to quit my job in frustration, and I need some perspective. A few months ago, after a great decade as a salesperson at a manufacturing company, I took a sales-management job at a major accounting firm. I hate it. All I do all day, it seems, is listen to complaints about obnoxious clients. But I have no idea how to make our customers less difficult. What am I doing wrong?

A. Probably nothing. You can't wave a magic wand and make your customers shape up. You can, however, go along on a few sales calls with your most chronic complainers and quietly observe what goes on. Then, drawing on the experience that got you this job, make specific suggestions for reducing the friction. Taking an active coaching role, rather than just letting people vent, might reduce your own frustration—and give you a pretty good idea of who your best (and worst) salespeople are.

put it: "I've worked in start-ups and big corporations, and what is clear to me is that capabilities, trust, fairness, and vision will trump age every time."

In an ideal world, no manager—young, old, black, white, or Martian—would be put in the position of having to oversee a drastic shift in strategy without first being allowed to handpick the people who'll be doing the heavy hauling. Here on Earth, though, the vast majority of managers have to make do with the people already in place. "People are a company's biggest asset, but they're also its biggest obstacles when it comes to changing strategy," says David Hofrichter, a PricewaterhouseCoopers partner who has been studying this problem for twenty-three years. "Companies need to be quick, flexible, and innovative, and changing a stodgy corporate culture into a nimble one is a herculean challenge. But if companies don't have the right people in place, their strategy is doomed." Gulp.

Q. What do you do when you have an important business decision to make and the available research doesn't help—that is, there are as many facts supporting one choice as the other? Do you try to stick to one set of facts, or go with your instinct?

A. A fascinating question! Psychiatrists and psychologists dating back to Freud and Jung have made detailed studies of the role of "gut feeling," or intuition, in decision making. Michael Ray, who teaches creativity in the graduate business school at Stanford, says, "Another word for intuition is 'recognition,' which literally means 'to know again.' When you've worked long and hard to build experience in any given area, the right decision often comes very quickly as a sort of emotionless recognition" of factual information that has perhaps been partially or completely forgotten by your conscious mind. Ray also says that in situations such as you describe, where key facts are contradictory, intuition is "mistake free": "Since equally good reasons exist to support either choice you make, you'll probably have no trouble explaining—or defending—your intuitive decision on a logical basis." So go with your gut.

Drawing on his work with thousands of companies, Hofrichter

has identified four basic types of employees found in every organization, and has pinpointed how each type contributes (or doesn't) to maximum nimbleness. I'm usually skeptical of formulaic approaches to managing people. Humans are infinitely various, and endlessly resistant to categorization, thank heavens. But Hofrichter's analysis strikes me as worth pondering. See how it jibes with what you see around you in your own company.

The first of the four employee types is the "superstar." Says Hofrichter: "These are the most desirable ones. They've 'got it'— that is, they understand where the company's trying to go and they deliver results in the right way." You need them, so don't hesitate to spoil them rotten: "Do whatever it takes to keep them, and reward them exceptionally well. Set them up as examples for the rest of your company." The second group comprises what Hofrichter calls "open-minders"—people who, although they may have underperformed in the past, are ready to align themselves with change and eager to be part of the new order. "They're worth investing in. Get them trained and up to speed fast," he says. "This group is where your training-and-development dollars will get the biggest payoff."

Next we come to the "skeptics," a tricky bunch. They're doubtful about the need for change or about top management's plans for achieving it, so—for the moment anyway—they're dragging their feet: "With the right coaching, where you tie rewards to specific changes in attitudes and behaviors, about half of this group will 'see the light' and turn into superstars. The other half will fall into the fourth grouping." Ah, that fourth grouping, dubbed "recalcitrants." These are the folks who are so entrenched in the way things have always been done that they will resist, or even sabotage, your efforts. About 15 percent of any company's workforce is made up of recalcitrants. What should you do with them? "Show them the door as soon as possible," Hofrichter says.

"They're not worth developing. If you try to 'save' them you'll be wasting your investment—and sending the wrong message to the rest of the organization. You're far better off replacing them with new hires who are already in sync with the culture you're trying to create."

Although nobody breaks out the numbers along these lines, I suspect that a fair amount of the churning described in Chapter 4—the currently widespread corporate practice of laying off and hiring large numbers of people simultaneously—springs from the desire (or the need) to replace recalcitrants with superstars, or at least open-minders. Hofrichter recommends that before you try to make any new strategy a reality, you'd be smart to identify your employee types and begin right away to take decisive action. Above all, don't let recalcitrants hang around long enough to drag down any salvageable skeptics.

Sounds good in theory, and if you can manage to do it in real life, then great. As already noted, however, sometimes you're stuck with the people you've got—often because simply showing them the door would violate an

Q. I'm in charge of customer service at an e-commerce company. Most of my staff are young and inexperienced. I'm trying to persuade them that it's important to be prompt, courteous, and responsive to customers, but I'm not getting through. Do you know of any proof that politeness and responsiveness can actually increase sales, or am I dreaming?

A. In 1999, an etiquette-consulting company called Eticon, based in Columbia, South Carolina, surveyed 1,281 people across the United States and found that 80 percent think rudeness in business has been increasing lately. Where it gets interesting is that when asked how they reacted to bad manners or lousy attitudes, 58 percent said they "take business elsewhere, even if [the competitor] is out of my way or charges higher prices." So here's an idea. Get your surly staff together and write your company's current revenues on a big blackboard. Then subtract 58 percent, and explain that this lower number is where you may be headed. If they don't get the message, maybe they're in the wrong line of work. That's fixable.

employment contract or union agreement; or because, recalcitrant though they may be, a large number of them have technical skills that would be difficult or impossible, or just too expensive, to replace. Now what do you do?

Well, you're in a tough spot. But you might consider taking a page from Jaguar of North America, which pulled off one of the most surprising, and roaringly successful, turnarounds of the past decade. After Ford acquired the then-sputtering British luxury car-maker in 1990, it embarked on a massive reorganization aimed at producing better, more reliable cars in far less time. If you're a car buff, you know that in those days the words "Jaguar" and "reli-able" scarcely ever appeared in the same sentence, unless it was the punch line of a joke. Dale Gambill, then vice president of cus-tomer service, was charged with improving the relations between Jaguar and its dealers and customers. Antagonism ruled, mistrust was rampant, and there was all too clearly no point in spending tens of millions on reengineering the car if no one in his or her right mind would either sell the thing or buy it—or for that mat-ter, take it as a gift. Jaguars, always breathtakingly beautiful inside and out, did nonetheless earn their reputation as a car that spent lots of time in the shop.

Now, picture Dale Gambill on a mission perhaps not so differ-ent, in essence, from your particular crusade. When he stood up in front of a gathering of seasoned Jaguar employees, many of whom predated the Ford acquisition, his only aim was to exhort them to think harder about pleasing dealers and customers. Instead, he got what he later told me was "the shock of my life." The reorganization (which included mass layoffs of about 35 per-cent of the company's North American workforce) had created a huge cadre of what Hofrichter would call recalcitrants. In Gambill's words: "They said, 'Hey, let's forget the customer for a minute here and focus on the fact that you aren't taking care of us.' I hadn't realized how much pent-up frustration there was. These people spent two whole days venting. They said we had no clear vision for the future. They said we had too many competing sets of values among the departments. They said we never learned anything from our mistakes and were just constantly going around putting out fires. And—here was the big thing—*they* told *me* we had to get a lot more customer-focused.

"I went there thinking I was going to do all the talking. But I barely got a word in edgewise."

Gumbill, with the support of Jaguar's then-president Mike Dale, responded with a tactic that might work for you, too. He put the loudest dissenters in charge of creating solutions. Then, he got out of the way. Teams called employee-involvement groups fixed so many problems that within three years Jaguar zoomed from its dismal number 24 slot on J. D. Power's annual survey of customer satisfaction (see www.jdpower.com) into the top ten. Since then, the make has consistently leaped to the heights of the list—which, among carmakers, Wall Street auto-industry analysts, and serious car shoppers, holds enormous sway. In

Q. I am a brand-new supervisor and am having trouble with an employee who will not follow directions. How should I deal with this?

A. Are you sure that your directions are as clear as they could be? I ask this because supervisors (especially new ones) often assume that subordinates know much more than they actually do about what is expected of them. Sit down with this person and say: "You know, I'm getting the impression that you and I aren't quite on the same wavelength about how this job should be done. Is there something you're having trouble with that you'd like to talk about?" The answer or answers may surprise you. On the other hand, the person may just say, "No, everything's fine"—which in turn gives you the chance to reply, "Well, actually, I have to disagree with you there"—and then explain precisely why. This way, you get your point across, but you've first given your recalcitrant underling a chance to air whatever he or she may think the problem is. Sometimes, of course, a person who simply refuses to cooperate at all just does not belong on your team. But before making that decision, try listening.

1999 (the most recent available ranking as of this writing), Jaguar was number one, ahead of fearsome competition like BMW, Mercedes, and Lexus.

You see my point. Before you sack your recalcitrants (assuming that you can or would like to), maybe it wouldn't hurt to listen to them. There is always the outside chance they might be right. After all, if Gambill had insisted on doing all the talking at that two-day meeting, as he'd originally planned, it's unlikely that Jaguar would be where it is today.

And while we're on the subject of hearing people out, every change-management guru I've ever met has made one point I'd be remiss not to pass along here: Beware of "yes men" (or, to bring that old expression up to date, "yes persons"). No strategy in the world has ever been without its share of snarls. However, if nobody tells you the truth about what's really going on, you won't find out about snags and setbacks until it's too late. Encourage your people to deliver bad news, if there is any, immediately. Then listen as calmly as you can.

This isn't easy, especially if the subordinate ringing the alarm bell is someone (a recalcitrant, perhaps) whose personality rubs you the wrong way. But consider what Thomas Watson, Jr., who turned IBM from a quirky little computer company into the thousand-pound gorilla known as Big Blue, once told *Fortune:* "I never hesitated to hire someone I didn't like. The comfortable assistant—the nice guy you like to go fishing with—is a great pitfall. I looked for those sharp, scratchy, harsh, almost unpleasant guys who see and tell you about things as they really are."

Got any scratchy people working for you? Have you sat down for a long chat with them lately? Asked them lots of detailed questions? No? Well, why not give it a try? You might be surprised at what you find out, especially if you're willing to listen like an open-minder instead of speaking as a superstar.

Or, as my dad used to tell his houseful of chatterbox kids (yours truly in particular): "Nobody ever learns anything while they're talking."

"How Can I Hire the Best (and Avoid the Rest)?"

It's hard to think of any management task more urgent or important than hiring the right people and putting them in the right jobs. "We spend all our time on people," legendary General Electric CEO Jack Welch once told *Fortune*. "The day we screw up the people thing, this company is over." Unfortunately, hiring well is also one of the most elusive arts there is—and yes, it is more art than science, as you've probably discovered if you've tried to do it. That doesn't mean it can't be mastered. Luckily, some very smart people have studied the problem and come up with a few suggestions for improving your chances of bringing terrific people on board.

Consider the situation of a reader signed "Second Chance," whose hiring dilemma is fairly typical. After a few years of running his own firm, he was all set to line up an office manager, a human-resources director, and a sales manager, "and finally start delegating some of the work around here." The problem? "In my old corporate job, I wasn't very good at hiring people. That is, I would hire somebody who seemed great but who then just couldn't get the work done, or couldn't get along well enough with the people who were already there. Occasionally I hired people who were not challenged enough by their jobs, I assume, since they left after a short time. Now that I have all these very promising résumés on my desk and am about to start interviewing candidates, how can I avoid making the same old mistakes?"

Lou Adler is a veteran recruiter who has developed a system he calls Power Hiring (see his Web site at www.powerhiring.com). He

Q. Please settle an argument. I'm trying to persuade higher-ups in my company that if we want to recruit the best people, we have to invest in fixing up our boring Web site. My boss keeps insisting that this is not an important priority. Who is right?

A. You are—especially if you're hoping to attract the best and brightest new college grads. A survey of several thousand of them, in the summer of 2000, by JobTrak (www.jobtrak.com) found that 77 percent say the quality of a company's Web site is either "somewhat important" or "very important" in deciding whether to apply for a job there.

wrote a whole book about it. Based on his two decades of experience at culling the sheep from the goats, the book is called *Hire with Your Head: A Rational Way to Make a Gut Decision*. In Adler's view, anyone who wants to choose wisely needs to use a four-point method. First, if you've ever made the kinds of misjudgments that the reader signed "Second Chance" describes, cheer up, you're only human. "We are preprogrammed to make hiring mistakes, because our brains have something I call a 'stupid switch' that causes us to react to other people on an emotional basis first and a rational basis later," Adler points out. "If you can disengage the 'stupid switch' for just thirty minutes—that is, consciously avoid or suppress any emotional response at all to a candidate in that first half hour—you can avoid about 50 percent of the most common hiring errors."

What might those errors be? Ah. The most insidious is believing that you are getting a clear picture of what someone is "really like." Says Adler, "Cultural fit and personality do count, of course. But they have to count second. Competence matters first and foremost and, unfortunately, the personality on display during an interview doesn't predict a thing about subsequent performance. It doesn't even predict real personality." Adler's solution: Concentrate on assessing job skills and competence first, then worry about a candidate's personality, or cultural "fit"—if you get that far.

How should you assess competence? "You don't need to ask a lot of clever questions. Just ask the person to describe in detail his or her most significant team and individual accomplishments in the past couple of jobs. People will tend to start out speaking in general terms, so you need to dig a bit for specifics," Adler says. Spend five to ten minutes exploring each past achievement, evaluating each in terms of the acronym SMART, which stands for: Specific details, Measurable information, Actual role the candidate played, Results achieved, and Time it took. Then compare what you learn with what is needed in the job you're trying to fill. Does it mesh?

"Always treat candidates as customers, not employees"— and that means starting with the way you word any help-wanted ads or on-line postings you may be putting out there. Adler notes that most ads and postings are "just lists of job requirements, designed to attract people who are looking for a job." So, what's wrong with that? "To get the very best candidates, you need to target those who are *not* looking. Focus the wording on where you and your ideal candidate are going, not where you or they have been in the past. Make it forward-looking. Describe the opportunity for growth, not the barriers to entry. If you do, you'll quickly start to see a better crowd of applicants." That in itself should improve your odds of getting the people you really want.

And take your time about it. As Merna Skinner sees it, many bosses—pressed for time themselves and in a rush to hire somebody quickly for a job that needs doing, oh, last week—approach job interviewing too haphazardly. Skinner is a coach at Exec/Comm, a New York City firm that specializes in turning managers into ace interviewers. "What happens

Q. In your column, you answer a lot of questions about job interviews. I'm just curious about something. What is the most interesting interview question you have ever heard of?

A. This one: "What cherished assumptions or beliefs have you had to give up in order to get where you are?"

in a face-to-face interview is the most important step in the whole evaluation process," she notes. "Yet most managers make two mistakes. They don't prepare adequately, and they don't pay attention to how they budget their time during the interview. As a result, they spend too much time talking and not enough time listening to the candidate for important clues."

In the preparation stage, Skinner recommends that all managers involved in the hiring decision sit down and agree on a complete description of the job, what educational or technical requirements are required, and—here's where it gets interesting—a list of the three most important skills the best candidate should bring to the table. Then, during the interview, look for specific evidence that the would-be employee is, in Skinner's words, "willing, able, and a match." The willing part may seem obvious, but isn't always: "You're looking for someone who's not only talented but also enthusiastic about using their capabilities." A prospective hire, for example, may have excellent analytical skills and a proven track record doing sales analyses, but may really be hoping to make a switch into working for a marketing group. And hiring someone to do a job that doesn't really interest him or her will, as Skinner says, "have a direct impact on their future performance." It will not be a good impact.

At the same time, pay attention to what you've established are the top three skills necessary for the job at hand. Does this candidate have them? "You really have to probe past a candidate's first response to get to this," says Skinner. For instance, let's suppose that one of the top three skills is a knack for forming cohesive teams, and you've got someone in front of you who claims to be a gifted group leader. You want to ask detailed questions, such as, "How did you interact with your group?" and "What specific results did your group produce, and how did you do that?" or whatever else elicits information beyond a pat answer. Says

Skinner, "A candidate who can't furnish persuasive proof of having used a particular skill in the past is not likely to suddenly start using it in a new job."

Like Adler, Skinner recommends taking a careful look at how a potential hire is likely to fit into the corporate culture—but saving this for last, after the person has shown both willingness and ability. "Are there any 'red flags' in this person's background that would make him or her inappropriate for the position? Short tenures in past jobs are worth examining in detail, to see why a candidate may have left different types of organizations," she says. If someone didn't stay long at a company that was culturally similar to yours, chances are that he or she will not linger with you, either.

What if you're charged with interviewing people who've never actually worked full time anywhere before, and thus have no track record at all—namely, new college grads? "This year, for the third time in a row, my department has put me in charge of hiring entry-level people right out of school," wrote someone signed "Hopeful in Houston," who wanted to know how to keep from "making the same mistake I made in the last two years, that is, hiring people who seem bright and eager and have all the right credentials (good colleges, high grades)—but who end up requiring so much time and attention from managers that we can barely get our own jobs

Q. I just interviewed someone who is talented, creative, full of great ideas, and would be a great addition to our team, but I can't get approval from my boss to hire her because he says she doesn't have enough experience. Do you have any suggestions for how to overcome this?

A. Well, you might ask your boss to consider what Charles "Boss" Kettering, who is widely credited with having helped build General Motors into the world's biggest car company, once said: "I don't want men of experience working for me. The experienced man is always telling me why something can't be done. He is smart; he is intelligent; he thinks he knows the answers. The fellow who has not had any experience is so dumb he doesn't know a thing can't be done—so he goes ahead and does it."

done. Do you have any suggestions on how to pick out the self-starters who will learn fast and not need quite so much hand holding?"

This isn't an unusual lament. Each spring I hear from bosses seeking to cull future stars from the ranks of the newly graduated, and the vicissitudes don't vary much from year to year—except that nowadays people in their twenties seem more inclined to stay with their first employer for shorter and shorter lengths of time. "I don't mind spending a lot of valuable time training young people. I see it as part of my job," wrote one fed-up financial manager. "What does make the investment seem wasted is that as soon as these kids finally learn the job, they leave the company, which makes those of us who taught them their (very marketable) skills feel like big chumps."

How to keep people around once you've trained them is another topic, which we'll get to shortly. But Jane Caryl runs a New York City–based firm called Focus Staffing that specializes in helping companies locate and hire independent thinkers. Caryl has a few ideas on how to find new college grads who will pick up the ball and run with it. Let's start with the criteria that "Hopeful in Houston" has been using (and maybe you have, too): "good colleges, high grades." Those things are nice, of course, but they don't automatically indicate that someone is a self-starter.

So what does? In reading résumés and doing interviews, Caryl says, "look for people who have pushed the envelope in some way. Ask questions like 'What kinds of special projects have you worked on, either academic or extracurricular? What did you seek out, or start up, yourself? What were you totally responsible for, and what excited you about that?' You are looking for a certain personality type—someone who is accustomed to taking on a challenge and working through twelve or fifteen steps on his or her own to get to the solution of a problem. And that personality type is not confined to the best schools by any means, nor does it necessarily have the highest grades," which may simply signify that a person was good at memorizing things and taking tests.

Sad to say, human-resources departments in big companies often do such an uninspired job of screening candidates that the most promising ones may never reach you. Notes Caryl, "In small, entrepreneurial companies, your chances of getting a 'direct hit'—a good fit quickly—are far greater than in a huge corporation, because you don't have so many layers of approval or so many arbitrary checklists imposed on job candidates." If you suspect that the human resources staff may (with the best intentions, of course) be sending you people who fit their own idea of what's needed rather than yours, go and talk with them about it. Explain that you don't want applicants with impressive credentials who nonetheless have no experience at crossing the street by themselves. A good HR person will understand what you mean and redefine his or her screening criteria accordingly.

Failing that, you may have to take the next step yourself: Ask that all candidates for the spots you need to fill be sent to you directly without passing through the corporate bureaucracy at all. This will give you a lot more work to do up front, obviously, which is probably the last thing you need right now. But if it lets you bring in entry-level people who can get up to speed fast, it will save you a whole lot of time and aggravation later.

And that is, after all, a crucial piece of what smart hiring is all about.

"Help! My Best People Keep Quitting! How Can I Block the Exits?"

Amid all the reengineering, restructuring, streamlining, repositioning, and reshuffling that companies have been doing since the mid-eighties, it's clear that many of them failed to notice until it was too late that a quiet revolution was spawned by all that change: Employees no longer feel any loyalty to the enterprises where they work and have no qualms about quitting at the drop of a hat or the flourish of a stock option. *Fortune* began predicting this turn of events about sixteen years ago. Was anybody listening? Bosses seem no more loyal than anybody else, by the way. A recent survey of 3,800 U.S. companies, by Management Recruiters International, found that about 60 percent have resorted to using hefty sign-on bonuses to swipe middle managers from rivals.

> Q. If you had to give just one piece of advice on how to keep star employees from leaving, what would it be?
>
> A. Ask them what it would take to make them happy. Beverly Kaye (www.careersystemsintl.com) and Sharon Jordan-Evans (www.jeg.org) are career-development coaches who wrote a great book called *Love 'Em or Lose 'Em: Getting Good People to Stay*. They write: "[Many managers] dance around this subject for fear of putting someone on the spot or putting ideas into someone's head (as if they never thought about leaving on their own). . . . What if you don't ask? You will guess right sometimes. The Christmas bonus might please them all. Money can inspire loyalty and commitment for the near term. But if the key to retaining Tara is to give her the chance to learn something new, whereas Mike wants to telecommute, how could you ever guess that? Ask—so you don't have to guess."

Consider this all-too-typical comment, which appeared on my Web site after a discussion about why people quit their jobs with such abandon these days: "After the mass layoffs and firings of the past fifteen years, you expect loyalty?! I was working as a C++ programmer when [my department was] cut at the end of a pay period and had the doors locked behind us with thirty minutes of advance notice. I've managed to restructure my career, but no thanks to any employer I've ever worked for. I know now that I'm a free agent—free to be fired, free to leave, free to sell my skills and knowledge to whoever provides more potential for advancement and the chance to work with new technologies. There's *no* reason to put up with poor management or lack of opportunity."

As noted back in Chapter 2, Americans in their twenties and early thirties—having learned from their parents that no one spends a whole career in one company anymore—now switch employers roughly every three years. In high-tech, it's more like every thirteen months, and average turnover at computer and software companies is now running at 20 percent a year, or more than double the rate in any other field. And that isn't just among the rank and file. Chicago outplacement firm Challenger Gray & Christmas, which tracks turnover among CEOs, reported in mid-2000 that 106 computer-company chief executives had quit (or been ousted) in the preceding nine months, far more than in any other industry.

If you're trying to run a tight ship with a crew that keeps going AWOL, none of this is news to you. I get dozens of letters a month from bosses in the same boat as a reader signed "Left in the Lurch," who wrote: "In the year and a half that I've been in charge of an important new-product-development project, I've hired two dozen people—and about one dozen have left within six months, usually with very little notice. (In one case, someone said he was going out for an hour to get an oil change on his car. He never came back.) We've started doing exit interviews to try and figure out why we keep losing so many. But in the meantime, any suggestions?"

So much thoughtful research has been lavished on this question recently—some of it on the pages of *Fortune*—that whole books could be devoted to it and indeed have been (see the Appendix). It's a classic good news, bad news situation. Let's start with the bad news: The costly and disruptive problem of rapid employee turnover will probably not go away entirely anytime soon, if ever; and there are signs that it may get worse before it gets better.

According to a study of two thousand employees by the Hudson Institute and Walker Information, 33 percent of people with full-time jobs are "high risk," defined as not committed to their present employer and not planning to stick around for two more years. Another 39 percent fall into a category labeled "trapped"—not committed to the company or its goals but likely to stay for two years anyway, for one reason or another (for example, until they finish night school, or get fully vested in the pension plan). Only 24 percent, or somewhat fewer than one in four, describe themselves as both committed and likely to stay for at least two years.

Let's say you manage a team of twelve. Look around. Within two years, nine of those familiar faces are likely to be history.

Now for the good news (and high time, too): If you're really determined to hold on to your best people, the odds are that—with some effort and ingenuity—you can. In fact, for reasons that we'll get to in a minute, you as a front-line manager may be the only one in your company with any real influence over whether your stars stay or go. And keeping them may not mean busting your payroll budget, either: Sometimes, yes, people do change jobs to get more money. But far more often, what they're after is something else entirely.

Since techies are the most slippery type of employees these days—and generally the hardest to replace—let's take a look at them first. What do they want? Says Vincent Milich, director of the Hay Group's information-technology consulting practice: "There is a stereotype about tech people—perhaps because they tend to be young—that they care a lot about 'quality of life' perks like flextime." But when Hay surveyed job-hopping techies, they found that the defectors' biggest complaint was "not being able to get ahead without becoming managers." Without any clear path to advancement—including interesting work that leads to new challenges, whether or not a new title is attached—these people often feel they are wasting their time. Then it's adios, amigo. In his letter to me, "Left in the Lurch" made note of the fact that his company offers excellent pay and benefits, and yours probably does, too. Great! But ask yourself: Are you also offering people a sense that they have an exciting future with you? And can they see clearly what they need to do to get there?

When Caliper, the Princeton-based human-resources experts, did a national study of 180 companies with high turnover in high-tech, "nearly 40 percent [of departing employees] said they were leaving because the work wasn't challenging, there was slim potential for advancement, and insufficient recognition," says Caliper president Herbert Greenberg. Interestingly, only 26 percent said anything at all about money; and just 11 percent said they were quitting because of a conflict with a coworker or a boss. Allen Salikof, president of Cleveland-based Management Recruiters International, has given a lot of thought to why so many techies leave big, established companies, opting to go sweat it out at a start-up instead. "Employees are interested in money, of course, but they're actually more interested in a job in which they're invited to sit at the table, so to speak, to be players in growth and success," he observes. "This is why so many people were willing to take a chance on a dot.com—even knowing full well that only one in ten dot.com start-ups will succeed."

Q. Help! I'm in charge of a team of highly talented people who frequently get job offers from other parts of our own company, as well as from outside. I'm already paying them as much as I can (which is a lot), and actively helping them move ahead in their careers. Is there anything else I can do (that won't cost any money) to keep them happy here?

A. If you're not already doing it, give them lots of praise, appreciation, and pats on the back. Says Alex Hiam, an expert on employee motivation whose clients have included Kellogg's, Coca-Cola, and General Motors: "Observe your people closely to 'catch' them doing something right. Then praise them immediately, in specific terms." Sounds simple, and it is. But it works—and it doesn't cost a dime.

There is ample and growing evidence that the desire for challenging work is what drives all kinds of employees, not just
techies, and in all age groups. In March 2000, Randstad, a recruiting, training, and outsourcing company headquartered in Atlanta,
released the results of an exhaustive survey of six thousand U.S.
workers aged eighteen to sixty-five. The conclusion: "Money is
not the magic bullet for recruiting or retaining talent. 77% of the
workforce prefer jobs where they have to learn new skills all the
time. 74%, given the choice, would opt to work at a place where
they received bonuses based on performance—compared to just
26% who would choose a job where deadlines are minimal and
stress is low."

How interesting is the work your people do? Does it give them
the chance—or, better yet, require them—to pick up new skills
and sharpen and refine old ones? Are they recognized in some
regular, systematic way for what they achieve—either with performance bonuses, acknowledgment and praise, or (ideally) both?

Bruce Tulgan is head of a firm called RainmakerThinking that
advises companies on how to manage twentysomethings, which is
the age group statistically most likely to run out on you. Tulgan
points out that performance bonuses need not always be in the
form of cash: "Every resource an employer can make available
should be viewed as an incentive." He notes that bosses often say
that employees nowadays are too demanding—"[My clients tell
me,] 'This one wants Thursdays off, that one wants her own office,
this one wants to bring his dog to work, that one wants to have
dinner with the senior VP . . .' But managers are wrong to complain. When you discover the wants and needs of an individual
contributor, you've found a needle in a haystack. Different people
are motivated, both to perform and to stay, by very different
incentives—and, in many cases, the desired rewards are so idio-
syncratic that you'd never guess them in a million years if the

employee didn't offer clues." This is a nice way of saying that exceptionally talented people are often a little, um, eccentric. Cater to their quirks. This is one thing that did very, very well. You can, too.

Tulgan suggests using each employee's particular wish as a bargaining chip: "You want Thursdays off? I'm glad to know that. Here's what I need from you in exchange for that. . . ." "You want your own office? We can arrange that. Now, here's what I'd like you to do for me. . . ." According to Tulgan, managers in the New Economy "must become purchasing agents. Just as purchasing agents negotiate with vendors to get the best deal for both sides, managers have to learn to negotiate with employees."

What if one of your special deals with a star employee draws charges of favoritism, or grumblings that it isn't "fair," from others in the office? Stand your ground. "There is nothing that could be less fair than compensating high performers and low performers at the same rate or in the same ways," says Tulgan. "Rewarding high performers at a higher rate is not only fair, it's the *only* fair way." It may also be the only way you'll hang on to the people you'd most hate to lose.

How can you tell if, despite your best efforts, someone you rely on is thinking about quitting? After all, it's unlikely this person will come right out and tell you that he or she is interviewing with a competitor, or has feelers out all over the Internet for a better job elsewhere. B. Lynn Ware, founder of a retention consulting firm called ITS Inc., told the *Harvard Management Update* in April 2000 that bosses need to be on the lookout for a few early-warning signs. These include a change in behavior, such as coming in later or leaving earlier; a decline in overall performance or a sudden withdrawal from the rest of the team; or a rash of complaints from a person who has never griped before. Pay attention to wistful references to far horizons ("Someone I know just got a

$30,000 signing bonus at XZY Corp.") or to other employees who left ("This place just hasn't been the same since Joe quit"). Says Ware: "One of the things we look at is the 'domino effect' that can follow when a manager who was a mentor, or a peer who was significant to others in the organization, suddenly leaves. That can trigger more departures."

As soon as you spot one of these signals, says Ware, don't hesitate to talk about it. "Meet privately with the employee right away. Explain what you've noticed and ask if there's a deeper concern behind the behavior." Then tell the employee how much he or she is valued, and ask for suggestions. "You might say something like 'I really want to see you have a better work experience than you've had recently. How can we solve these problems?' "

If this sounds like coddling, well, it is—but do you want to keep this person or don't you? Bear in mind what Curt Coffman and Marcus Buckingham told *Fortune* about what they learned in writing a book called *First, Break All the Rules,* which was based on Gallup Organization interviews with more than 80,000 managers and 1,000,000 employees (yes, a million): "It's not the company that the employee quits. It's the manager. . . . A great manager is someone who says, 'You come to work with me, and I'll help you be as successful as possible; I'll help you grow; I'll help you make sure you're in the right role. . . . And I want you to be more successful than me.' "

By that definition, would your employees describe you as a great manager?

Suppose that your honest answer is, well, no way. How can you get there from here? Caela Farren is president of MasteryWorks, an Annandale, Virginia, consulting firm that specializes in helping Fortune 500 companies keep their stars from wandering off. She has devised a list of ten questions, aimed at assessing just where you currently stand with your best people. Can you answer "yes" to all of these?

1. Do you know why a given employee works for your company instead of somewhere else?

2. Have you discussed several career options with this person, and does she feel she is moving in the right direction?

3. Do you know this person's number one career concern or worry? Are you working to address it?

4. Do you keep an eye out for signs of fatigue or burnout, and do you take action to correct the problem?

5. Do you and this employee have an open, trusting, respectful relationship?

6. Do you know this person's long-term goals?

7. Does the work environment meet the person's personal and professional needs?

8. Have his mood, physical health, and overall well-being been stable over the past six months?

9. Does she seem to have passion or enthusiasm for the work she's doing?

10. Does he know that you will promote his development by offering formal training, new challenges, or other kinds of learning opportunities?

The last question on the list may be the most crucial since, as already noted, the lack of fresh challenges is the main reason people quit. Trying to address it may demand more initiative and creativity from you than any other part of your job. But here's the beauty part: Being continually obliged to come up with terrific new opportunities for your people—or actively encouraging them to invent their own—will probably mean that you'll never be bored yourself. And, if one of your stars comes up with some brilliant idea that grows into, say, a big new line of business for the company, some of the glory is bound to rub off on you, too.

Of course, there will always be folks like the guy described by "Left in the Lurch," who went out for an oil change and never came back. There is just no accounting for those people; but, if you've ever been the victim of one, the Caliper job-changing study might make you feel a little bit better about it. In a post-script, Caliper's researchers listed The Ten Strangest Reasons Employees Gave for Leaving a Job. Among them: "The building temperature is much too cold." "There was a demon residing in our computer network." "To start a worm farm."

Um, okey-dokey, then. Let 'em go.

"Do We Really Need to Bring the Lawyers in Here?"

If you've ever had the slightly paranoid thought that the U.S. Supreme Court exists mainly to heap complications on your life, I can sympathize. It does seem as if every time I think I have a grip on the main legal issues that managers need to know about, some big new decision rearranges the landscape with all the force of a hurricane slamming into a barrier island. One example: On June 12, 2000, the nation's highest court handed down a decision, in a case called *Reeves* v. *Sanderson Plumbing Products Inc.* It gave every corporate lawyer in the land a bad case of the heebie-jeebies.

The facts were: Roger Reeves, a fifty-seven-year-old employee at Sanderson Plumbing Products in Mississippi, was told by his plant's director of manufacturing that he was "too damn old" to keep doing his job as a supervisor. Two months later, Reeves was fired. He sued, charging age discrimination, and a jury agreed with him, awarding him $70,000 in damages and $28,490 in back pay. That decision was overturned by an appeals court, on the grounds that Reeves had no concrete evidence his employer intended to discriminate against him based on his age. Writing for the Supreme Court, however, Justice Sandra Day O'Connor said that Reeves didn't need any such evidence in order to prevail, and that indirect evidence—that is, his boss's remarks about his age, among other "evidence of age-based animus"— was enough.

"This same reasoning could extend to ADA [Americans with Disabilities Act] and Title VII [civil rights] cases too," Michael Lotito, a partner in Jackson Lewis in San Francisco and a renowned employment-law expert, told me the day after the decision. "The new, looser standard of evidence will make it a lot harder for employers to get summary judgments from judges in discrimination cases of all kinds." The precedent set by *Reeves* could also snatch victory out of the hands of employers in thousands of cases now grinding their way through the state courts, since the Supreme Court's opinions often weigh heavily in state judges' decisions.

Said Lotito, "There will be more jury trials, and more employees and ex-employees will be emboldened to file lawsuits." To avoid a new avalanche of discrimination suits, "companies are going to have to demonstrate real, proactive efforts toward prevention. The burden will be on them to prove their intent was specifically *not* to discriminate."

But then, as someone with the power to hire and fire, you've probably already heard about this from your own legal department, right? And it's probably added a new list of headaches to what was already a hazardous enough aspect of your job. After all, it's not as if employers weren't being sued left and right even before *Reeves*. The past decade has been a busy one for lawyers. First came the Americans with Disabilities Act in 1990, followed by the Civil Rights Act of 1991. At least as significant but, oddly, little noted in the press, Congress amended Title VII in 1991 to allow all kinds of employment discrimination cases—formerly heard by judges—to go before juries, who are famously more emotional (and more concerned with commonsensical, as opposed to legal, definitions of "fairness") than judges. Plaintiffs began to win more cases: 36 percent in 1998 contrasted with 24 percent in 1990, according to the U.S. Department of Justice (DOJ). The same amendments permitted juries to give compensatory and punitive damages, so monetary awards, formerly limited to back pay, took off into the stratosphere.

Predictably, so did the number of lawsuits. DOJ statistics show that employment discrimination cases jumped from 8,400 in 1990 to 23,700 in 1998. In 1999, a poll by the Society for Human Resource Management showed that 55 percent of companies surveyed had been sued by employees (or ex-employees) in the preceding twelve months. By the time *Reeves* was handed down,

Q. Several women working for me have complained that our company's tuition-assistance policy is rather vague. It seems to offer 50 percent of tuition, books, and other expenses, but there are "exceptions." Many men here are getting reimbursed at 100 percent, although my female subordinates say they have been denied 100 percent reimbursement for pursuing degrees in similar fields of study. Do they have grounds for an EEOC complaint?

A. Before they contact the EEOC, your employees would be wise to have more detailed information at hand. As long as the tuition-assistance policy remains "vague," it will be hard to prove that anybody is violating it. On precisely what grounds are the "exceptions" granted? Can anyone document the assertion that only men are benefiting from them? Suggest to your people that they sit down with whoever in your company wrote this policy. Maybe they can explain (or fix) the apparent discrepancies. As a general rule, government lawyers should always be a last resort. Just ask anyone who's ever met one.

lawyers at Jackson Lewis estimated that 75 percent of all lawsuits against corporations involved employment disputes. Each action cost, on average, over $250,000 in judgments, court costs, and fees—even when the employer came out the winner or settled (without a trial) on the courthouse steps.

Here's hoping nobody ever sues your company over something you allegedly did or failed to do, because in many kinds of employment cases, you as a manager can be held personally liable, too. (You can also, of course, be fired.) No wonder I get so many letters from bosses in a state of panic over the merest suggestion, on the part of a current or former employee, that the lawyers may soon be getting into the act. What makes the specter of a suit so unnerving—especially after *Reeves*—is that even if you as a boss are in fact completely innocent, a jury can often be persuaded otherwise. And, partly because laws and precedents vary so widely from state to state, there is usually no surefire way to predict beforehand just which way any given case might go.

If top management at your company has the sense God gave a goose, you have already had some—perhaps even much—formal training in how to prevent employment lawsuits. In my personal opinion, the courts would be a lot less crowded if every new manager, on his or her first day in the job, were handed a copy of the *American Bar Association Guide to Workplace Law* (see the Appendix). It's not only great bedtime reading, but it's so clear and comprehensive that a working knowledge of its contents might just keep you out of hot water someday.

The list of stuff you can (theoretically at least) be sued for is virtually endless. Martin Aron, a distinguished labor lawyer and partner at Budd, Larner, Gross, Rosenbaum, Greenberg & Sade in Short Hills, New Jersey, has written extensively on what he calls "the four-headed monster": ADA, FMLA (the Family Medical Leave Act), OSHA (the federal Occupational Safety and Health

Q. If a male employee repeatedly calls a female employee a "heifer" in front of other employees (but in the woman's absence), is this hostile-environment sexual harassment?

A. I originally thought your question was some kind of a prank but, alas, you convinced me otherwise. The attorneys I spoke with about this suggested that while the circumstances you describe don't yet warrant legal redress, it might be prudent to put out a memo to the effect that comparing colleagues with barnyard animals is against company policy. Then fire the next oinker who violates it, before you have a real stink on your hands.

Act), and workers' compensation—all of which have a protean way of overlapping and becoming entangled with one another until you can scarcely tell where one leaves off and the next picks up.

The courts, including the Supreme Court, have thrown employers a few bones on ADA, often deciding against plaintiffs whose definitions of "disability" were either too "broad" or were "remediable." At the same time, FMLA has been a constant thorn in the sides of companies trying to deal with employees' inconvenient and ill-timed absences. Weirdly, FMLA defines a "serious" health condition as anything requiring "continuing treatment"—meaning one or more visits to a doctor. That's right, one or more. Two will do. According to FMLA, anyone who has worked for twelve continuous months for a company with fifty or more employees is entitled to twelve weeks of unpaid leave for any "serious" condition, at the end of which the employee can step back into his or her job without adverse consequences of any kind. Earnest critics of our employment laws have sometimes called FMLA the Job Security for Absentees Act, because that is what it sometimes seems like, much to the chagrin of bosses everywhere. Moreover, since 1999—when a jury in Maryland found in favor of a state trooper named Kevin Knussman, who was denied extended paternity leave and sued under FMLA—you'd be wise to let your male employees take up to twelve weeks off after the birth of a new baby.

Title VII meanwhile requires you to make "reasonable accommodation" for your employees' religious practices. The Pregnancy Discrimination Act of 1978 prohibits you from declining to hire someone because she's expecting a baby—even if you fear that filling the job with anyone, pregnant or not, who is planning a long leave of absence soon will throw a serious wrench into your business. Even asking your male employees not to flaunt body-piercings at work could bring trouble: Banning pierced earrings for men but not for women, San Francisco labor lawyer Victor Schachter told *The Wall Street Journal* recently, is arguably a form of sex discrimination.

The only bright spot in all this—and it is, luckily, a big one—is that you don't have to wade into these waters alone. In fact, you shouldn't try. If you're falsely accused of wrongdoing and the people upstairs believe your account of what happened (or didn't), it's customary for an employer to back you 100 percent, including covering all of your legal costs if both you and the company are sued.

Over the years, I've talked with many employment lawyers, on both the plaintiffs' and the corporate defendants' sides of the table. Obviously, each and every case is a different kettle of fish, depending partly on the specific circumstances and partly on

Q. I own a small business and have issued an employee handbook that calls for binding arbitration in the event one of my employees has a dispute with the firm. One of my key employees has refused to sign the arbitration agreement. I consulted a human-resources adviser who said the agreement will apply whether the employee signs it or not. Is that true?

A. Not necessarily. No offense meant to your human-resources adviser, but what you really need is an attorney who is up-to-date on case law in this area for the state where you're located. You might also want to rethink whether mandatory arbitration makes sense. Two prominent groups, the National Academy of Arbitrators and the American Arbitration Association, have come out with policy statements saying that arbitration is fairest and most effective—not to mention less subject to later challenge in court—when employees voluntarily agree to it.

which state of the union it's transpiring in. But most of these lawyers say that if you're hoping never to glimpse the inside of a courtroom, there are two general rules to follow. The first one is this: If you have to fire someone, be very, very careful how you do it. And the second; When in doubt about any situation that seems even remotely actionable, don't try to handle it on your own. Get help.

First things first. Reams of research support the notion that in the overwhelming majority of cases where ex-employees sue companies, the legal action is sparked by the plaintiff's resentment of how he or she was treated during a firing. Of course, for anyone with a shred of compassion (which of course includes you), firing someone is probably the hardest thing they will ever have to do as a manager. In fact, many bosses are tempted to rush through it in unseemly haste, just to get it over with.

Don't rush. Kate Wendleton, president of the Five O'Clock Club, a terrific career-counseling network in New York City, suggests that you prepare a "script"—either in your head or written down—with all the points you want (and need) to cover during what she calls the "termination meeting." Basic kindness is an essential part of this process. "Even in a 'no-fault' situation, like a merger or a downsizing, self-esteem can take a real beating," says Wendleton. A few positive comments can help to soften the blow. A couple of examples: "George, you've been a trouper for years, and we all appreciate that." Or, "Mary, you have such great people skills and have added so much to the group."

No matter what the circumstances, give the person at least one sincere compliment to hold on to. "A termination-for-performance should not be an occasion for abuse, or seen as a chance to settle old scores," Wendleton says. "The most generous severance package in the world won't erase bitter memories of uncaring or unkind words. The 'sharp stick in the eye' is likely to be remembered long after the separation money has been spent."

Obviously, money does matter, and you need to go into this meeting with complete, clear details about severance benefits. Be prepared to get a quick answer to any question you can't answer at the time. If outplacement counseling is available, be sure to emphasize that; and be ready to discuss references or any other help you'd be willing and able to provide. "After the initial shock, the employee is going to need to start formulating a strategy for moving forward," Wendleton notes. Try to move the discussion in that direction, rather than dwelling on the past (or allowing the firee to get mired there. At this point, regrets and recriminations help nobody). One concern people often have is, How is this going to look? Spell out how this parting of the ways is going to be announced to the rest of the team or the company—if indeed it needs to be announced at all. (If it does, it should probably be in one of those "So-and-So is leaving us to pursue other opportunities" memos, that leave purposefully vague just whose idea So-and-So's departure may have been. It's nobody else's business anyway.)

While we're on this grim subject, here are a few words that might help clear up a widespread confusion: Every once in a while, I get letters from people who want to fire an employee who has a "bad attitude," but who are under the impression that they might be sued for doing so. "I have a team of six people working for me, one of whom is so obnoxious—rude, sarcastic, hostile, and argumentative—that no one can stand working with him," went a typical entreaty. "His attitude is such a drag on morale and productivity that I want to fire him, but a colleague of mine says that it would open us (and me) up to a lawsuit. Is this true?"

No, it isn't. Says Thomas Schweich, an employment attorney at Bryan Cave in St. Louis, "Failing to get along with coworkers, to the point where morale and productivity are damaged, is ample grounds for firing—because dealing effectively with people is every bit as much a part of a job as the more technical

Q. I have a problem that is the exact opposite of sexual harassment. What would you do if you were me (young, single, female) and you had been in love with your boss (older, male, married) for several years? We get along very well, but he doesn't suspect how I really feel about him. Should I tell him? Or quit my job and then tell him? Or what?

A. Oh, dear. This could get very messy. Let's clear up a big misapprehension. If you tell your boss you're in love with him, it is not necessarily "the exact opposite of sexual harassment." If, as seems likely, this news would be unwelcome to him, it might very well be considered harassment, regardless of the fact that he outranks you. Do you want to take that chance?

aspects." Where it does get a little confusing is that the federal Equal Employment Opportunity Commission (EEOC) issued a set of guidelines in 1997 that extended the protections of the Americans with Disabilities Act to cover people with mental illnesses. One example would be a person who is clinically depressed—hence lethargic, apathetic, and unable to concentrate on work (three common symptoms of depression)—who consequently gets fired for having a "bad attitude." Over the past three years, EEOC complaints arising from mental illness have skyrocketed to more than 15 percent of the total, making this the single largest category of complaints.

William Walsh, who has taught a course for the American Management Association called "How to Legally Fire People with Attitude Problems," explains: "It's important to pinpoint what you mean by 'attitude.' If the problem comes from anything that could be classified as a disability, firing the person could be actionable." Partly for this reason, many employers try hard to get people with serious attitude problems into counseling, usually through the corporate employee assistance program. Then, even if the company ends up letting the problem employee go, at least it can show in court that some effort was made to fix the problem first. Besides, notes Walsh, even in a recession, trained talent can be costly to replace, so companies figure that even a troublesome person is a bird in the hand."

The other action that you as a manager must take to protect yourself, and the company, is to document exactly how the employee's so-called bad attitude affected the business. Keep a detailed log of specific instances where other team members' ability to get their work done was harmed by the obstreperous party, or any and all other concrete, measurable ways in which the attitude problem translated into a performance problem. You need to be able to show that the person's performance was below par by some objective standard. Just saying, "Nobody could stand working with the guy" is not going to cut it.

Document everything. You need to lay a paper trail of precisely what happened when. And at every step of the way, in any predicament where you suspect some legal issue could arise, don't forget to follow the lawyers' second bit of counsel: Keep the human-resources department informed of what's going on.

Let's say one of your employees has accused another one of sexual harassment. Before filing a sexual-harassment lawsuit, a would-be plaintiff first has to lodge a formal complaint with the EEOC. Such complaints tripled, from about five thousand in 1990 to more than fifteen thousand in 1997, and then leveled off—but they're still common enough to be a real cause for concern. As Susan Crawford, vice president and general counsel at Scitor in Sunnyvale, California, told me: "I've found that managers too often are reluctant to refer a [sexual harassment] complaint to human resources. Instead they get enmeshed in trying to handle it themselves, which can lead to some real disasters. Bosses need to see that this is a complicated area with a lot of pitfalls, and it is not a sign of failure on their part to say, 'Hey, I need a hand with this. I'm not the expert here.' "

In this or any other legal matter, the people who do know

where all the pitfalls are—and who will try to be fair to every-body—are not in your department. They are in human resources, or legal, or both. Do yourself a favor that could well spare you a truly awful adventure with our legal system: Rather than delude yourself that you can practice law without a license, consult the pros. Proceed according to their instructions.

Then breathe easy. Once you've called in the heavy artillery, the problem is out of your hands.

Isn't it nice to know that something is?

ACKNOWLEDGMENTS

First and foremost, thanks to the wonderful, smart, thoughtful, funny readers of my columns in *Fortune* and on the Web site, without whose intriguing questions and astute comments this book could never have existed. You make my job a pleasure. I'm also unspeakably grateful to the many consultants, lawyers, educators, executives, recruiters, psychologists, career coaches, and experts of every other stripe who have kindly shared their time and their knowledge with me, so that I could pass it along. Thank you all.

At *Fortune,* I'm indebted to the indefatigable Research Center staff: Patricia Neering, Doris Burke, Susan Kramer, Mary Danehy, Fran Gretes, Zoraida Matos, Helen Whatford, and everybody else up there on the twenty-sixth floor who cheerfully chases down even the most arcane fact or reference, day in and day out, with speed and grace. Likewise, to Suzanne Barlyn and Joe McGowan, for making the Appendix comprehensive, accurate, and up-to-the-minute, my hat is off. And to William Nabers, photo guy extraordinaire, what can I say? The phrase "patience of a saint" springs to mind; but how many saints would put up with me? So far, only people do. Talk about blessed.

Among the editors of *Fortune* and fortune.com, past and present, I'd like to thank Ken Labich and Chris Peacock, for your encouragement, wit, and laughter; Brian Dumaine, Rik Kirkland, Geoff Colvin, Rick Tetzeli, Vera Titunik, and Gabrielle Solomon for your constant support; and John Huey, for (accidentally, but still . . .) giving me the idea to write a career-advice column in the first place. I know some people thought it was a goofy idea, and maybe they were right. But thanks for letting me stick with it.

To Kris Dahl at ICM: I'm glad you talked me into writing this book, and I still owe you three beers. To my editor, Henry Ferris: Due to your inimitable combination of forbearance, frankness, and fun, you may be stuck with me for a while. To my parents, Julie and Phil, my biggest fans for four decades now and counting. And to my wiser (and sweeter) half, Dave Lounsbury: You are a marvel for putting up with my crankiness over the past year and a half. I'll make it up to you, honest. In fact, I'm going down to the kitchen right now to bake you a pie.

A. F.

APPENDIX

CHAPTER ONE: SO YOU'VE GRADUATED FROM COLLEGE. NOW ALL YOU NEED IS . . . MORE ADVICE?

Books

Baldrige, Letitia. *Letitia Baldrige's New Complete Guide to Executive Manners.* New York: Simon & Schuster, 1993.

Bolles, Richard Nelson. *What Color is Your Parachute? A Practical Manual for Job-Hunters & Career-Changers.* Berkeley, Calif.: Ten Speed Press, 1997.

Farr, J. Michael. *America's Fastest Growing Jobs.* Indianapolis: JIST Works, Inc., 1999.

———. *America's Top Jobs for College Graduates.* Indianapolis: JIST Works, Inc., 1999.

Farr, J. Michael, and LaVerne L. Ludden. *Best Jobs for the 21st Century.* Indianapolis: JIST Works, Inc., 1999.

Harkavy, Michael. *101 Careers: A Guide to the Fastest-Growing Opportunities.* New York: John Wiley & Sons, 1999.

Jandt, Fred J., and Mary B. Nemnich. *Cyberspace Job Search Kit.* Indianapolis: JIST Works, Inc., 2000.

Kador, John. *Internet Jobs! The Complete Guide to Finding the Hottest Internet Jobs.* New York: McGraw-Hill, 2000.

Kahr, Julia, and the staff of the *Yale Daily News. Working Knowledge: 150 Successful Professionals Tell You How to Use College to Get the Job You Want.* New York: Simon & Schuster, 1999.

Karl, Arthur, and Shannon Karl. *How to Get Your Dream Job Using the Web.* Scottsdale, Arizona: Coriolus Group, 1997.

Katzanek, Frank. *Reality 101: The Ultimate Guide to Life After College.* New York: Simon & Schuster, 2000.

Kuiper, Shirley, and Gary F. Kohut. *Write to Win!* Florence, Kentucky: Thomson Learning, 1999.

Lessard, Bill, and Steve Baldwin. *NetSlaves: True Tales of Working the Web.* New York: McGraw-Hill, 1999.

Linkemer, Bobbi. *Polish Your People Skills.* New York: AMACOM New Media, 1999. (Includes an interactive CD-Rom on building positive, enjoyable relationships at work.)

Maxwell, Bruce. *The Congressional Quarterly Insider's Guide to Finding a Job in Washington.* Washington, D.C.: CQ Press, 1999.

Montauk, Richard. *How to Get Into the Top MBA Programs.* Paramus, N.J.: Prentice Hall, 1997.

Perkins, Anthony B., and Michael C. Perkins. *The Internet Bubble: Inside the Overloaded World of High-Tech Stocks and What You Need to Avoid the Coming Shakeout.* New York: HarperBusiness, 1999.

Schaffer, William A. *High-Tech Careers for Low-Tech People.* Berkeley, Calif.: Ten Speed Press, 1999.

Veruki, Peter. *The 250 Job Interview Questions You'll Likely be Asked . . . and the Answers That Will Get You Hired.* Holbrook, Mass.: Adams Media Corporation, 1999.

Wolfinger, Anne. *Quick Internet Guide to Career and Education Information.* Indianapolis: JIST Works, Inc., 1999.

Internet Sources

Resource Tools

JobStar: California Job Search Guide *(http://jobstar.org)*: Library-sponsored guide, not limited to California, providing links to job-search resources on the Internet. Includes links to nationwide salary surveys, career guides, résumé advice, listings of employer hotlines, and extensive database of middle and senior management jobs and recruiting services.

JobTrak *(www.jobtrak.com):* A nationwide electronic network that links students, alumni, and career-counseling centers at 900 colleges and universities with potential employers. Includes job-posting boards, job-search tips, an on-line career fair, and advice on relocation.

National Association of Colleges and Employers *(www.jobweb.org):* Source of information on career planning and employment for college graduates. Operates as liaison among universities and colleges, Fortune 500, medium-sized and start-up companies, governmental agencies from all levels, HR and other employment professionals, and college students and alumni. Provides research on job trends, legal issues in the workplace, and salary surveys. Extensive links to job-search information, career fairs, and professional associations.

The Riley Guide *(www.rileyguide.com):* Employment opportunities and job resources on the Internet. Annotated links to career fields and job opportunities, researching companies, résumé and cover-letter aids, salary surveys. Information for job recruiters. Updated weekly.

Jobs Directories and Databases

Monster.com *(www.monster.com):* One of the newer jobs databases as well as one of the largest, with more than 150,000 job opportunities. Search by company name, location, and job title. Brief company profiles. Résumés are posted for viewing by potential employers who pay for access to job seekers.

CareerMosaic *(www.careermosaic.com):* One of the first employment sites on the Internet, CareerMosaic lists 100,000 jobs across all industries and professions. The site features positions (no more than 30 days old) ranging from entry-level to manager to CEO; detailed descriptions of leading corporations; and customized job searches by description, title, company, and location. A database of some 140,000 résumés allows employers to scroll for résumés sorted by category, location, and key word. The Career Resources Center combines *Fortune* magazine's editorial content with CareerMosaic's JOBS database.

JobBank USA *(www.jobbankusa.com)*: Provides extensive and easily accessible job information in a wide variety of fields and occupations. Posts résumés for employers and recruiters. Links to news groups.

America's Job Bank *(www.ajb.org)*: A free on-line recruitment center, posting 1.3 million job openings with an average 400,000 searches conducted daily. Includes comprehensive job listings, at all levels of expertise and interest, from all 50 states, the District of Columbia, Puerto Rico, and the Virgin Islands. An extensive database of information from various sources, including the U.S. Bureau of Labor Statistics, enables job seekers to gain insights to occupational trends, state and employer profiles, and other resources for planning career moves.

Top Electronic Recruiters *(www.interbiznet.com)*: Interbiznet.com analyst of electronic recruiting industry, examines and reviews job recruiting Web sites. Sites organized for HR managers, job hunters, and third-party recruiters. Daily on-line newsletter follows the industry and reports on trends.

EscapeArtist.com *(www.escapeartist.com)*: Major overseas job directory. Links to information on moving and living overseas, including tax implications, job listings by country. World newspapers and detailed links to individual countries.

CEO Express *(www.ceoexpress.com)*: Career links in a variety of professions, including banking, finance, health care, advertising and marketing, legal, and technology. Links to recruiter directories and professional organizations. Links to company and business research, stock exchanges, and major media.

JobOptions *(www.joboptions.com)*: Comprehensive searchable database of jobs and employers, updated daily. Other services include résumés forwarded to employers, career tools such as résumé writing, articles on interviewing, resources for working parents. HR and employer information include HR and legal resources, diversity and salary information.

thepavement.com *(www.thepavement.com)*: A Web site for young adults, ages 20 to 26, that offers career-and life-building services to assist in

the transition from college to the real world. Offers free access to services and tools needed to find a first job, begin a career, or continue
building one. Services include entry-level and early-career job listings,
car and apartment classifieds, relocation information, personal finance
advice, and more.

enVISION *(www.womenconnect.com/loclink/COLC)*: A Web site for young
women starting their professional lives. Offers career advice on topics
that include how to craft a killer résumé and cover letter; real-life career
success stories; ways to consider an offer; networking and finding a
career coach; and tips on enjoying your "after hours." The site's
Paycheck Check-up helps determine the average earnings of women
and men in specific professions.

eLance *(www.eLance.com)*: An on-line job site where freelancers can list
skills and search for job opportunities. Users can search for work via
industry categories like Legal, Marketing, Medical, and Education. Site
includes advice on starting your own business, personal finance tips for
freelancers, and how to build a Web site for your freelance business.

FreeAgent *(www.FreeAgent.com)*: Web site listing job opportunities for
freelancers and their résumés for employees. Freelancers can create a
free, interactive résumé/portfolio with their own URL, find deals on
business supplies, and receive expert advice on topics like "keeping a
corporate front while working at home," and how to fight burnout.

dice.com *(www.dice.com)*: One of the largest job-search Web sites for
computer professionals. Organized for access by recruiters and job
seekers. Offers regional searches in key high-technology markets. Lists
thousands of permanent, contract, and consulting jobs. Extensive links
to career resources such as résumé writing, interviewing skills, and
associations and user groups. Recruiter directory available.

BrassRing.com *(www.brassring.com)*: Web site for professionals in high-
tech industry. Services include extensive job databases, customizable
searches, company profiles, stock information, and industry news.
Companies that have posted positions on BrassRing include Compaq,
Dell, Intuit, Oracle, and Sony.

New York Times CareerPath *(www.nytimes.com.jobmarket)*: Search *New York Times* classifieds and other major newspapers for jobs. Listings of *New York Times* advertisers. Company profiles, columns on managing your career, and Dilbert, for a chuckle, are also available.

ACCESS *(www.accessjobs.org)*: Comprehensive resource for jobs, internships, and career development in nonprofit organizations. Provides nonprofits with a national pool of job seekers.

CoolWorks *(www.coolworks.com)*: Jobs available at national and state parks, resorts, guest ranches, amusement parks, and summer camps. Paid, seasonal, and volunteer jobs.

USAJOBS *(www.usajobs.opm.gov)*: Administered by the U.S. Office of Personnel Management, USAJOBS is one of four electronic systems listing job positions and data on internship programs in the federal government. Jobs are listed by category: entry-level professional, senior executive, clerical, and so on. Site includes a feature that enables job seekers to look up any opening that may exist in a given agency; an on-line résumé-builder that provides advice on how to create a federal-style résumé; and information about salaries, benefits, and other topics.

BrilliantPeople *(www.brilliantpeople.com)*: Run by Management Recruiters International, a giant global headhunting firm, the site links job seekers with one of 5,000 recruiters at more than 1,000 MRI offices worldwide. Includes résumé-writing tips, advice on interviewing techniques, and data on hiring trends in various regions of the United States.

Researching Companies

CompaniesOnline *(www.companiesonline.com)*: Information on over 100,000 public and private companies with a Web presence. Search for individual company or browse by industry.

EDGAR *(www.sec.gov/edgarhp.htm)*: Full-text documents filed by publicly traded companies with the U.S. Securities and Exchange Commission.

Hoovers Online *(www.hoovers.com)*: Company profiles, including financials and industry snapshots, on U.S. public and private companies.

Corporate Report Card *(www.cepnyc.org/index.htm)*: Sponsored by the Council on Economic Priorities, site rates more than 300 companies on their corporate social responsibility, including environment, minority advancement, charitable giving, women's advancement, and community outreach.

Salaries

Crystal Report *(www.crystalreport.com)*: On-line newsletter edited by Graef Crystal, provides information on corporate compensation for executive recruiters, compensation consultants, institutional investors, boards of directors, and stock analysts. Subscription access required.

Inflation Calculators *(www.jsc.nasa.gov/bu2/inflate.html)*: Calculate how far your salary will go with these inflation calculators, adjusting cost-of-living index, employment-cost index, or producer-price index from one year to another. Cost of living is compared among major U.S. and international cities.

Occupational Employment Statistics *(http://stats.bls.gov/oes/oes_data.htm)*: Presented by the Bureau of Labor Statistics, offers national, state, and metropolitan-area wage estimates by occupation. Links to *Occupational Outlook Handbook (http://stats.bls.gov/ocohome.htm)*, with employment projections, salary levels, and educational requirements.

Career Development

The Black Collegian *(www.black-collegian.com)*: Electronic edition of professional and career-development magazine devoted to African Americans. Career-planning information and job opportunities, employer profiles actively recruiting African Americans, and a Minorities Job Bank.

Careers WSJ *(http://careers.wsj.com)*: Career information, with content from *Wall Street Journal and National Business Employment Weekly*. Articles and columns on workplace issues, HR news and trends, analysis of legal issues affecting the workforce and executive recruiting. Job listings for technical, management, and other professional positions.

Go For IT! *(www.go4it.gov)*: U.S. Department of Commerce resource for developing America's IT (Information Technology) workforce. Reports on job trends, the business environment, and congressional testimony are available. Analysis and debate on shortage of skilled IT workforce.

JobHuntersBible *(www.jobhuntersbible.com)*: Internet version of career guide classic *What Color is Your Parachute?*

Periodicals

2000

"New Ethics or No Ethics? (Doing Business the Dot-Com Way) [cover story]," J. Useem, *Fortune*, March 20, 2000.

1999

"Résumés, Applications, and Cover Letters [cover story]," O. Crosby, *Occupational Outlook Quarterly*, Summer 1999.

"For Sale Online: You [cover story]," J. Useem, *Fortune*, July 5, 1999.

"References: A Two-way Street," *Nation's Business*, May 1999.

"Searching the Net for Your Next Gig," E. C. Baig, *Business Week*, May 17, 1999.

"The Network Way to a Better Job," M. Schulhof, *Kiplinger's Personal Finance Magazine*, May 1999.

"Interview Tips and Bloopers," J. A. Cantore, *Career World*, April/May 1999.

"Dealing with Job Rejections," M. Masikiewicz, *Career World*, March 1999.

"Six Tricky Interview Traps," P. Stock, *Mademoiselle*, February 1999.

"What Are Employers Really Looking For?" H. Neuman, *Career World*, February 1999.

"How to Write a Résumé a Computer Will Love," H. Neuman, *Career World*, January 1999.

"Starting Over: Interviewing for a New Job After 50," A. M. Scheele, *Modern Maturity*, January/February 1999.

1998

"Taking Charge in a Temp World," A. Harrington, *Fortune,* December 21, 1998.

"The Job Hunt," J. A. Cantore, *Career World,* November/December 1998.

"Phone Tips for the Job Hunter," J. A. Cantore, *Career World,* October 1998.

"High-tech Tolls Shorten the Job Search," P. R. Brotherton, *Black Enterprise,* September 1998.

"What Do You Want Out of a Career?" J. Arenofsky, *Career World,* September 1998.

"You and Your Job. Should You Still Be Together?" E. Mall, *Glamour,* July 1998.

"The Essentials of an Effective Job Search," T. Coelho, *We,* May/June 1998.

"Finding a Job Online," L. Touby, *Working Mother,* April 1998.

"How to Build a Network," M. Masikiewicz, *Career World,* April/May 1998.

"Finding the Job You Should Want [Harvard Business School quiz]," J. Waldroop and T. Butler, *Fortune,* March 2, 1998.

"Super Effective Interview Tactics," R. Ryan, *Working Woman,* February 1998.

"Informational Interviews: Get the Inside Scoop," B. L. Malone, *Career World,* January 1998.

1997

"Customizing Your Résumé," T. J. Saftner, *Career World,* November/December 1997.

"Cover Letters That Get You in the Door," A. M. Sitley, *Career World,* April/May 1997.

"Make Your First Impression Count [job fairs]," A. Arthur, *Black Enterprise,* April 1997.

"How to Sell Yourself to an Employer," M. Pratt, *Career World,* January 1997.

"Job Surfing: Move On to Move Up," J. Martin, *Fortune,* January 13, 1997.

Chapter Two: Moving Up: How to Travel Vertically in a Horizontal World

Books

Axtell, Roger E. *Do's and Taboos Around the World.* New York: John Wiley & Sons, 1985.

Boreham, Roland S. *The Three-Legged Stool: Relationships First—Success Follows.* Danbury, Conn.: Rutledge Books, 1998.

Bright, Deborah. *On the Edge and In Control: A Proven 8-Step Program for Taking Charge of Your Life.* New York: McGraw-Hill, 1998.

Bruzzese, Anita. *Take This Job and Thrive.* Manassas Park, Va.: Impact Publications, 1998.

Chambers, Harry E. *Getting Promoted: Real Strategies for Advancing Your Career.* Reading, Mass.: Perseus Books, 1999.

Claxton, Guy. *Hare Brain Tortoise Mind.* Hopewell, N.J.: Ecco Press, 1997.

Fortgang, Laura Berman. *Take Yourself to the Top.* New York: Warner Books, 1998.

Frankel, Lois P. *Jump-Start Your Career.* New York: Three Rivers Press, 1997.

Goleman, Daniel. *Working with Emotional Intelligence.* New York: Bantam Books, 1998.

Kelley, Robert E. *How to Be a Star at Work.* New York: Times Business, 1998.

Krannich, Caryl, and Ron Krannich. Get a Raise in Seven Days. Manassas Park, Va.: Impact Publications, 1999.

Morin, William. *Total Career Fitness: A Complete Checkup and Workout Guide.* San Francisco: Jossey-Bass, 2000.

Nolen, Roland. *Beyond Performance: What Employees Really Need to Know to Climb the Ladder of Success.* Wheaton, Ill.: New Perspectives Press, 1999.

O'Malley, Michael. *Are You Paid What You're Worth? The Complete Guide to Negotiating the Salary, Benefits, Bonus, and Raise You Deserve.* New York: Broadway Books, 1998.

Yeomans, William N. *Seven Survival Skills for a Reengineered World.* New York: Dutton, 1996.

Internet Sources

Vocational Guidance

CareerLeader *(www.careerdiscovery.com)*: Subscription-based, interactive career self-assessment program developed by the directors of MBA career-development programs at the Harvard Business School. Offerings include discussions of key elements of corporate culture and how your personality will fit in; how to recognize—and cure—your career "Achilles heels"; ratings of your entrepreneurial attributes; and specific career paths for you to explore. Site includes personal career counseling and coaching service and links to Career Central and CareerPath.com.

CareerZone *(www.careerzone.com)*: Backed by thousands of career coaches, the site includes features that help users assess professional strengths and weaknesses, identify career goals, prepare for performance evaluations, negotiate a raise, evaluate job offers, and more.

Fortune *(www.fortune.com)*: The Career Resource Center pages of the site offer self-assessment quizzes, such as "How High Is Your Work E.Q.?" and "Do You Deserve a Raise?" The site also includes detailed information on *Fortune*'s annual list of the "100 Best Companies to Work For."

International Coach Federation *(www.coachfederation.com)*: Web site of the International Coach Federation (ICF), a nonprofit professional organization of personal and business coaches. Provides free coach-referral service drawing from ICF members in most states and 10 countries. Corporate, small-business, personal (life planning and enrichment), and Career (career transition and major career moves) coaching is available.

The Five O'Clock Club *(www.FiveOClockClub.com)*: A national career-counseling network based in New York City, the site can connect job seekers with certified counselors who specialize in targeting the job you want, résumé development, job-search strategy, salary negotiations, and more.

Miscellaneous Resource Tools

Accredited College Degrees through Distance Learning
(www.accredited degrees.com): Offers a frequently updated directory of more than 350 U.S. universities and colleges with "distance learning" (on-line or by video and/or correspondence) degrees—from bachelor's to doctorates—in 900 fields.

CEO Express *(www.ceoexpress.com)*: Career links in a variety of professions, including banking, finance, health care, advertising and marketing, legal, and technology. Links to recruiter directories and professional organizations. Links to company and business research, stock exchanges, and major media.

The Conference Board *(www.conference-board.org)*: Research publications and reports on workplace issues such as diversity, work and family, employee motivation, performance enhancement, and compensation. Web site provides access to "Across the Board," monthly Conference Board publication that deals with management and economic issues for senior-level executives.

The Economic Press *(www.epinc.com)*: Web site of the Economic Press, publisher of over 40 periodicals, books, audio, and subscription publications aimed at helping people improve their skills, get along better with coworkers and colleagues, and be inspired to enjoy their work.

Employee Benefit Research Institute *(www.ebri.com)*: Offers surveys, research studies, and reports on all aspects of employee benefit programs, such as retirement plans, social security, health insurance, and pension plans.

The Executive MBA Council *(ww.emba.org)*: Provides a list of accredited schools nationwide, for managers interested in pursuing an executive MBA degree.

Salaries

Crystal Report *(www.crystalreport.com)*: On-line newsletter edited by Graef Crystal, provides information on corporate compensation for executive recruiters, compensation consultants, institutional investors, boards of directors, and stock analysts. Subscription access required.

Inflation Calculators *(www.jsc.nasa.gov/bu2/inflate.html)*: Calculate how far your salary will go with these inflation calculators, adjusting cost-of-living index, employment cost index or producer-price index from one year to another. Cost of living is compared among major U.S. and international cities.

Occupational Employment Statistics *(http://stats.bls.gov/oes/oes_data. htm)*: Presented by the Bureau of Labor Statistics, offers national, state, and metropolitan-area wage estimates by occupation. Links to *Occupational Outlook Handbook (http://stats.bls.gov/ocohome.htm)*, with employment projections, salary levels, and educational requirements.

Salary.com *(www.salary.com)*: This site is a comprehensive guide to earning what you're worth, with a feature called "Salary Wizard" that lets you compare your current pay to the average at your level, in your field, and in your geographic region. Also offers solid advice on salary negotiations, how to evaluate stock options, and much more.

Periodicals

1999

"Six Big Career Mistakes and How to Avoid Them," D. B. Hogarty, *Reader's Digest,* May 1999.

"Career Survival Guide," J. Connelly, *Working Woman,* April 1999.

"Managing Oneself," P. F. Drucker, *Harvard Business Review,* March/April 1999.

"Andy Grove on Navigating Your Career," A. S. Grove, *Fortune,* March 29, 1999.

"The Big Payoff," M. J. Harris, *Working Woman,* March 1999.

"Ten Tips for Career Success," J. Arenofsky, *Career World,* January 1999.

"Want More Money?" E. Seideman, *Glamour,* January 1999.

1998

"This Way Up," J. Matus, *Men's Health,* November 1998.

"The Global Glass Ceiling [10 women who broke through it]," J. Guyon, *Fortune,* October 12, 1998.

"What Do You Want Out of a Career?" J. Arenofsky, *Career World,* September 1998.

"The Grass Isn't Always Greener," C. Jones, *Black Enterprise,* November 1998.

"Believing in Yourself [career success]," J. Portillo, *Career World,* October 1998.

"Facing the Fear of Risk," T. J. Saftner, *Career World,* April/May 1998.

"Get More Out of Your Career," J. White, *Black Enterprise,* October 1998.

"A Sounding Board in Cyberspace [on-line career counseling]," S. Harrington, *Fortune,* September 28, 1998.

"Managing Your Long-term Success," R. M. Kanter, *The Futurist,* August/September 1998.

"What Are You Really Worth?" B. Goodman, *Money,* September 1998.

"Career Coach," A. Weintraub, *Working Mother,* June 1998.

"It's Time for a Career Workout," P. R. Brogherton, *Black Enterprise,* June 1998.

"The 10 New Rules for Strategizing Your Career," R. L. Knowdell, *The Futurist,* June/July 1998.

"Six Dangerous Myths About Pay," J. Pfeffer, *Harvard Business Review,* May/June 1998.

"Sixteen Ways to Succeed in a New Workplace," A. Perryman, *Working Woman,* April 1998.

"Ingratiate Your Way to a Raise?" M. Schulhof, *Kiplinger's Personal Finance Magazine,* March 1998.

"Work Smart: Get Organized for Success," J. Arenofsky, *Career World,* February 1998.

"How to Succeed in Business Without an MBA," K. Bruce, *Forbes,* January 26, 1998.

"Career Guidance from the Federal Government: Helping Workers Help Themselves," M. Barkume, *Occupational Outllook Quarterly,* Winter 1998–1999.

1997

"Are You (More Than) Ready for a Pay Raise?" R. Henkoff, *Fortune,* December 8, 1997.

"Stand Out from the Crowd [career success]," G. Marshall, *Reader's Digest,* October 1997.

"The Game of Raw Ambition: From Cubicle to Corner Office in 10 Shrewd Moves," L. Morice, *Mademoiselle,* April/May 1997.

"Job Surfing: Moving On to Move Up," J. Martin, *Fortune,* January 13, 1997.

"Take Control of Your Life—and Your Career," J. A. Cantore, *Career World,* January 1997.

CHAPTER THREE: DIFFICULT BOSSES, TOXIC COWORKERS, AND OTHER IRRITANTS

Books

Axelrod, Alan, Jim Holtje, and James Holtje. *201 Ways to Deal with Difficult People (Quick Tip Survival Guides).* New York: McGraw-Hill, 1997.

Bell, Arthur H., and Dayle M. Smith. *Winning with Difficult People.* Happauge, N.Y.: Barrons Educational Series, 1997.

Brinkman, Rick, and Rick Kirschner. *Dealing with People You Can't Stand: How to Bring Out the Best in People at Their Worst.* New York: McGraw-Hill, 1994.

Cava, Roberta. *Difficult People: How to Deal with Impossible Clients, Bosses and Employees.* Ontario, Canada: Firefly Books, 1997.

Crowe, Sandra. *Since Strangling Isn't an Option—: Dealing with Difficult People—Common Problems and Uncommon Solutions.* New York: Perigee Books, 1999.

Delisser, Peter. *Be Your Own Executive Coach.* Worcester, Mass.: Chandler House Press, 1999.

Gabor, Don. *Speaking Your Mind in 101 Difficult Situations.* New York: Fireside, 1994.

Gill, Lucy. *How to Work with Just About Anyone: A 3-Step Solution for Getting Difficult People to Change.* New York: Simon & Schuster, 1999.

Haden Elgin, Suzanne. *The Gentle Art of Verbal Self-Defense at Work.* Paramus, N.J.: Prentice Hall, 2000.

Kaye, Kenneth. *Workplace Wars and How to End Them: Turning Personal Conflicts into Productive Teamwork.* New York: AMACOM, 1994.

Lichtenberg, Ronna. *Work Would Be Great If It Weren't for the People: Ronna and Her Evil Twin's Guide to Making Office Politics Work for You.* New York: Hyperion, 1999.

Littauer, Florence. *How to Get Along with Difficult People.* Eugene, Ore.: Harvest House, 1999.

Lundin, Kathleen, and William Lundin. *Working with Difficult People: A Worksmart Guide.* New York: AMACOM, 1995.

Lundin, William. *When Smart People Work for Dumb Bosses: How to Survive a Crazy and Dysfunctional Workplace.* New York: McGraw-Hill, 1998.

Mannering, Karen. *Managing Difficult People: Proven Strategies to Deal with Awkwardness in Business Situations.* Philadelphia, Pa.: Trans-Atlantic Publications, 2000.

Pachter, Barbara. *The Power of Positive Confrontation: The Skills You Need to Know to Handle Conflicts at Work, Home, and in Life.* New York: Marlowe & Co., 2000.

Pardoe, Blaine L. *Cubicle Warfare: Self-Defense Tactics for Today's Hypercompetitive Workplace.* Rocklin, Calif.: Prima Publishing, 1997.

Simmons, Annette. *Territorial Games: Understanding and Ending Turf Wars at Work.* New York: AMACOM, 1998.

Stone, Douglas, Bruce Patton, and Sheila Heen. *Difficult Conversations: How to Discuss What Matters Most.* New York: Viking, 1999.

Toropov, Brandon. *The Complete Idiot's Guide to Getting Along with Difficult People.* New York: Alpha, 1997.

Wheeler, Marilyn. *Problem People at Work: The Essential Survival Guide to Dealing with Bosses, Coworkers, Employees, and Outside Clients.* New York: St. Martin's Griffin, 1995.

Williams, Redford, and Virginia Williams. *Anger Kills: Seventeen Strategies for Controlling the Anger That Can Harm Your Health.* New York: Times Books, 1993.

Internet Sources

BrainwareMedia.com *(www.brainware.com)*: On-line store that specializes in workplace training videos, CDs, audiocassettes, and books. Materials include self-study courses in handling difficult people, conflict management, effective communication, and customer service skills.

Daniel Robin & Associates *(www.abetterworkplace.com)*: Web site for a workplace consulting firm, featuring free articles about coping with and addressing workplace conflict. See list under "Essential Leadership and Organizational Development Tools" on home page.

Difficult Conversations Inc. *(www.difficultconversations.com)*: A site for the Cambridge, Massachusetts–based consulting firm Difficult Conversations Inc., which helps clients overcome corporate conflict and emotional situations to achieve effective communication. Includes a free, downloadable worksheet (click on "Need Help Now?"), designed to help clients tackle difficult conversations and negotiations.

The Management Assistance Program for Nonprofits *(www.mapnp.org)*: Source of information on managing nonprofit organizations from national nonprofit management-support organization. Includes free on-line library relevant to all types of businesses. Click on "Free Management Library" in left column of home page. Topics include interpersonal relations, conflict management, office politics, etiquette, and leadership skills.

Occupational Safety and Health Administration, United States Department of Labor *(www.osha.gov)*: Source of government information on workplace issues, including articles and manuals about workplace violence and prevention. Click on "Site Search" near top of home page. Enter "workplace violence" at search prompt for articles and guidance.

Plainsense *(www.plainsense.com)*: A health site that provides general information about day-to-day issues affecting human well-being. A section dedicated to stress-coping skills features articles about difficult people, conflict resolution, anxiety, forgiveness, and work habits. Click on "Stress Skills" on home page.

Smart Business Supersite *(www.smartbiz.com)*: Source of information for small-business development and management. An extensive database includes free articles on workplace politics, difficult coworkers, interpersonal skills, and conflict management. Materials are also available for purchase. Enter search terms at prompt on home page. Other resources include business news and trade show information.

The Stress Doc *(www.stressdoc.com)*: On-line home of Mark Gorkin, a social worker, speaker, and humorist. Provides extensive information about coping with stress both on the job and in life. Features numerous Q & A's about coping with workplace issues, including difficult personalities on the job. Click on "Work Stress" in left column of home page for articles about control freaks, defensive managers, lame-duck managers, and nitpickers. Selecting any story in this section generates a list of difficult personality types with easy access to more articles.

Work 911 *(www.work911.com)*: Web site of Bacal & Associates, a Winnipeg, Canada–based business consulting firm specializing in workplace conflict and communication. Provides a collection of articles and ideas pertaining to the workplace. Includes both free and fee-based information about difficult people, hostile customers, conflict at work, workplace violence, and conflict resolution. Discussion lists on difficult people and workplace conflict provide forums for venting frustrations.

Periodicals

2000

"Dealing with Difficult People on the Job," M. Rafenstein, *Current Health*, January 2000.

1999

"The Human Moment at Work," E. M. Hallowell, *Harvard Business Review*, January/February 1999.

"How to Make Conflict Work for You," M. Rowh, *Career World*, February 1999.

"Flak Attack: How to Get Better Feedback from Your Boss," A. Weintraub, *Working Mother*, March 1999.

"10 Tricks for Winning Over Impossible People," S. Woodman, *McCall's*, April 1999.

1998

"Putting a Lid on Conflicts," M. Barrier, *Nation's Business*, April 1998.

"The Art of Communication," K. Charles, *Black Enterprise*, August 1998.

"Keeping Your Cool with Difficult People," B. Repp, *Nation's Cities Weekly*, October 1998.

1997

"Chill Out—Coping with Conflict," M. Pratt, *Career World*, February 1997.

"Let's Get Critical," H. Roome, *Home Office Computing*, June 1997.

1996

"Breaking Bad News to a Client," S. M. Pollan and M. Levine, *Working Woman*, May 1996.

"Reaching and Changing Frontline Employees," T. J. Larkin and S. Larkin, *Harvard Business Review,* May/June 1996.

"Easy Ways to Avoid an Argument," S. Horn, *Reader's Digest,* October 1996.

1995

"How to Tell the Boss You're Overworked," S. M. Pollan and M. Levine, *Working Woman,* May 1995.

"Office Conflicts: When No Win is Win-Win," D. L. Jacobs, *Working Woman,* May 1995.

"Ratting on a Colleague," S. M. Pollan and M. Levine, *Working Woman,* June 1995.

"The Skill Every Manager Must Master," N. Austin, *Working Woman,* June 1995.

"Run the Business Like a Business," C. E. Aronoff and J. L. Ward, *Nation's Business,* November 1995.

CHAPTER FOUR: NOBODY EVER TOLD YOU IT WAS GOING TO BE THIS COMPLICATED

Books

Asker, S. *Plan B: How to Get Unstuck from Work, Family, and Relationship Problems.* New York: Perigee Books, 1999.

Bailey Reinhold, Barbara. *Toxic Work: How to Overcome Stress, Overload, and Burnout and Revitalize Your Career.* New York: Dutton, 1996.

Berglas, Steven, and Roy F. Baumeister. *Your Own Worst Enemy: Understanding the Paradox of Self-Defeating Behavior.* New York: Basic Books, 1993.

Carnoy, M. *Sustaining Flexibility: Work, Family, and Community in the Information Age.* New York: Russell Sage Foundation, 2000.

Douglas, A. *The Unofficial Guide to Childcare.* New York: Macmillan,1998.

Galinsky, E. *Ask the Children: What America's Children Really Think About Working Parents.* New York: William Morrow, 1999.

Gleeson, K. *The Personal Efficiency Program: How to Get Organized to Do More Work in Less Time.* New York: John Wiley & Sons, 2000.

Godfrey, N., and C. Cartwright. *Working Mother's Time: How to Take It, Make It, Save It, and Enjoy It.* New York: St. Martin's Griffin, 2000.

Gordon, J. *Stress Management.* Philadelphia, Pa.: Chelsea House Publishers, 2000.

Goulston, Mark, M.D., and Philip Goldberg. *Get Out of Your Own Way: Overcoming Self-Defeating Behavior.* New York: Berkeley Publishing Group, 1996.

Hurst, G., M. Kachura, and L. Sides. *Time Out: Daily Devotions for Workaholics.* Nashville, Tenn.: T. Nelson Publishers, 1991.

Jukes, Jill, and Ruthan Rosenberg. *Surviving Your Partner's Job Loss: The Complete Guide to Rescuing Your Marriage and Family from Today's Economy.* Washington, D.C.: National Press Books, 1993.

Kofodimos, J. R. *Balancing Act: How Managers Can Integrate Successful Careers and Fulfilling Personal Lives.* San Francisco: Jossey-Bass, 1993.

————. *Why Executives Lose Their Balance.* Greensboro, N.C.: Center for Creative Leadership, 1989.

London, M. *Career Barriers: How People Experience, Overcome, and Avoid Failure.* Mahwah, N.J.: Lawrence Erlbaum Associates, 1998.

McDonald, Kathy, and Beth Sirull. *Creating Your Life Collage: Strategies for Solving the Work-Life Dilemma.* New York: Three Rivers Press, 2000.

McGee-Cooper, Ann, with Duane Trammell and Barbara Lau. *You Don't Have to Go Home from Work Exhausted!: The Energy Engineering Approach.* Dallas: Bowen & Rogers, 1990.

Marshall, Susan A. *How to Grow a Backbone: 10 Strategies for Gaining Power and Influence at Work.* Lincolnwood, Ill.: Contemporary Books, 2000.

Maxwell, John C. *Failing Forward: Turning Mistakes into Stepping Stones for Success.* Nashville, Tenn.: Thomas Nelson Publishers, 2000.

Merrill, Deborah M. *Caring for Elderly Parents: Juggling Work, Family and Caregiving in Middle and Working Class Families.* Westport, Conn.: Auburn House, 1997.

Reeves, Martha E. *Suppressed, Forced Out and Fired: How Successful Women Lose Their Jobs.* Westport, Conn.: Quorum, 2000.

Rich, P., Stuart A. Copans, and Kenneth G. Copans. *The Healing Journey Through Job Loss: Your Journal for Reflection and Revitalization.* New York: John Wiley & Sons, 1999.

Sack, Steven Mitchell. *Getting Fired: What to Do if You're Fired, Downsized, Laid-Off, Restructured, Terminated, or Forced to Resign.* New York: Warner Books, 1999.

Sklover, Alan L., Esq. *Fired, Downsized, or Laid Off: What Your Employer Doesn't Want You to Know About How to Fight Back.* New York: Henry Holt, 2000.

Watson, Charles E. *What Smart People Do When Dumb Things Happen at Work: Hundreds of Tips for Dealing with All the Blunders, Glitches, Traps, and Setbacks That Sabotage Your Road to Success.* Franklin Lakes, N.J.: Career Press, 1999.

Internet Sources

Family and Work Institute *(www.familiesandwork.org)*: Web site of a New York City–based nonprofit organization that addresses the changing nature of work and family life. Free information includes tips about navigating transitions from work to home and talking to children about work-family issues.

Legal Information Institute *(www.law.cornell.edu/lii.html)*: This resource of legal materials administered by Cornell Law School includes a comprehensive overview of unemployment compensation. Enter the word "unemployment" in the "key word search" field for information about the topic.

Lycos Calendar by Anyday.com *(http://anyday.lycos.com)*: A free on-line organizer, address book, and reminder service. Input your personal events into the calendar and the on-line system will send you a reminder as the time approaches. In exchange for using this organizational tool, you will also receive additional reminders of Internet chats, television shows, trade shows, and other events. You can add them to your calendar, or ignore them and just use the calendar for your own personal appointments and birthdays.

Martindale-Hubbell Law Directory *(www.lawyers.com)*: A comprehensive national directory of lawyers, including attorneys who specialize in employment issues, with information on finding and hiring the right legal help.

Mindtools *(www.mindtools.com)*: An on-line resource center featuring information about achieving your personal goals in life and learning skills such as effective thinking and time management. One section of this site *(www.mindtools.com/page5.html)*: includes a free, extensive series of articles about how to achieve more with your time. You can learn about concepts such as goal setting, planning, prioritizing, coping with delays, and action plans. The section also features links to time-management books. Mindtools also offers users access to Life Plan for a $25 registration fee, a shareware program that assists with setting goals and maintaining focus on personal objectives.

National Partnership for Women and Families *(www.nationalpartnership.org/workandfamily/workmain.htm)*: Web site for the Work and Family Program of the National Partnership for Women and Families, a national nonprofit organization originally founded as the Women's Legal Defense Fund. The program promotes workplace fairness, flexibility, and family economic security. Its free on-line resource includes free information on family and medical leave, choosing caregivers, and striking a balance between work and home.

Parent Soup *(www.parentsoup.com)*: A comprehensive resource for families, covering issues as varied as sleeping habits and childhood progression. The site includes a wealth of child-care information, including directories and articles about choosing a caregiver.

The Productivity Institute *(www.balancetime.com)*: This Web site for a Connecticut-based time-management consulting firm features free articles about how to balance your life. A stress test (click on "Take the

Stress Test") can help you pinpoint your personal effectiveness. A free e-mail newsletter about time management is also available.

Single Rose.com *(www.singlerose.com)*: An on-line resource and community for single mothers. Features include chat rooms, articles, and support for women who single-handedly manage the responsibilities of work and child rearing. Other topics include divorce, recovery, and anger management. Visitors must register to use the site, but it's free.

Work and Family Connection *(www.workfamily.com)*: This clearinghouse on life and work issues was developed by the Work and Family Connection, a Minnesota-based work-family consulting firm. Extensive, free information includes articles about integrating work and life, trend reports, news briefs, suggestions for corporate work-family practices, and information about caregivers. Additional information is available to subscribers.

Periodicals
2000

"Work and Family Stress-Busters," *Family Life,* March 2000.

"Working Parents' Strategies for Balancing Employment and Child Care," *Jet,* April 3, 2000.

"Take That, Sitters: Business Travelers Taking the Kids," R. Hill, *San Francisco Business Times,* March 10, 2000.

"Part-Time Work for Women: Does It Really Help Balance Work and Family?" C. Higgins and L. Duxbury, *Human Resource Management,* Spring 2000.

1999

"Fair Shares [job sharing]," S. Caminiti, *Working Woman,* November 1999.

"Making Peace in the Workplace," R. Walker, *Christian Science Monitor,* August 9, 1999.

"Home Stress on the Job," E. Bloch, *Parenting,* February 1999.

"Stress," J. Adler, *Newsweek,* June 14, 1999.

"Stress Busters: What Works;" G. Cowley, *Newsweek,* June 14, 1999.

"Leave It at Home," *Management Today,* November 1999.

1998

"Fired up Over Getting Fired," P. Bart, *Variety,* November 23, 1998.

"Getting Fired—It Isn't the End of the World," K. Bruce, *Forbes,* April 20, 1998.

"How to Recover from a Firing," A. Faircloth, *Fortune,* December 7, 1998.

1996

"How Do I Tell My Boss I'm Overworked Without Getting Fired?"
   S. Piperato, *Executive Female,* January/February 1996.

"Never Fire Your Father [family business]," T. Eiben, *Fortune,* June 10, 1996.

1995

"So You Fail. Now Bounce Back!" P. Sellers, *Fortune,* May 1, 1995.

CHAPTER FIVE: NOW THAT YOU'RE THE BOSS . . .

Books

On Employee Retention

Coffman, Curt, and Marcus Buckingham. *First, Break All the Rules.* New York: Simon & Schuster, 1999.

Cook, Mary (ed.). *The AMA Handbook for Employee Recruitment and Retention.* New York: American Management Association, 1992.

Dibble, Suzanne. *Keeping Your Valuable Employees: Retention Strategies for Your Organization's Most Important Resource.* New York: John Wiley & Sons, 1999.

Kaye, Beverly L. *Love 'em or Lose 'em: Getting Good People to Stay.* San Francisco: Berrett-Koehler Publishers, 1999.

McConnell, John H. *Hunting Heads: How to Find and Keep the Best People.* Washington, D.C.: Kiplinger Books, 2000.

Parker, Glenn, Jerry McAdams, and David Zielinski. *Rewarding Teams: Lessons from the Trenches.* San Francisco: Jossey-Bass, 2000.

Saratoga Institute, The. *Retention Management: Strategies, Practices, Trends.* New York: American Management Association, 1997.

Schreyer, Ray, and John McCarter. *Recruit and Retain the Best: Key Solutions for the HR Professional.* Manassas Park, Va.: Impact, 2000.

On Hiring and Firing

Adler, Lou. *Hire with Your Head: A Rational Way to Make a Gut Decision.* New York: John Wiley & Sons, 1998.

Graham, Donna. *Online Recruiting: How to Use the Internet to Find Your Best Hires.* Palo Alto, Calif.: Davies-Black Publishing, 2000.

Repa, Barbara K. *Firing Without Fear.* Berkeley, Calif.: Nolo.com, 2000.

Rosenberg, DeAnne. *A Manager's Guide to Hiring the Best Person for Every Job.* New York: John Wiley & Sons, 2000.

Senn, Larry E., and John Childress. *The Secret of a Winning Culture: Building High-Performance Teams.* Los Angeles: The Leadership Press, 1999.

On Leadership

Aldag, Ramon J., and Buck Joseph. *Leaderhip & Vision: 25 Keys to Motivation.* New York: Lebhar-Friedman Books, 1999.

Blanchard, Ken, Bill Hybels, and Phil Hodges. *Leadership by the Book: Tools to Transform Your Workplace.* New York: William Morrow, 1999.

Harkins, Phil. *Powerful Conversations: How High-Impact Leaders Communicate.* New York: McGraw-Hill, 1999.

Loeb, Marshall, and Stephen Kindel. *Leadership for Dummies: Your Step-by-Step Guide to Building Leadership Skills.* Foster City, Calif.: IDG Books, 1999.

O'Toole, James. *Leadership A to Z: A Guide for the Appropriately Ambitious.* San Francisco: Jossey-Bass, 1999.

On Legal Matters

American Bar Association. *American Bar Association Guide to Workplace Law.* New York: Times Books, 1997.

Cope, Thom K., JD. *The Executive Guide to Employment Practices*, 3rd ed. Lincoln, Neb.: Dageforde Publishing, 1999.

Petrocelli, William, and Barbara Kate Repa. *Sexual Harassment on the Job: What It Is & How to Stop It.* Berkeley, Calif.: Nolo.com, 1998.

Powers, Dennis M. *The Office Romance: Playing with Fire Without Getting Burned.* New York: AMACOM, 1999.

Steingold, Fred S. *The Employer's Legal Handbook: A Complete Guide to Your Legal Rights & Responsibilities*, 3rd ed. Berkeley, Calif.: Nolo.com, 1999.

Weiss, Donald H. *Fair, Square & Legal: Safe Hiring, Managing & Firing Practices to Keep You & Your Company Out of Court*, 3rd ed. New York: AMACOM, 2000.

On Managing

Deep, Sam, and Lyle Sussman. *Act On It! Solving 101 of the Toughest Management Challenges.* Cambridge, Mass.: Perseus Publishing, 2000.

Gebelein, Susan H., et al. *Successful Executives' Handbook: Development Suggestions for Today's Executives.* Minneapolis: Personnel Decisions International (Reference Series), 2000.

Herbelin, Steve. *Work Team Coaching: An Interpersonal Approach to High Performance.* Riverbank, Calif.: Riverbank Books, 2000.

Zemke, Ron, Claire Raines, and Bob Filipczak. *Generations at Work: Managing the Clash of Veterans, Boomers, Xers, and Nexters in Your Workplace.* New York: AMACOM, 1999.

Internet Sources

On Managing and Leadership

American Express Small Business Exchange (*www.home3american-express.com/smallbusiness***):** This showcase for American Express services features a library of free information that is useful for all aspects of small-business management. Click on "Expert Advice" toward the bottom of the screen to find articles about day-to-day management, hiring and firing employees, on-line marketing, and legal issues. A free e-mail newsletter, offering practical advice from a small-business expert, is also available.

American Management Association (*www.amanet.org*): Presented by the nation's premier management association, this Web site features a free archive of management-related research, including information about workplace testing and monitoring, job-skill testing, managerial skills, competence, and career advancement. Click on "Research Reports" on the home page to access this section. The site also has information about seminars, conferences, and AMACOM books.

Breakaway Management (*www.breakawaynow.com.*): A Web site for a California-based management consulting firm founded by Tom E. Jones, a nationally renowned organization development specialist. This on-line treasure is a minicourse in management. Visitors can access a wealth of free articles authored by Dr. Jones, addressing issues such as retention, recruiting, changing behavior of underachievers, and overcoming workplace conflict. An on-line "toolbox" features quick management tips.

BusinessTown (*www.businesstown.com*): A small-business advice and assistance site. Free articles include hiring and firing tips, management psychology, teamwork, planning, and marketing. A free small-business e-mail newsletter is also available.

The Christian Businessman (*www.christianbusinessman.com*): The on-line version of the print magazine includes free articles about managing, hiring, and firing. See directory on left side of screen for content listing.

DBM Knowledge Communication Library (*www.knowledgecom.com*): This e-learning center features on-line management courses developed by Drake Beam Morin, an international human-resources consulting firm, and Harcourt Professional and Corporate Development company.

Curriculum, which is available for a fee, includes team building, leadership, human-resources and project management.

On Legal Matters

Equal Employment Opportunity Commission (*www.eeoc.gov*): Everything you need to know about federal employment discrimination laws and regulations, direct from the federal agency in charge of fielding complaints. The site's home page is updated regularly to include recent legal developments.

Find Law (*www.findlaw.com*): A free, voluminous resource of legal materials in all subject areas, including labor and employment law and small businesses. Articles include in-depth analyses of sexual harassment, family leave, disability discrimination, and firing people. A message board and e-mailing list are also available to visitors who are interested in these particular topics. The site also includes an extensive directory of links to employment and human-resource organizations as well as journals, newsletters, government agencies, and databases. To access the employment-law directory, click on "legal subject index" on the home page, and then click on "labor and employment law" or "small business."

HRLawForum.com (*www.hrlawforum.com*): This free Web site, developed and edited by Kollman and Sheehan, P. A., a Baltimore, Maryland–based civil-law practice, includes free legal information relevant to human-resource and management professionals. Articles address topics such as disabilities in the workplace, defense strategies for discrimination charges, and family medical leave.

Law Offices of David H. Greenberg, Esq. (*www.DiscriminationAttorney.com*): A comprehensive resource developed by a Los Angeles–based labor lawyer. Free information includes Q & A's about discrimination based on race, gender, pregnancy, sexual orientation, and other categories. Articles about wrongful termination, breach of contract, and workers' compensation are also on-line.

Nolo *(www.nolo.com)*: Nolo, a Berkeley, California–based legal publisher, has been transforming complex legal matters into user-friendly materials since 1971. The comprehensive Nolo Web site is an extension of the company's self-help legal guides and software. Employers and employees will find access to a vast array of legal materials pertaining to the workplace in Nolo's "Employees and Contractors" center *(www.nolo.com/category/emp_home.html)*. This section includes a legal encyclopedia of articles about job discrimination, sexual harassment, losing or leaving a job, and independent contractors. The site is updated regularly to provide the latest employment-law information.

Sexual Harassment Information from the University of Maryland, Department of Women's Studies
http://www.inform.umd.edu:8080/EdRes/Topic/WomensStudies/GenderIssues/SexualHarassment): An overview of facts and resources about sexual harassment in the workplace. The site also includes some public documents pertaining to the notorious Tailhook and Clarence Thomas/Anita Hill matters.

United States Department of Labor *(www.dol.gov)*: Web site of the federal agency that oversees the nation's labor matters. Information includes laws, regulations, labor statistics, training programs, and compliance matters.

Periodicals
2000
On Employee Retention
"10 Strategies to Attract and Keep Top-Quality Staff," A. Graham, *Folio: The Magazine for Magazine Management,* May 2000.
"How to Keep Your CFO," D. Bedell, *Corporate Finance,* April 2000.
"Employee Retention: What Managers Can Do," *Harvard Management Update,* April 2000.
"Keeping Your Employees—It's Not Just About the Money," M. Rittenberg, *Manager's Intelligence Report,* April 2000.

"Hire Power: Nine Tips for Taming Employee Turnover," J. Sullivan, *Nation's Restaurant News*, March 2000.

"Holding Onto Talent: The Best Defense Is a Pre-Emptive Strike," C. Hymowitz, *Wall Street Journal* (eastern edition), March 14, 2000.

"Are You Spending Too Much on Employee Retention?" *HR Focus*, February 2000.

"A Market-Driven Approach to Retaining Talent," P. Cappelli, *Harvard Business Review*, January/February 2000.

On Firing and Hiring

"Friendly Firing," C. Dannhauser, *Working Woman*, April 2000.

"When Young Managers Deliver the Pink Slips," C. Butler, *New York Times*, February 16, 2000.

"Executions Corporate Style [firing]," J. Segal, *HR Magazine*, January 2000.

"Hold Resume Truths to Be Self-Evident? No Way," C. Butler, *New York Times*, March 22, 2000.

"Using References as a Hiring Resource," P. DeCallier, *San Diego Business Journal*, March 13, 2000.

"How to Avoid Hiring the Prima Donnas Who Hate Teamwork," C. Hymowitz, *Wall Street Journal* (eastern edition), February 15, 2000.

"The Jungle [recruiting]," R. Silverman, *Wall Street Journal* (eastern edition), January 25, 2000.

On Leadership and Managing

"Follow the Leader: Why Leadership Talks Work," B. Filson, *Public Relations Tactics*, January 2000.

"Grooming Employees for Success," T. Kuczmarski, *Crain's Chicago Business*, April 10, 2000.

"Tips for Managing Employees Through a Merger," *Manager's Intelligence Report*, February 2000.

On Legal Matters

"Harassment Suits Hit the Dot-Coms," M. Ligos, *New York Times,* April 12, 2000.

"The Thin Line Between Love and Hate: Same Sex Hostile Environment Sexual Harassment," M. DelPo, *Labor Law Journal,* Spring 2000.

"Office Romances May Court Trouble," J. Greenwald, *Business Insurance,* April 14, 2000.

"Sexual Harassment on the Job," T. J. Wallis, *Career World,* February/March 2000.

1999

On Firing

"You're Fired!" S. Branch et al., *Your Company,* February/March 1999.

On Legal Matters

"Women Face 'Blue Wall' of Resistance [sexual harassment]," A. Marks, *Christian Science Monitor,* August 18, 1999.

"Harassment Grows More COMPLEX," C. O'Blenes, *Management Review,* June 1999.

"Why an Office Romance May Endanger Your Job," *Management Today,* February 1999.

"Minimize Liability by Implementing Policies," J. Hall, *Workforce,* November 1999.

"Beware of Illegal Interview Questions," J. Thomas, *Women in Business,* July/August 1999.

"Differently Disabled [discrimination]," D. Savage, *ABA Journal,* April 1999.

"Job Bias on the Basis of Parenthood," S. Coolidge, *Christian Science Monitor,* February 16, 1999.

"A Fair Workplace? Not Everywhere [discrimination]," D. McDonough and R. McNatt, *Business Week,* April 26, 1999.

On Managing

"You Can't Motivate Everyone," M. McCormack, *Management,* December 1999.

"The Art of Wooing Gen Xers," J. Cole, *HR Focus,* November 1999.

"Managers Keep Making the Same 'Stupid' Mistakes Over and Over Again," G. Cebrzynski, *Nation's Restaurant News,* June 14, 1999.

Miscellaneous

"Is Your Office Bully Proof?" A. Cox, *Mother Jones,* May/June 1999.

1998

"You Can Say Good Riddance to Bad Attitudes," G. Flynn, *Workforce,* July 1998.

"Ready, aim—fire!" M. Donley, *Crain's Chicago Business,* March 9, 1998.

"Failure to Post Job Lands Employer in Bias Suit," L. Atkinson, *HR Focus,* May 1998.

INDEX